Data Engineering for AI

Enhance data persistence strategies for optimal AI and analytical workload performance

Sundeep Goud Katta

Lav Kumar

bpb

www.bpbonline.com

First Edition 2025

Copyright © BPB Publications, India

ISBN: 978-93-65893-403

To View Complete
BPB Publications Catalogue
Scan the QR Code:

www.bpbonline.com

iii

Dedicated to

My parents, wife and son
                    - Sundeep Goud Katta

My parents, wife and son
                    - Lav Kumar

About the Authors

- **Sundeep Goud Katta** is a seasoned technology leader based in California, with over 13 years of experience in AI-driven solutions, cloud-based architectures, and scalable CRM platforms. As a lead, he has spearheaded enterprise-grade initiatives that streamline deployment pipelines, enhance system resilience, and drive intelligent automation through GPT-powered models and predictive analytics. Sundeep's technical expertise spans across CRM experience platforms, Azure cloud ecosystems, and modern web technologies, including Three.js, Revit, and WPF. He has played a pivotal role in large-scale platform migrations, performance tuning, and the creation of robust validation and monitoring frameworks that power secure, high-performing, and user-centric systems. An active contributor to the tech community, Sundeep has served as a reviewer for IEEE COMPASS, judged prestigious industry awards such as Globee and Brandon Hall, and reviewed technical publications for leading publishers including O'Reilly and Manning. His passion for innovation, technical excellence, and knowledge-sharing positions him as a leading voice in the evolving landscape of scalable data engineering.

- **Lav Kumar** is a seasoned full-stack developer with over 12 years of experience architecting and delivering scalable, enterprise-grade software solutions. Based in Fremont, California, Lav currently serves as a lead member of technical staff at a leading CRM company in San Francisco, where he plays a pivotal role in advancing AI-powered search capabilities. His work focuses on enhancing user experience through personalized search results and the optimization of intelligent search algorithms. Lav's professional journey includes impactful tenures at Nokia and Samsung, where he contributed to the development of core features and applications that helped shape the commercial success of flagship products. His technical expertise spans Java/J2EE, modern UI development, microservices architecture, and the integration of AI/ML technologies into production systems. A passionate advocate for data science and big data, Lav is dedicated to building innovative, data-driven solutions that scale. His contributions have earned him multiple awards for excellence and innovation across his career. As a Salesforce Trailhead Ranger and an Accelerate Program Graduate, Lav demonstrates an ongoing commitment to professional growth and technical mastery.

About the Reviewers

❖ **Anusha Reddy Narapuredddy** is a senior software engineer at Apple, where she leads the development of Apple's largest observability platform. With deep expertise in building large-scale distributed systems, AI/ML applications, and observability platforms and infrastructure that power critical AI/ML services used by billions of users worldwide, Anusha has played a pivotal role in the development and deployment of several industry-leading technologies. Her work ensures the reliability of Apple's flagship services like Siri, Search, and iOS.

As CNCF OpenTelemetry contributing member, Anusha is recognized for her contributions to the field of computer science, particularly in advancing observability platforms. She holds patents and has published scholarly articles in the field of distributed systems and AI-enhanced observability.

❖ **Gaurav Khare** is a seasoned senior data engineer with 16 years of experience in the finance domain. He is an expert in Python, Hadoop, Spark, NLP and big data technologies, specializing in data analysis, data science. Throughout his career, he has built scalable data infrastructure and implemented advanced analytics solutions to improve banking operations and decision-making. An avid reader and technical reviewer, he stays at the forefront of emerging technologies. He actively contributes to technical communities, sharing insights and mentoring peers, earning a strong reputation as a skilled professional and thoughtful leader.

❖ **Vipin Kataria** is a seasoned data and machine learning engineer with over 20 years of experience in designing and implementing customer and data-centric products. As an enterprise architect, he currently focuses on building cloud data platforms that help businesses develop applications providing timely, trusted, and actionable data. He is also dedicated to building Gen AI platforms leveraging large language models to transform business operations and enhance customer experiences.

His technical expertise spans building scalable real-time streaming platforms using Apache Kafka, Spark Streaming, and event-driven architectures that process terabytes of IoT data. His expertise extends to designing comprehensive ML platforms that provide end-to-end capabilities from data preparation to model deployment, featuring automated pipelines for continuous training, A/B testing, and model monitoring using MLflow and Kubeflow.

Beyond technical architecture, he is passionate about mentoring teams and building data-driven cultures, fostering innovation and excellence in every organization he serves. He is also an active independent researcher in machine learning and a technical reviewer for various books and journals.

❖ **Raghavendra Patlolla** is a full-stack engineer with over 10 years of experience in web and API development. He specializes in database management, using DynamoDB and PostgreSQL to design scalable and efficient solutions for complex applications. He also has extensive expertise in deploying applications on AWS and Azure, leveraging tools like AWS Cognito, API Gateway, and Lambda functions to create secure, serverless architectures. His back-end development skills include building robust APIs with Node.js, Express.js, and GraphQL, ensuring seamless data interactions. Additionally, he is skilled in front-end development, creating intuitive user interfaces with frameworks such as ReactJS, Vue.js, Angular, and Svelte. Known for optimizing workflows and reducing costs, he brings a blend of technical expertise and practical problem-solving to every project.

Acknowledgements

We would like to express our sincere gratitude to everyone who played a role in the completion of this book.

First and foremost, our heartfelt thanks go to our family and friends for their unwavering support and encouragement throughout this journey. Their love and motivation have been a constant driving force behind our efforts.

We are especially thankful to Rajeev Reddy Vishaka, Raghav Patlolla, and Anusha Narapureddy for their valuable input and contributions. Your insights and feedback have been instrumental in shaping the content and elevating the quality of this book. We truly appreciate your support.

Our sincere appreciation goes to BPB Publications for their continued guidance and expertise in bringing this book to life. Their support throughout the publishing process has been indispensable.

We would also like to acknowledge the contributions of the reviewers, technical experts, and editors whose thoughtful feedback helped refine and enhance the manuscript.

Lastly, we extend our deepest thanks to our readers. Your interest and encouragement mean the world to us.

Thank you to everyone who helped turn this book into a reality.

Preface

We live in an age awash with data. Every app click, sensor reading, and customer interaction generates a new stream of information. For a modern professional, the ability to collect, organize, and transform this flood of raw data into meaningful insights is not just a niche skill, it is a career-defining advantage. In a world where data drives decisions, those who can harness that data to build intelligent solutions are leading the charge.

The book was written with working professionals in mind. Whether you are a seasoned data engineer, a solutions architect, or an AI enthusiast, this book speaks to your goals of leveling up and staying ahead in a rapidly evolving field. It is for anyone who wants to go beyond the buzzwords and understand what really makes scalable, AI-ready data systems tick. As you turn these pages, you will find a relatable, no-nonsense exploration of the technologies, principles, and patterns that empower high-performance data infrastructure in real-world scenarios.

Consider this book your hands-on roadmap for building robust data platforms. No matter your current focus, designing batch or real-time data pipelines, wrangling streaming data in motion, or preparing features for the next machine learning model, you will find guidance tailored to your needs. The chapters ahead break down complex topics into approachable lessons so you can apply them directly in your daily work and if you are eyeing a transition into an AI-focused role, the practical knowledge here will demystify the backbone of AI projects and give you the confidence to contribute from day one.

You will learn how to design and optimize data pipelines that can efficiently manage large-scale workloads. The course will guide you in streamlining real-time data flows, ensuring your analytics and AI models consistently receive fresh and reliable inputs. You will also explore techniques for engineering high-quality data features that strengthen the effectiveness and robustness of your machine learning models. Additionally, you will gain the skills to secure and govern data throughout its entire lifecycle, from ingestion to storage and beyond, enabling you to trust and confidently share your data.

Chapter 1: Introduction to Data Engineering in AI- This chapter traces the evolution of data engineering alongside AI, covering the shift from early infrastructure to big data and distributed systems. It explains key concepts like data types, pipelines, and tools, while emphasizing data engineering's role in scalable AI systems and its growing importance in modern organizations. It also introduces the intersection of business intelligence and AI, highlighting how well-orchestrated data enables smarter decision-making. Whether you are new to the field or experienced, the chapter provides a solid foundation and context for what follows. It concludes with a forward-looking perspective on data engineering's expanding influence across industries.

Chapter 2: Managing Data Collection- Data collection is the critical first step in any AI pipeline, and this chapter discusses the scalable methods for acquiring data from APIs, databases, sensors, and user-generated content. It covers the architectural differences between real-time and batch data collection, and how tools like Kafka and Flume support large-scale ingestion. You will explore best practices for ensuring reliability, high throughput, and fault tolerance. The chapter also emphasizes early data validation to minimize downstream issues and outlines strategies for optimizing latency and cost, particularly in cloud-native setups. Key topics like data formats, logging, and security are discussed, establishing a foundation for efficient, high-quality data collection.

Chapter 3: Data Ingestion in Action- Once data is collected, it must be ingested efficiently into processing systems. This chapter breaks down the ingestion process across modern data stacks. You will explore pipeline designs for structured, semi-structured, and unstructured data. Tools like AWS Kinesis, Apache NiFi, and Kafka Connect are introduced with context. The chapter discusses architectural choices for ingestion: stream vs. micro-batch vs. batch. You will learn how to optimize ingestion for parallelism, buffering, and error recovery. It highlights strategies to ensure schema enforcement, deduplication, and real-time transformation. Best practices for ingesting data into data lakes and warehouses are also shared. Whether it is IoT or logs, ingestion is where speed meets structure, and this chapter shows you how.

Chapter 4: Data Storage in Real-time- Modern analytics and AI require real-time access to clean, consistent data. This chapter walks through architectures like Lambda, Kappa, and Lakehouse models. You will discover how to architect for low-latency queries and scalable data growth. Topics like time-based partitioning, data versioning, and compaction are covered. It also introduces file formats like Parquet, Avro, and ORC in a real-time context. The chapter helps you choose between hot and cold storage and manage costs effectively. You will learn how to ensure ACID compliance or eventual consistency depending on your use case. Streaming storage systems like Apache Hudi and Delta Lake are explored. The goal is to help you build real-time data lakes that serve both operational and analytical needs.

Chapter 5: Data Processing Techniques and Best Practices- Data must be processed before it becomes useful for AI or business intelligence. This chapter starts with a comparison of ETL and ELT workflows and where each fits best. You will learn how to scale processing using tools like Apache Spark, Flink, and Beam. The chapter discusses the trade-offs of SQL-based vs. NoSQL-based processing engines. It discusses stream processing, windowing functions, and join strategies at scale. Special focus is given to managing cost and reducing redundancy in multi-stage pipelines. It explores how to ensure data quality, auditability, and lineage during transformations. You will also see how to design pipelines for retraining machine learning models. Whether you are processing terabytes or petabytes, this chapter gives you a playbook to do it right.

Chapter 6: Data Integration and Interoperability- AI pipelines often rely on data coming from different systems; this is where integration matters. This chapter explains how to connect disparate data sources using APIs, ETL tools, and message queues. Technologies like Apache NiFi, Talend, and MuleSoft are introduced with architectural examples. You will understand how to deal with schema evolution, latency mismatches, and data duplication. The chapter covers integration across on-prem, cloud, and hybrid environments. It also explores the role of metadata, data contracts, and standard formats like JSON, XML, and Avro. Interoperability in an enterprise setting means building trust across systems, and that is emphasized here. Whether integrating legacy systems or modern SaaS platforms, this chapter provides actionable insights. Real-world data mapping and synchronization strategies round out the discussion.

Chapter 7: Ensuring Data Quality- Even the most scalable pipeline fails if the data is unreliable. This chapter dives into ensuring data quality at every step of the pipeline. It introduces key quality metrics like accuracy, completeness, consistency, and timeliness. Tools like Great Expectations, Deequ, and Apache Griffin are examined with practical examples. You will learn how to automate validation rules and handle edge cases in real-time. The chapter outlines strategies for managing schema drift and alerting on anomalies. There is a strong focus on integrating data quality checks into CI/CD pipelines. Use cases from finance, healthcare, and retail demonstrate what can go wrong and how to prevent it. By the end, you will see data quality not as an afterthought, but as a built-in feature of modern engineering.

Chapter 8: Understanding Data Analytics- With clean data in place, the next step is turning it into insights. This chapter explores data analytics frameworks and how they support AI models and dashboards. It starts with a taxonomy of analytics: descriptive, diagnostic, predictive, and prescriptive. You will learn how scalable analytics platforms handle real-time and batch data. Concepts like OLAP cubes, query optimization, and caching strategies are demystified. Performance tuning, cost optimization, and governance are all addressed. You will see how analytics pipelines power business KPIs and machine learning features. The chapter also covers metadata management and data lineage tracking. It is a bridge between raw data and the decisions that drive the enterprise forward.

Chapter 9: Data Visualization and Reporting- Insights are only useful when they are understood. This chapter explores how to visualize data so stakeholders can act on it. It explains chart types, design principles, and storytelling techniques for effective dashboards. Tools like Tableau, Power BI, Looker, and D3.js are compared. Real-world scenarios demonstrate how visualizations influence business outcomes. The chapter dives into common pitfalls like misleading axes and cognitive overload. Accessibility, interactivity, and personalization are emphasized. AI's role in auto-generating visual insights and anomalies is also explored. Whether you are presenting to executives or monitoring ML models, clear visuals matter and this chapter shows how to deliver them.

Chapter 10: Operational Data Security- Security is not just an IT function, it is foundational to trustworthy data platforms. This chapter provides a comprehensive view of securing data in motion and at rest. It covers encryption standards, key management systems, and RBAC implementations. The shared responsibility model in cloud platforms is explained in detail. You will explore security architectures using VPNs, firewalls, and private endpoints. The chapter also outlines how to build threat models for data pipelines. Real-time alerting, access audits, and compliance automation are emphasized. Case studies from regulated industries demonstrate what is at stake. Secure data pipelines are critical to safe, ethical AI, and this chapter makes sure you know how to build them.

Chapter 11: Protecting Data Privacy- As data volumes grow, so do privacy concerns. This chapter covers how to design pipelines that respect user privacy and comply with regulations. You will explore principles from GDPR, CCPA, and HIPAA in a practical context. Anonymization, pseudonymization, and data masking techniques are explained clearly. The chapter outlines how to manage user consent, access controls, and audit trails. It highlights privacy-preserving machine learning techniques like federated learning and differential privacy. Real-world examples show the impact of privacy lapses and how to prevent them. You will also learn how to integrate privacy policies into agile data teams. Privacy is not just legal, it is ethical, and this chapter shows you how to embed it from day one.

Chapter 12: Data Engineering Case Studies- To tie it all together, this chapter presents real-world case studies from leading industries. You will walk through how an e-commerce giant scaled its feature store using Spark and Redshift. A financial services company's fraud detection pipeline using Kafka and Flink is detailed. Healthcare use cases showcase privacy-respecting integration with EHR systems. Each case study includes architecture diagrams, tool choices, and key lessons learned. The chapter reflects on how trade-offs were managed under pressure. Whether scaling for billions of events or optimizing for real-time AI, these stories bring theory to life. You will know about patterns, anti-patterns, and inspiration for your systems.

Code Bundle and Coloured Images

Please follow the link to download the
Code Bundle and the *Coloured Images* of the book:

https://rebrand.ly/py6bjvm

The code bundle for the book is also hosted on GitHub at
https://github.com/bpbpublications/Data-Engineering-for-AI.
In case there's an update to the code, it will be updated on the existing GitHub repository.

We have code bundles from our rich catalogue of books and videos available at
https://github.com/bpbpublications. Check them out!

Errata

We take immense pride in our work at BPB Publications and follow best practices to ensure the accuracy of our content to provide with an indulging reading experience to our subscribers. Our readers are our mirrors, and we use their inputs to reflect and improve upon human errors, if any, that may have occurred during the publishing processes involved. To let us maintain the quality and help us reach out to any readers who might be having difficulties due to any unforeseen errors, please write to us at :

errata@bpbonline.com

Your support, suggestions and feedbacks are highly appreciated by the BPB Publications' Family.

Did you know that BPB offers eBook versions of every book published, with PDF and ePub files available? You can upgrade to the eBook version at www.bpbonline.com and as a print book customer, you are entitled to a discount on the eBook copy. Get in touch with us at :

business@bpbonline.com for more details.

At **www.bpbonline.com**, you can also read a collection of free technical articles, sign up for a range of free newsletters, and receive exclusive discounts and offers on BPB books and eBooks.

Piracy

If you come across any illegal copies of our works in any form on the internet, we would be grateful if you would provide us with the location address or website name. Please contact us at **business@bpbonline.com** with a link to the material.

If you are interested in becoming an author

If there is a topic that you have expertise in, and you are interested in either writing or contributing to a book, please visit **www.bpbonline.com**. We have worked with thousands of developers and tech professionals, just like you, to help them share their insights with the global tech community. You can make a general application, apply for a specific hot topic that we are recruiting an author for, or submit your own idea.

Reviews

Please leave a review. Once you have read and used this book, why not leave a review on the site that you purchased it from? Potential readers can then see and use your unbiased opinion to make purchase decisions. We at BPB can understand what you think about our products, and our authors can see your feedback on their book. Thank you!

For more information about BPB, please visit **www.bpbonline.com**.

Join our book's Discord space

Join the book's Discord Workspace for Latest updates, Offers, Tech happenings around the world, New Release and Sessions with the Authors:

https://discord.bpbonline.com

Table of Contents

CHAPTER 1
Introduction to Data Engineering in AI

Introduction

This chapter provides an overview of data engineering from its early days to the modern-day stack, emphasizing the role of data in **artificial intelligence** (**AI**) and **machine learning** (**ML**). It covers key concepts, tools, and the evolution of data management and processing frameworks. You will explore the historical shift from traditional data management to the big data revolution, uncovering how technological advancements have reshaped the way organizations handle vast and complex datasets. We will delve into the essential role of data engineering in modern businesses, highlighting its impact on operational efficiency, strategic insights, and competitive advantage. The chapter also bridges the connection between data engineering and AI, illustrating how well-engineered data pipelines empower machine learning models to deliver accurate and actionable results.

By the end of this chapter, you will have a comprehensive overview of the data engineering's past, present and future, enabling you with the knowledge to navigate its core principles and its synergy with AI. This chapter will set the stage for deeper exploration in the chapters to come.

Structure

The chapter discusses the following topics:

- Early days of big data revolution

- Role of data engineering in modern business
- Intersection with AI and ML
- Understanding data types, structures, and sources
- Navigating the data landscape
- Databases, data warehousing, and data lakes
- ETL processes
- Importance of data quality and integrity

Objectives

By the end of this chapter, you will have an idea of how data engineering has evolved from the early days of big data to how it plays the most important role in today's business landscape. We will look at how data engineering intersects with AI and ML, showing how these fields work together to make smarter decisions. In this module, you will be learning different types of data, their structure, and sources in a way that will provide a very strong foundation for any person entering the world of data. Core concepts such as databases, data warehousing, and data lakes would be explained in an understandable way with respect to how they support and help in storing large bulks of information. We will also cover ETL processes, showing the difference between traditional ways and how things have changed with time. Finally, the importance of data quality and integrity will be underlined to make sure that the insights one draws from data are reliable and actionable.

Early days of big data revolution

During the early days of big data, massive data generation overlapped with emerging technologies for storage, processing, and distributed computing. This inflection points not only changed how organizations utilize and make sense of big data but also provided many fundamental principles that still spur innovation in data science, ML, and AI today.

Historical background

In the early days, most organizations used to rely on bulky mainframes occupying entire rooms to store and process the data. Early systems lacked capacity and functionality compared to what was needed, mainly targeting large organizations like governments and research institutions. Entry of data was a labor-intensive task, and storage was costly making businesses selective about the data they maintained. Businesses used to have to decide what data was worth storing due to storage and maintenance costs. The era of mainframes also made sure that the data was stolen or locked up, therefore making it hard for any organization to share or integrate information with other departments.

As technology improved, these issues were solved by relational databases. Relational databases introduced a structured form of data storage in tabular forms with relationships between those tables. This introduced more usability and flexibility to the data. Initial innovators like *IBM DB2* and *Oracle* started shaping data management in such a way that allowed organizations to store larger amounts of information more proficiently. Relational databases introduced sophisticated querying capabilities, therefore allowing users to identify specific datasets and conduct analytics atop them. Thus, the era of the digital revolution in data engineering began through the movement from manual to more automated data management systems.

Transition to digital

The digital revolution marked the beginning of a great transformation in data storage and processing. Relational databases became the order of the day and with this mainstream adoption came organizations that had begun to realize the power of structured data. This transition offered businesses a chance to enhance efficiency in their operations through access to data that earlier was not easy to deal with. SQL was developed as the standardized means of interacting with these databases, allowing for more intuitive, useful querying, and data manipulation.

It was during this era that demands for data access in real-time increased. Data retrieval speed was also further improved by the evolution in storage technology, for example, from the tape-based system to the use of disk drives. More organizations started adopting digital processes and data was no longer confined to printed forms or physical records. A sudden influx in the volume of data rose after digitalization. It was the time when enterprises needed more complex systems capable not only of storing massive data but also of retrieving and analyzing it with efficiency. The relational database model proved to be trustworthy yet showed its inability under the influx that rose due to several new sources.

Big data revolution

As the digital internet evolved, the influx of data increased and so did the concept of big data. The traditional relational databases that had served companies well for years began to struggle with the increasing volume, velocity, and variety of data. The rise of social media, e-commerce, and digital services meant that organizations were generating more data than before and much of it was unstructured. Storing them in relational databases did not serve the purpose. It was becoming heavily complex to keep adding data neatly into relational tables; it came in the form of videos, images, sensor readings, and complex transactional records.

The big data revolution was driven by the need for more robust tools capable of handling massive datasets across distributed systems. Enter *Hadoop*, a distributed computing framework that enables businesses to process vast amounts of data across clusters of commodity hardware. Hadoop revolutionized the way large datasets were managed by breaking them down into smaller chunks and distributing them across multiple servers.

This distributed approach allowed companies to take advantage of cheaper hardware rather than relying on expensive, high-end systems. Hadoop's power stemmed from its ability to process data in parallel which speeds up tasks that would have taken days, if not weeks, on traditional systems. Built on the principle of scale-out architecture, Hadoop could effortlessly handle everything from simple logs to complex datasets. This newfound capacity for processing data opened a world of possibilities for businesses, allowing them to tap into new insights and build data-driven strategies. Hadoop combined with its **Hadoop Distributed File System (HDFS)** ensured that data remained redundant and available, even if some of the hardware failed. In short, Hadoop became a key player in the big data revolution, empowering organizations to handle and analyze massive data at an unprecedented scale.

> **Note: Hadoop was not the first big data technology but it played a significant role in popularizing the concept of big data due to its ability to handle massive datasets in a distributed and scalable way. Before Hadoop, companies were using other distributed computing technologies like Google's MapReduce and Bigtable which inspired Hadoop's creation.**

Hadoop's ability to store unstructured data in its HDFS and its processing power through *MapReduce* marked a turning point in data engineering. Companies like *Facebook* and *Google* led the way in harnessing the power of big data technologies, enabling them to build personalized services and optimize their operations through data-driven insights. This revolution unlocked new possibilities but it also introduced new complexities in terms of managing, securing, and analyzing such large volumes of information.

Data explosion

The growth of the Internet along with the rapid increase in mobile devices and the rise of the **Internet of Things (IoT)** further accelerated the explosion of data. By the mid-2000s, companies were collecting terabytes, if not petabytes, of data daily. Every click, swipe, and purchase generated data that could be captured and analyzed, opening new opportunities for businesses to understand their customers in real-time. However, this data explosion also presented tougher times for data engineers and data scientists to make effective use of.

> **Note: A data engineer focuses on building and maintaining the infrastructure and pipelines that handle large datasets, ensuring data is clean, reliable, and accessible. In contrast, a data scientist analyzes this data to extract insights, develop predictive models, and inform decision-making. While data engineers prioritize architecture and data flow, data scientists concentrate on statistics, machine learning, and deriving value from the data. Both roles are essential in the data-driven ecosystem, complementing each other to unlock data's full potential.**

This era of data explosion set the stage for the next phase of innovation in data engineering where the focus shifted from merely storing and processing data to leveraging it for advanced analytics and AI. The convergence of big data technologies with AI created a fertile ground for ML and predictive modeling, unlocking new opportunities across industries.

Role of data engineering in modern business

Data engineering plays a crucial role in modern business by ensuring that vast amounts of data are efficiently collected, processed, and made accessible for analysis. This discipline enables organizations to transform raw data into valuable insights, driving informed decision-making and innovation across all sectors.

Data-driven enterprise

The current business world uses more and more data to drive strategy and decision-making across organizations. It is not an innocent byproduct of operations but has transformed into an asset at the very core of businesses and organizations. Businesses that make priorities related to data as a core resource are being referred to as data-driven enterprises nowadays. These organizations believe that the information they will gather from customer interactions, operations, or external sources will offer them insights to inform future growth and improvement in day-to-day operations. The key to tapping into the power of data will be through effective usage of the data pipelines that enable businesses to collect, process, and analyze data in a structured and meaningful way.

Data-driven enterprises have advantages over traditional businesses in many different aspects, they are better positioned in the knowledge of market trends, identification of customer preferences, and timely response to changes in their environment. This is possible because a data-driven enterprise enables one to make decisions based on up-to-date information rather than intuition or reports compiled some time ago. A retail company can therefore continually readjust its inventory levels in accordance with monitored customer purchasing trends to avoid stockouts, increasing customer satisfaction. Conversely, financial service firms may leverage big data to detect the potential risks of their portfolio and change their strategy before that to avoid an issue.

Being one of the top facilitators in data engineering, its role is to ensure that data from different sources moves seamlessly into a position where it can be analyzed. This involves the creation of pipelines that bring data in from sources such as transaction systems, sensors, and social media, treating it like some sort of raw material that needs transformation into an easily analyzable format. The aim is to harness the power of continuous flows for real-time analysis and decision-making. This enables businesses to be agile, adapting to new information and trends as they arise rather than waiting for quarterly reports or annual reviews.

Additionally, data-driven companies can make sure that innovation in culture is assured through the usage of data to test new ideas and measure their impact. Instead of intuition, they are driven by data in making decisions on product development down to strategies for marketing. This is a way of increasing their chances of success while allowing them to experiment even more freely knowing that they can always easily pivot if the data suggests a different approach could be more effective.

Business value of data engineering

The business value of data engineering cannot be overestimated. With data at the heart of today's business processes, the ability to leverage and efficiently exploit has become a prime source of competitive advantage. Letting organizations unlock the real value of the data means using tools and processes that make innovation and growth a reality in ways unimaginable before.

Data engineering has an edge concerning predictive analytics. Predictive analytics deals with what is more likely to take place in the future due to historical data, from there, businesses get informed concerning customer needs, market trends, and probable risks. Predicting the behavior of entities is therefore useful in many sectors, such as banking, medicine, and retail where it helps in devising an optimal outcome, for instance, predictive analytics would be applied by a health provider to risk-profile how likely patients are to develop grave chronic diseases before that usual occurrence or take remedial actions. Similarly, this technology in the retail sector can predict the demand for certain products during peak seasons so that the retailer is better placed to have adequate stocks. Thus, data engineering plays an extremely important role in the development of AI applications.

ML models fuel AI work on huge volumes of clean and structured data. Data engineers develop the pipelines to feed those models with data, having all the information accurate, complete, and ready to analyze. If appropriate engineering practices are not followed in managing the data, ML models may deduce biased or incorrect results and poor decisions. Data engineering will not be the last in the list of any business powered by AI, through automation of processes, personalization of customer experiences, or innovation of new products. Besides making AI and predictive analytics possible, it gives businesses insight into their customers' behaviors. Businesses will know more about what customers want, how they behave, and what leads them to buy by collecting data and analyzing information about customer interactions. The given type of information will help in increasing the level of customer satisfaction, formulating advertisements that are targeted at the right people, and creating products that fit the needs of the customers, for example, it can analyze customer browsing behavior data to determine which products tend to be purchased together to make personalized suggestions to its customers.

It is in the realm of business outcomes, but data engineering also drives innovation by enabling the experimentation of new ideas and facilitating change in a business through impact measurement. It could also be argued that with the right data infrastructure in place, businesses will have the ability to quickly test new products and services, and new business models using data to define whether they are successful or not. This gives any business better agility and responsiveness to the market than its competitors.

It also ensures that data is handled in a secure and compliant manner. A good framework of data governance is necessary in today's world where data breaches and privacy rank among the top concerns for businesses and end consumers alike. The data engineer implements the processes and technologies that undertake protection against sensitive data, hence ensuring adherence to regulations like the **General Data Protection Regulation (GDPR)** and the **California Consumer Privacy Act (CCPA)**. This not only saves businesses from potential fines and reputational damage but also builds trust with customers.

The symbiotic relationship between AI and data engineering is evident in modern architectures that enable seamless data processing for ML applications. For instance, **feature stores** play a critical role in managing and serving features for ML models, ensuring consistency between training and inference. Additionally, **data validation pipelines** help maintain data integrity by detecting anomalies and inconsistencies before AI models consume them. In real-time AI systems, architectures like **streaming data pipelines** enable real-time inference by continuously processing and transforming data, allowing AI models to make instant decisions. These concrete examples highlight how data engineering underpins AI success by providing reliable, scalable, and high-quality data pipelines.

Overall, data engineering provides a basis for businesses to leverage data effectively in innovation, enhancement of decision-making, and favorable competition. In a data-driven enterprise, the role of a data engineer becomes very critical in ensuring that the data is clean, accessible, and ready for analysis, helping the business enterprises to unleash full power from their data assets.

Intersection with AI and ML

The intersection of AI and ML within the realm of data engineering is where innovation truly thrives. As we explore scalable data engineering in AI, the synergy between these fields is foundational to building systems that not only manage large datasets but also extract meaningful insights from them. Data engineering provides the framework like scalable pipelines, distributed systems, and optimized storage solutions, that empowers AI and ML models to learn from vast amounts of data.

At this intersection, data engineers ensure that the data-feeding AI and ML models are clean, well-structured, and readily available, while also managing the infrastructure to handle rapid growth in data volume. AI and ML, in turn, bring intelligence to the data engineering process by automating data preparation, anomaly detection, and predictive maintenance in pipelines. Together, they create a feedback loop where AI systems continuously improve as data engineers design systems that can scale alongside the evolving demands of ML applications, ensuring that both operate in harmony.

AI and data engineering symbiosis

Data engineering is the underlying guarantee of effectiveness and accuracy for any AI or ML system. The relationship existing between data engineering and AI or ML is close; one depends on the other for good performance. In other words, AI and ML models make predictions, classifications, or decisions according to the quality of the data inputs they receive. In return, it is the data engineers who organize a clean dataset ready for consumption by these models, for instance, a huge amount of data is involved in the training phase of AI models.

If the data is not well organized, incomplete, or full of errors, then nothing can be learned from it, and it probably will yield wrong results. The more structured and clean the data is, the more efficient the learning process of AI models will be, hence higher accuracy and better performance. The initiative of AI and ML imperatively brings out the need for a strong data engineering foundation that would support the initiative. Precisely, data engineers are the gardeners who grow the data so that AI models may thrive.

Data engineers have the most responsibility when it comes to the streamlining of data across the system. This involves constructing and maintaining the infrastructure that provides for seamless transitions of data from various sources to its destination in AI or ML models. This entails cleaning the data, transforming it, removing noise, and ensuring it is in a format that can easily be used by the models. This is an important step for the models to perform well but if the quality of data is poor, then the prediction would come out biased or not generalize well to new data.

Without any data engineering, AI and ML would fall into inaccurate, incomplete, or badly formatted data. Therefore, both come together and play a vital role in forming an important partnership that aids businesses in extracting insights from their data, as well as making smarter decisions. Data engineering hence provides the base on which AI or ML builds to offer high-powered, data-driven solutions. For this reason, high-level collaboration between data engineering and AI is one of those key factors which guarantee high performance, from recommendation systems to autonomous vehicles.

Building data pipeline for AI

Putting a solid data pipeline in place is one of the most significant ways to ensure AI and ML models do their jobs to the best of their abilities. In very broad terms, a data pipeline can be defined as an end-to-end process that takes data from its source, such as customer transactions, social media activity, sensor readings, and more, through a series of cleaning, transformation, and storage stages before it finally passes into an AI or ML model.

Having a data pipeline in place serves to guarantee that data is good in quality, consistent, and can be presented for training and predictive purposes. Contrarily, ill-designed pipelines are showpieces of delays, errors, and poor-quality data, which in turn may have the AI models perform poorly. As would naturally go without saying, *the making of a well-*

designed data pipeline is paramount in the AI development process. The data ingestion function is typically indicative of the start of a standard data pipeline where raw data is ingested from various sources, this could be unstructured data, like social media posts or video files, or structured, data maintained in relational databases. Each of these stages should be able to capture and store this data in some form of a pipeline which can be accessed and manipulated with ease.

From data cleaning to model predictions, refer to the following points for a better understanding:

- **Cleaning and transformation after the ingestion**: It is the responsibility of a data engineer to clean them from all inconsistencies and inaccuracies in the data. For example, imputation of missing values, outliers' removal, or textual information transformation in some understandable format for the AI model. This step is very critical because AI models learn on clean and consistent data. If the data is unclean or incomplete, then the model performance will suffer, hence unreliable predictions. Pre-processed and transformed data will be moved to an access-optimized AI and ML model storage. It may be a data lake, a data warehouse, or some other large-scale data processing-based proprietary store.

- **Model predictions**: AI application needs to, respect the data size, speed of processing, or the complexity of the analysis to be done. Finally, it overflows into the train and predicts parts of the AI model. Training of models is a process of learning from the available data and adjusting parameters in such a way that reasonable predictions can be obtained. Once trained, it can make predictions on new examples, and thus, fraud detection, customer segmentation, and personalized recommendation predictions are done.

The well-designed data pipeline bears a great deal of importance to the successful improvement of AI and ML models over time. The quality and monitoring of the flow within these pipelines are entrusted to the data engineers who ensure continuity in the flow of data and rapid detection of problems that may affect data quality or bottlenecks in the system.

The following figure provides an overview of how raw data transforms to drive business decisions for organizations:

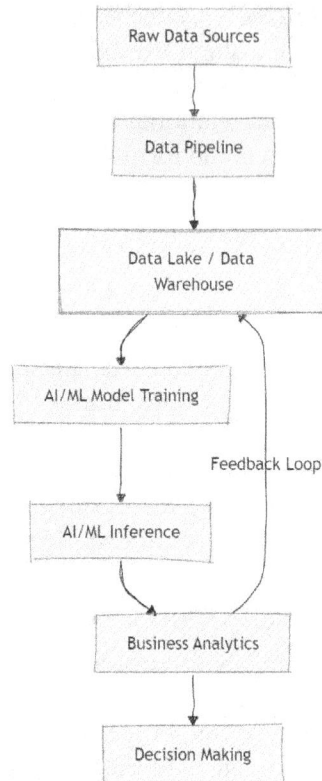

Figure 1.1: *AI or ML data pipeline with user integration*

In other words, data engineering and AI are deeply connected. Data engineering offers the necessary infrastructures and processes for high-quality data that feed AI models, without this base, AI would not be able to work properly, and correspondingly, firms would fail to unleash the full potential of their data assets. These range from building to the maintenance of strong data pipelines, some of the critical realizations during the development process in AI, ensuring that the models are re-trained continuously, and optimized for accurate and reliable insights. This is where the synergy between data engineering and AI will come in, two areas important toward innovation and growth in business today.

Understanding data types, structures, and sources

The evolution of data has shown the data comes in different forms such as structured, semi-structured, and unstructured, each one needing a different approach for processing and storage. From relational databases through to NoSQL systems, handling data formats such as JSON, XML, or just raw text is important. Sources also range from traditional transactional systems to real-time streaming data from IoT devices.

Data classification

The most important thing in understanding data engineering and AI would be knowledge about the different data types. All these forms of data contribute differently to how AI models will be built, trained, and applied. As discussed above, broadly, data can be divided into three basic types: structured, semi-structured, and unstructured data.

The easiest to work with is structured data. This is the type of data that fits neatly into tables and columns, like what you would find in a traditional relational database. The examples of structured data include customer information like names, addresses, or transaction histories. This type of data is highly organized and follows a defined format, which makes it easy to search, query, and analyze. Due to its organized nature, structured data is most often used in business intelligence, reporting, and analytics. Concerning AI applications, structured data will be used to train models for tasks of classification and prediction.

Not all data, however, is neat. Unstructured data lies at the other end of this spectrum. There is no pre-defined format for this kind of data, and handling can be trickier. Examples include e-mails, postings on social media sites, images, videos, and even audio recordings. Unstructured data is messy, and extracting meaningful insights from it requires specialized techniques, for example, NLP for text data or computer vision for images and videos but despite the complexity, unstructured data is increasingly important in AI applications because it gives rich information that structured data on its own cannot provide. For instance, AI can do sentiment analysis on social media or detect objects in pictures, both tasks requiring the processing of large amounts of unstructured data.

Sitting somewhere in the middle is semi-structured data. It does not apply to a strict table format, such as structured data does, but at the same time, it retains some properties that make it easier to work with than completely unstructured data. A common representation of semi-structured data is **JavaScript Object Notation (JSON)** or **Extensible Markup Language (XML)**, mostly used in web applications or exposed application programming interfaces. Here, the data is preserved in a hierarchical structure with labels or tags that make it easier to parse and retrieve specific pieces of information than in raw, unstructured data.

For instance, a web service may return information about customers in JSON format, and any system that reads this information to seek out certain fields, such as a customer's name or address, may process it.

Each of these data types has its place in AI applications, depending on what kind of problem a developer is trying to solve. Structured data might be useful in AI exercises, such as, predicting customer churning, whereas historic records would be rated against unstructured data for the discovery of patterns in user interactions from social media. Semi-structured data might come in handy during scenarios where one has to integrate external web services or **application programming interface (APIs)** with AI systems.

There are various data types that one needs to learn to make AI systems work with all kinds of information in today's digital world.

Data sources

The sources of data may vary corresponding to the type of data. It majorly recommends that any AI system is only as good as the quality of the data and in terms of diversity and reliability of the sources from which it is drawn. Most fundamentally, there exist two main types of data sources: internal and external.

Internal data sources are generated from within an organization. This simply refers to the system that a business would generally use to manage its core processes, such as enterprise resource planning, customer relationship management systems, or databases tracking sales and inventory among others. An example could be an **enterprise resource planning** (**ERP**) system engaging in the provision of highly detailed information about a company's supply chain, beginning from raw materials to finished goods, while a **customer relationship management** (**CRM**) system may track customer interaction, preferences, and purchase history.

Internal structured data can be generated through systems for operational improvements or fed into AI for better decision-making. This could be, for example, sales data from a CRM system to train an AI model for the prediction of purchasing behavior in the future. For example, machine logs or data from IoT sensors form another couple of good cases of internal data sources. Machines and sensors in the manufacturing or logistics industries emit streams of data related to operational performance, temperature readings, or the condition of their equipment. Apart from regular monitoring, this data could be leveraged into prediction and optimization with regard to system health and process performance. In this sense, usually, continuous and volumetric data becomes relevant in building AI apps endowed with real-time monitoring and predictive maintenance capabilities. External data sources are derived from outside the organization, and they offer great information that supplements data from inside an organization. They also include *Twitter*, *Facebook*, and other social media websites, public datasets, and third-party service providers. For example, such a system developed for brand sentiment tracking purposes could draw information from data scraped from social media posts and online reviews. External data can provide context and a broader view of the marketplace that cannot be delivered by internal data. For example, competitive pricing data scraped from websites could help a retail company in AI models for dynamic readjustment of their pricing strategies.

Another important external source is publicly available data sets. Several governments, institutions, and international organizations make the collected data available to the public for use.

Such datasets can range from the mundane, like demographics or economics, to a variety of weather patterns or even global health statistics. AI applications can use such data to further focus their predictions or model trends arising, perhaps, outside the view of available internal data. For example, an AI application might predict crop yields by combining weather data from a public meteorological service with internal agricultural records. Another trend in using external data sources includes payment to third-party providers for access to their carefully curated data streams. For example, financial institutions might purchase stock market data feeds that will fuel AI algorithms to forecast changes in the stock market or suggest the best investment option. Equally, an e-commerce platform might buy customer behavior data from a third-party provider to enhance skills in product recommendation. This goes a long way in making an AI system have holistic knowledge about the various data sources. The more the sources of data, the richer the insights could be. On the downside, dealing with external data sources raises huge challenges connected with data quality, privacy, and integration. The data engineer ensures that information flows in from these sources and is reliable and up to date, thus ensuring compliance with regulations like GDPR. Besides, integrating any external data with such an internal system is observationally complex, data transformation and validation are carefully done so that the complete set maintains a consensus. In a nutshell, data classification and sources are what underpin data engineering. Structured, unstructured, and semi-structured data all find their places in AI applications, from the simplest prediction to the most complex image or text analysis. Meanwhile, data can originate from internal systems, such as ERP and CRM platforms, or external sources like social media and third-party APIs. The type and source of data are both very critical in the design of AI systems since they directly impact the performance, accuracy, and relevance of the kinds of insights generated.

Navigating the data landscape

Modern data-driven organizations generate and store vast amounts of data every day. Dealing with these vast reams of data and making sense of all the information requires sturdy systems and strategies, here is where some of the central concepts of databases, data warehousing, and data lakes step in. Each one of them serves a different role in handling and processing data with approaches quite distinct and suited for various types of data and use cases.

Database

Databases have been used for the past several decades and form the underpinning of most data systems for storing and managing information. A database is an organized collection of data that is easily accessed, managed, and updated. There are two major categories of databases: relational and NoSQL.

Relational databases are designed to accommodate related data in tables. These tables have rows and columns; each row, in turn, holds a record, while each column shows a data attribute, a customer name, or the price of a product. The data is structured according to a pre-defined format called a **schema** which stipulates how these tables are related. Some examples of relational databases include: MySQL, PostgreSQL, Oracle, and Microsoft SQL Server.

The greatest advantages of relational databases are in the way they ensure data integrity and consistency by primary and foreign keys, hence keeping data correct and properly interlinked within a system. In cases where data is highly structured and relationships between these types of data need to be maintained, relational databases come in handy. For example, a relational database in an e-commerce application would store customer, order, and product information in different tables but with relevant relationships to each other. Such table relationships facilitate complex queries that draw out all orders placed by a given customer or calculate the total sales of a particular product. However, with the further development of data types and use cases, it became obvious that relational databases were not fit to treat unstructured or semi-structured data. That is where NoSQL databases fit in. Unlike relational databases, NoSQL databases do not require a fixed schema and hence prove to be quite flexible and powerful in handling a wide array of data formats.

This is particularly useful for state-of-the-art applications processing unstructured data, such as social media feeds, sensor readings, or multimedia streams.

NoSQL can be document stores like MongoDB, key-value stores like Redis, wide-column stores like Cassandra, or graph databases like Neo4j. Each of these models of NoSQL is targeted to serve a particular kind of data and query, for example, document stores excel at storing complex data structures, such as customer profiles, and retrieving them in a very flexible way without the need for a strict schema. Graph databases are another example, they are designed to establish relationships between data points hence, an application like social networks or recommendation engines would be quite appropriate.

The great thing about NoSQL databases is that they natively support horizontal scaling, making them able to distribute data across multiple servers, so the handling of large volumes of data and high-traffic applications will fit very well in such databases. This feature is highly important in modern systems where data is being created at an unprecedented rate and must be processed in real-time.

Databases form the backbone of data engineering, evolving to meet the demands of scalability, availability, and consistency in modern AI-driven systems. **Cloud-native databases** like Amazon Aurora and Google Cloud Spanner exemplify this shift by offering managed, highly available, and automatically scalable solutions. Meanwhile, **NewSQL systems,** such as, CockroachDB and Google Spanner blend the scalability of NoSQL with the strong consistency of traditional relational databases. Understanding these advancements requires a look at distributed consensus mechanisms like Paxos and Raft, which help coordinate distributed transactions. Additionally, the CAP theorem remains a fundamental concept, highlighting the trade-offs between consistency, availability, and partition tolerance in distributed database design. These trends reflect the ongoing evolution of databases to support AI and large-scale data applications.

All data systems require databases, either relational or NoSQL. Relational databases are appropriate for structured data and those cases in which the consistency of data and the relations between the data points are vital. NoSQL databases provide flexibility and scalability; therefore, they will be applied in modern high-demand applications with unstructured or semi-structured data.

Data warehousing and data lakes

As organizations grew and began to generate a lot of data, more sophisticated methods for storing, managing, and analyzing this data arose: data warehousing and data lakes have been two of the most critical components in modern data architecture.

Data warehouses are specially developed databases engineered to store huge volumes of structured data from different sources at a central location. Unlike traditional, transactionally oriented databases, for instance, those used for updating customer records, data warehouses are specially optimized for querying and reporting. They are therefore very appropriate for business intelligence applications where the purpose is analysis of historical data to gain insight and strategic direction. This means that a data warehouse will normally aggregate all the data from several sources, like transactional databases, ERP, and CRM systems, and put it into one format. Typically, data will be cleaned and transformed and then stored in pre-optimized schemas for querying. Such a consolidation process, along with preparing data for querying, is termed quite simply **extract, transform, load** (**ETL**).

After the data has been stored, the warehouse is then queried to generate reports, dashboards, and insights with SQL that help businesses understand trends, performance, and opportunities.

The following figure illustrates the typical flow of data within a modern data-driven organization, showcasing how databases, data warehouses, and data lakes interact to support analytics and business decisions:

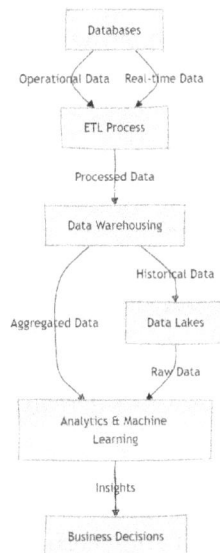

Figure 1.2: Databases vs. data warehouse vs. data lakes

Some major advantages of data warehousing include the quick processing of large historical data and the execution of several queries running across different data sets. For instance, a retail company may be using a data warehouse to store several years of sales data that will be used in running trend analysis, finding best-selling products, and even demand forecasting. Since the data is structured and organized in a warehouse, such queries can be run efficiently over huge datasets. However, when the data became more diverse and plentiful, especially in the case of unstructured data from sources like social media, IoT devices, and logs, data warehouses alone could not do the job. That is when data lakes entered the mainstream.

A **data lake** is a central repository that enables any organization to store all types of structured and unstructured data at scale. While a data warehouse needs to transform the data and organize it according to a pre-defined schema before storing it, in a data lake, there is no transformation of raw data. That means organizations can ingest any source of data, structured data from databases, semi-structured data such as JSON files, or unstructured data like videos and images, and store everything in one place.

The truly awesome fact about a data lake is its flexibility. Since the data that is stored is in native form, it can be processed and analyzed in many ways, depending on organizational needs, for instance, data scientists may use ML algorithms to scan unstructured data housed in the lake for specific patterns or trends.

Meanwhile, traditional **business intelligence** (**BI**) could still be used by analysts to run queries against the structured data in the lake. Another important point is that data lakes perform low-cost storage of huge volumes of data which makes them good at hosting huge data sets holding data that would never find space within traditional data warehouses. However, data lakes do come with their own problems because all data is stored in their raw form, it can be difficult to manage and organize. Without proper governance and metadata management, it becomes a data swamp, whereby all of your data becomes a jumbled mess, hardly useful for analysis. This will be mitigated by the investment in the proper tools and processes to ensure the data within the lake is properly cataloged, tagged, and easily accessible to the right users.

In summary, data warehouses and lakes perform complementary roles in modern data architecture. More specifically, data warehouses primarily serve as a means of retention and analysis of structured data, typically business intelligence and reporting. By bringing flexibility to store and process a vast amount of structured, semi-structured, and unstructured data, data lakes become a critical component of big data and AI applications. To that very end, both will allow an organization to exploit its assets in data for operational insights, predictive analytics, or advanced AI-driven applications.

ETL processes

ETL processes are the backbone of data engineering, enabling the efficient movement of data from various sources to storage systems. In scalable data engineering in AI, we will highlight how these processes clean, transform, and prepare data for use in AI and ML models, ensuring data quality and readiness for analysis.

ETL fundamentals

ETL is one of the most fundamental processes in the world of data engineering. It simply encapsulates all source-to-destination operations that move data to a location where it is efficiently and effectively analyzed. ETL process is very critical in ensuring that your data is clean, organized, and ready for analysis, particularly with very large business, AI, or ML datasets.

Extraction is the initial step of gathering data from independent sources. These can be as simple as traditional databases and spreadsheets or as complex as systems, CRM platforms, sensors, social media feeds, and web scraping services. Here, raw data is collected and then moved to some staging area for further processing. One of the major challenges that need to be overcome here is to ensure that the extraction process does not negatively impact the source system performance, particularly if this should be a live production system.

Once the data is extracted, it passes into the **transform** phase. This is where raw data is cleaned, filtered, and formatted for the target system's needs. These operations may embrace a wide span of tasks: eliminating redundancy, error correction, changing the data type, and aggregating values. Quite often, normalization or standardization of data will be necessary to make it homogeneous for the system under consideration, for instance, if one was drawing data from a variety of customer databases, the Transform phase would ensure that all records have a standard way of writing names, addresses, and dates.

Finally, in the **load** phase, the transformed data is loaded into the target system, which might be a data warehouse, a data lake, or some other database. Once loaded, the data is prepared for use in analytics, reporting, or as an input to machine learning models. The goal of the load step is to ensure that the transfer of data to the target system is effective and lossless, with minimal loads on the performance of the target system.

Traditional vs. modern ETL tools

In the early days of data engineering, traditional tools like Informatica were responsible for the ETL process. Informatica and other such tools were designed to help businesses master the intricacies of moving data between disparate systems. Most of such traditional tools involve a lot of manual setup and configuration and would generally be deployed on-premises. While they were powerful and flexible, they were not particularly designed for the size and complexity of today's data systems, especially with the onset of cloud computing and big data.

As the field of data engineering evolved, so have the tools used to manage this ETL process. Modern ETL tools are designed to handle data at scale and have flexibility, speed, and scalability in mind. For example, Apache Kafka is a new generation tool for handling real-time data streams; therefore, it would be very fitting for applications that need near real-time data processing and analysis. Kafka does not work like traditional ETL tools; it is not about moving data from A to B, rather it provides the capability of inter-system walkability through publishing and subscribing to data streams. It becomes scalable for several use cases.

Another modern ETL tool is **data build tool** (**dbt**). This ETL tool breaks the traditional ETL tool approach, focusing on the T of ETL. It views data engineers and analysts' transformation logic, usually written in SQL to transform the raw data into formats fit for analysis. Modularity and integrations with modern cloud data platforms such as Snowflake, BigQuery, and Redshift set dbt apart from Informatica and other tools like it. dbt lets teams manage their data transformations in a way that scales with the intricacy of their data systems.

ETL in a retail business

For example, consider a retail company that sells online and in-store. The company has a variety of data sources to capture sales information, customers' behavior, and the level of inventory available for the respective products. The online sales data may be maintained in a cloud-based e-commerce platform while in-store sales data is stored in the local POS system. Customer data is stored in a CRM and the inventory data is in a different supply chain management system.

All these disparate systems combine to present the retail company with a complete view of the business, moving data into a unified data warehouse, something that falls under the ETL process.

In the extract phase, data is pulled to a staging area from the e-commerce platform, **point of sale** (**POS**) system, CRM, and supply chain management system. The way data is stored through APIs, database queries, or file transfer, determines the pulling method. For example, the e-commerce platform may expose an API from which the company pulls order data while extraction from the POS system may need a direct database query to extract sales data.

During the second phase, transform, the data is cleaned and standardized. For example, the company might have to standardize date formatting between source systems, *MM/DD/YYYY* to *YYYY-MM-DD*, or the format of customer IDs between the CRM and e-commerce systems. The organization would also start filtering at this stage duplicate entries, wrong entries, and people who canceled the orders or returned merchandise.

Apart from the cleaning of data, the transformation stage may also involve aggregating data to come up with summary tables. For instance, a company might want to add sales data daily to have weekly or monthly totals to review trends more easily. In this case, if the goal of the company is to make future sales predictions using ML, then the transformation step might also include feature engineering, whereby extra variables are created from the raw data.

Finally, in the load phase, the company loads the source system data onto the company's data warehouse. With the data now in the warehouse, the company's analysts will run queries over the data and generate reports to derive business insights. This may be for the analysis of the trends of customer purchases to decide on the marketing strategies, or it may be for tracking the level of various products' inventory to make sure that the maximum-selling products never run out of stock. These datasets can further be used for training ML models to predict future sales or to identify potential customer churn.

By doing so, moving from traditional ETL tools like Informatica to modern ones like Kafka and dbt; the retail company will be better placed to handle scale and data complexity. With Kafka, they can process this data in nearly real-time, a very relevant factor in applications, such as, personalized marketing or dynamic pricing. And with dbt, they can modularize and scale their data transformations to ensure that their data warehouse is always topped up with clean, organized data ready for analysis and subsequent decision-making.

Importance of data quality and integrity

Data quality and integrity have become the pillars of modern data-driven businesses. The quality of data is at the core of any project that survives on data, most especially on AI and ML. Poor quality data produces wrong conclusions, biased models, and then bad decisions. Ensuring that the input data is correct, consistent, and complete becomes important in any AI application and business analytics.

Data quality is not strictly a technical problem but one of the business must-haves. The result of using poor-quality data could be flawed analytics, lost opportunities, and even regulatory penalties. Accordingly, high-quality data is critical for any business to have trust in the data and make correct decisions based thereon. If your data is of poor quality or not intact, AI models are likely to make inaccurate predictions or have innate biases, resulting in poor business decisions, not forgetting the severe damage to the company's reputation. Data quality has to be taken seriously at all levels of an organization.

For instance, a health provider uses AI to predict an outcome for a patient based on medical records and data from the patient. This could then mean that an AI system that is fed incomplete or inaccurate data will yield misleading diagnoses or set wrong treatment plans. There is when the need for quality data comes into play because people's lives and health outcomes hang in the balance. If the quality of the data is bad, the most sophisticated AI algorithms in the world also fail to execute a correct, actionable inference.

Data quality frameworks

A data quality framework is an organized way of producing data of certain standards. A comprehensive data quality framework will evaluate data for different dimensions such as accuracy, completeness, consistency, and timeliness. For example, accuracy ensures that data represents an accurate snapshot of the real-world scenario it is supposed to denote while completeness checks the capture of all necessary data points.

The majority of data quality frameworks normally specify some processes for data profiling, monitoring, cleansing, and remediation. This will be the first step in this strategy, data profiling, it may include studying existing data to determine the structure, content, and relationship of the data. In doing so, some problems, such as missing values, outliers, or inconsistencies, could be detected at an early stage. Data monitoring is the process that checks if the quality of data remains consistent over time while cleansing is correcting errors or inconsistencies of data. Last but not least, processes for remediation are put in place to try and prevent poor quality from entering the system in the first place, preventive measures so to speak, for instance, an e-commerce company needs customer transaction data for it to understand the behavior of buying and personalize marketing efforts. In this case, a data quality framework would ensure that all customer records are accurate in contact details and transaction histories so that AI models could predict future purchases or make effective recommendations.

Bad data, for instance, product details that are not correct or missing transaction histories would throw off defective predictions and produce bad customer experiences.

Data governance frameworks

Governance for data means the overall management of data availability, usability, integrity, and security across every organization. A data governance framework is important to ensure data quality, which must ensure conformance of data practices to business objectives and regulatory requirements. At its core, data governance provides guidelines about the proper handling of data regarding quality and security.

A sound framework of data governance helps businesses stay in control of their data by defining clear policies, roles, and responsibilities associated with the management of data. It defines the system of governance over data ownership, access control, and retention and compliance with applicable laws and regulations, such as GDPR, HIPAA, or CCPA, ensuring appropriate protection for sensitive data and an organization to face regulatory audits or potential breaches, for example, a large financial institution that deals with thousands of transactions daily needs an effective governance framework to align the institution with industry regulations.

The majority of these regulations require financial data to be accurate, securely stored, and accessed by authorized personnel only. A properly implemented data governance framework will set out processes for data handling and access, thereby enabling the institution to meet such requirements by ensuring that the data is reliable and that security breaches are minimized.

An effective governance framework also spells out issues related to data integrity, ensuring that a given dataset has not been tampered with or otherwise manipulated in ways not authorized, for instance, this is highly relevant in both the financial and health sectors, where tampered data may mean serious legal and operational implications. For instance, in healthcare, accurate and consistent patient data instills the best care across multiple systems; a robust data governance framework can ensure that integrity.

Data quality and governance in retail

Imagine a retail company running physical stores and an online marketplace. The company collects an enormous amount of data from various sources, such as POS systems in the stores, activity on their website, customer reviews, and interactions on social media. In this case, if the number of data sources is huge, one would need to take complete care of the quality and integrity of data.

In order to deal with this, a data quality framework is implemented by the company. They regularly profile and monitor their customer data for its accuracy. Suppose the address of a customer is missing or his e-mail is mis-formatted; it will flag the system and correct the data before it gets into the analytics pipeline. Checks are run to ensure that all critical customer details, including purchase history, are fully captured. It ensures that the customer segmentation models of the company are accurate and that marketing efforts go to target markets.

The company will be establishing a data governance framework in parallel. This would spell out the roles and responsibilities of who gets to manage which level of customer data. For example, the marketing department might have access to anonymized customer data for campaign development. More sensitive information, such as payment details, may rest within the finance department alone. The data governance framework stipulates further policies on how long the data can be held, along with compliance requirements as dictated by privacy laws like GDPR.

The company can now trust its data to be accurate, complete, and securely managed. It will also be better positioned to derive more reliable insights from its data, enhance its marketing efforts, and improve customer satisfaction. They can confidently pass a regulatory audit with the robust data governance framework in place and reduce the risks associated with data breaches.

Conclusion

Data engineering is at the core of the success of AI and ML systems. It is not just large volumes of data but also that the data needs to be clean, structured, and ready for use in the effectiveness of AI applications. As we have seen throughout this chapter, the quality of that data directly affects the performance of AI models; hence, data engineering is effectively the backbone of any modern AI-driven business. It lays the foundations for everything else, from an understanding of different data types and structures to building robust pipelines and maintaining data integrity.

Imagine you are building with LEGOs, you will need all the right pieces, collected carefully, to create something amazing. In the next chapter, we will learn the best ways to gather those pieces, whether they are in big bins or coming in constantly. We will explore how to get the data you need, make sure it is useful and see how it powers things like smart apps and business decisions.

Join our book's Discord space

Join the book's Discord Workspace for Latest updates, Offers, Tech happenings around the world, New Release and Sessions with the Authors:

https://discord.bpbonline.com

CHAPTER 2

Managing Data Collection

Introduction

Data collection is the systematic process of gathering raw data from various sources to capture useful information in view of analysis, processing, or decision-making. It is the starting point of this data pipeline from where the data is acquired, either from external or internal sources, such as IoT devices, sensors, applications, websites, APIs, logs, or databases.

This includes the scoping of relevant data points, how their capture is to be affected, and the quality of the collected data in terms of correctness, completeness, and readiness for ingestion, processing, and storage. Data collection may be done in real-time, continuous feeds, or in batches, i.e., intermittent data, depending on the nature of the data or what the organization requires.

Structure

The chapter discusses the following topics:

- Scalable data collection techniques
- Performance optimization
- Ensuring reliability and data quality

- Checks on data quality

- Data governance and cost management

- Impact of AI and BI

- Real-world case studies

Objectives

By the end of this chapter, readers will have a comprehensive understanding of the essential principles that underpin effective data collection, recognizing its pivotal role in building a successful data strategy. They will learn how to identify and select the right tools and technologies tailored to their specific business needs, ensuring that the data collected is both relevant and actionable. Additionally, the chapter will also grab readers' attention on best practices for maintaining data quality, focusing on accuracy, consistency, and completeness, which are critical for deriving meaningful insights. Ethical considerations will also be highlighted, guiding readers in how to responsibly collect data while respecting privacy and complying with legal requirements. Furthermore, readers will explore strategies for managing challenges associated with data collection, such as handling large volumes of data and integrating data from diverse sources. By the end of the chapter, readers will be well-prepared to approach data collection with a thoughtful, strategic mindset, ensuring that their data initiatives are built on a solid and ethical foundation.

Scalable data collection techniques

Data forms the lifeblood of the modern enterprise in this digital era. Each interaction, each transaction, and every process generate data. It is in a business's ability to collect and analyze that data where the key differentiator lies. As businesses grow, the volume of data they generate and the challenge of collecting data at a scale become increasingly complex. Big data puts a greater demand that often cannot be matched by the traditional methods, considering that these may or may not work well in small datasets. This is where scalable data collection techniques come into play. Scalability is not just a technical requirement but also a strategic necessity. This would be what helps the organization to efficiently process lots of data and, therefore, remain capable of extracting more value from their data as their growth goes on.

Key aspects of data collection include:

- **Source identification**: Identifying the source from which data is obtained, such as devices, applications, or APIs.

- **Data acquisition**: It involves the capturing and extracting of data from various sources, such as the use of APIs, web scraping, or direct inputs from devices.

- **Data validation**: It means the validation of the correctness, completeness, and reliability of data collected before the data passes into the pipeline for further usage.

Good data collection lies at the heart of any decent data strategy in today's data-driven world. From gathering customer feedback to monitoring website interactions, right down to capturing sensor data from smart devices, how we collect data informs and shapes everything else afterward. However, managing this process is far from straightforward. It is not just about tool and technology selection, but also about the validity, relevance, and ethics of the data being captured.

This chapter discusses the collection process. It discusses challenges and best practices that would help you lay a solid foundation for your data initiatives.

Scalability in data collection

Scalability, in relation to data collection, is the ability of a system to process increased volumes of data without performance or efficiency compromise. As organizations grow, the demands for data collection sometimes increase exponentially. What began as a rather manageable process, collecting data from perhaps a few sources can become unmanageably large when the number of data points, varieties, and sources multiplies. Scalability refers to the assurance that when demands are higher, data collection systems could be scaled up by adding more resources or optimizing the already used ones without performance compromise.

There are quite a number of key factors impacting scalability in the collection of data. First and foremost, comes the system's architecture through which data collection is performed. A typical scalable architecture is one that is distributed; hence it can share the workload across multiple servers or nodes. Distributed, the system can scale data volumes by adding nodes to the network rather than depending on a single server. The processing of data should be efficient. A system that can process data in real-time, or near real-time is bound to be more scalable since it processes the flow of coming data without batching up the processes.

Scalable data collection techniques

There is a need for efficient management techniques to deal with ever-increasing volume and variety for an organization to be truly scalable in data collection. One of the high recommendations is the use of a distribution system for data collection. The latter allows for the distribution in a distributed system since data collection tasks are divided among several nodes or servers, and each node performs some share of the workload. This approach has an advantage not only regarding performance by parallelizing tasks of data gathering but it also by improving fault tolerance, whereby the system can function even if one or several nodes fail.

Another key technique is to balance real-time and batch data collection. Real-time data capture involves collecting and processing data as soon as it is generated. This kind of data is necessary for applications in which the captured information requires immediate analysis, such as the continuous monitoring of sensor data or user behavior on a website. In contrast, batch data collection requires gathering data over a period of time and then processing it in bulk. Although less resource-intensive, batch processing is best for applications where data freshness is less critical. Combining both real-time and batch processing can strike a balance that best fits the scalability requirements being targeted by an organization.

Figure 2.1 illustrates an end-to-end data collection architecture, showcasing the entire data pipeline from data sources to processing, storage, AI applications, and monitoring. It begins with data ingestion, where raw data from APIs, IoT devices, and logs is captured via streaming or batch pipelines. This data flows into real-time and batch processing layers, where it is transformed and stored in a data lake or warehouse. From here, the processed data is used in feature stores, BI analytics, AI model training, and real-time AI applications. To ensure data integrity, a monitoring and data quality system is in place, handling schema validation, anomaly detection, dashboards, and alerts.

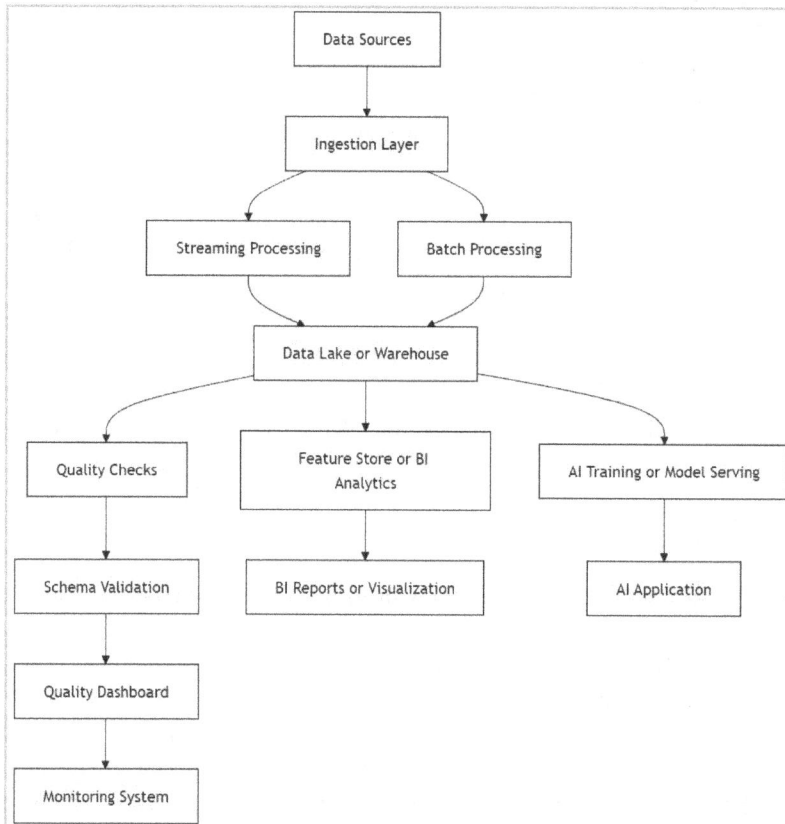

***Figure 2.1**: End-to-end data collection architecture*

Cloud-based solutions are another avenue for scalable data gathering. The cloud makes dynamically scaling resources up or down available on demand, based on volume. It might be that an organization, for instance, starts with a small amount of cloud storage and computing resources. As the data grows, it can easily ramp up because there is no longer a need for hefty upfront investments in hardware. Secondly, many big data cloud services are oriented to collect data on a large-scale. In that respect, it is much easier for an organization to implement scalable solutions by using those tools and services out-of-the-box, rather than creating them from scratch.

Further insights

AWS Kinesis data streams are an example of a distributed data collection system. The typical processing times and throughput depend on the stream configuration.

The following are the performance and scaling considerations for Kinesis streams:

- **Shards**: Each shard in a Kinesis stream supports up to 1 MB/second data write and 2 MB/second data read with a limit of 1,000 records per second.

- **Latency**: Kinesis usually has a latency of sub-second to a few seconds for processing data from the moment it is ingested to when it is made available for consumption.

- **Scaling**: In order to handle higher throughput, more shards can be added, but this requires balancing cost and complexity as each shard incurs additional charges.

Best practices in scalable data collection

Scalable data collection involves more than the selection of appropriate tools but also encompasses best practices that ensure the system is efficient, even as it grows bigger and bigger. Among the most important of these is the assurance of data quality when scaling. As the volume of information increased, so did the possibility of errors, inconsistencies, and duplication. These could be mitigated if the organization instituted strong data validation and cleansing as part of its data collection workflows. It may include automated checks for missing or malformed data, outlier handling, and error correction processes.

Other best practices include scaling performance and designing a system to support large volumes of data, but it is crucial to ensure efficient access to that data. It will entail optimally collecting data with minimal latency, thereby reducing resource use. Techniques for this include data compression, efficient encoding of data, and the use of in-memory processing.

Another consideration is the handling of different formats and sources of data. Any scaled-up setup for data collection may contain immense variation in data format, from structured data like JSON and XML to unstructured data like text and images. Given this diversity, the organization should select tools that can support most data formats and easily integrate with other data sources. This also allows the system to be versatile and open to whatever new kinds of data may emerge.

Third and last, monitoring of the data gathering system ensures scalability. As it grows, the complexity of managing and tracking various issues also increases. By instituting strong procedures for monitoring and logging, this helps in the early detection of problems before they affect performance or reliability. Maintenance like regular updating of software, optimization of configuration, and scaling of resources will go a long way in ensuring continued high performance of the system.

The following figure shows various data sources, collection mechanisms, and data collection layer of scalable data collection:

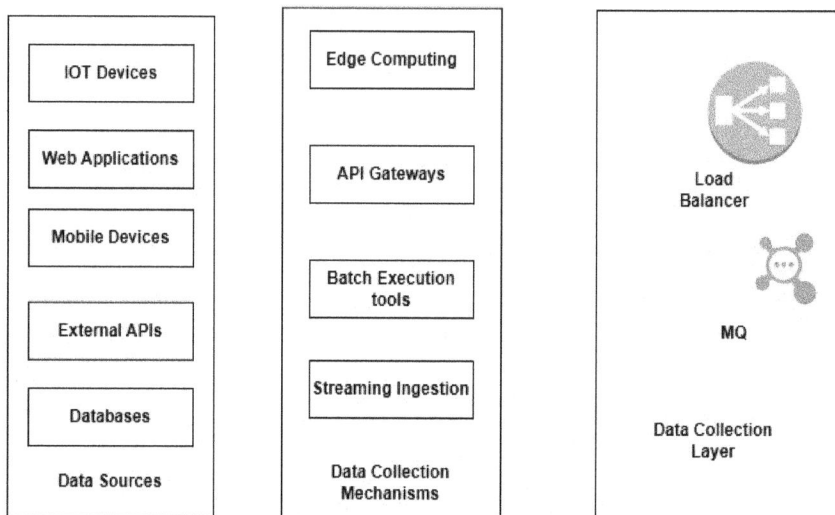

Figure 2.2: Scalable data collection

Technology tools for scalable data collection

Selecting the appropriate technology tools is a key activity in the implementation of a scalable data collection system. There are several tools and platforms in the market that address the challenges of scalable data collection, each catering to different needs and offering unique features.

Apache Kafka is one of the most popular tools used in scalable data collection. It is an open-source platform for distributed streaming that enables organizations to collect and process big streams of data in real-time. Kafka architectures are designed for high-throughput, low-latency data streams which renders Kafka quite suitable in an environment where speed and reliability matter. This provides a minimum delay in handling big volumes of data, ensuring that while the data grows, Kafka scales up with demand and does not sacrifice performance.

Amazon Kinesis is a cloud service that collects and processes data in real time. Part of Amazon Web Services, it tightly integrates with other AWS services, positioning Kinesis as a good option for customers who use the AWS ecosystem. With Kinesis, one can capture, process, and analyze data streams in real-time. The pricing of Kinesis is followed by a pay-as-you-use model, offering users cost-effective scalability. This flexibility in function makes Kinesis particularly useful for things like IoT device monitoring, log analysis, and clickstream data processing.

For organizations focused on batch-oriented data processing, **Apache NiFi** provides a robust and flexible solution. NiFi is an open-source tool for data integration, automating data movement between systems. It works especially great for environments where there is a need for collecting big volumes of data and transforming or routing them to various destinations. With vast support for multiple data formats and protocols,NiFi's drag-and-drop interface allows for use by the most technically inexperienced user to the most advanced while its highly scalable architecture allows it to grow to demands for increased data.

Another strong engine for batch and real-time data processing, **Google Cloud Dataflow** is a part of the Google Cloud Platform. Dataflow provides fully managed, auto-scaling data processing pipelines to process large amounts of data. Its integration with other Google Cloud services, including BigQuery and Cloud Storage, simply boosts its scalability and makes it one of the top contenders to consider as part of an organization's strategy to utilize cloud computing for its intake requirements.

Flume is a tool in the Apache ecosystem created to collect, aggregate, and move large volumes of log data from various sources into some sort of centralized data store. The architecture of Flume can be scaled up significantly, hence it can handle high volumes with low latency. This makes Flume especially useful in environments where log data coming from distributed systems needs to be collected and, in turn, analyzed in real-time such as in monitoring and security applications.

Each of these has variable strengths and tool selection should be informed by the specific needs of the organization, the types of data collected, and the scalability requirements of the data collection process. If an organization selects the right tools and deploys best practices in place, then a truly scalable data collection system is developed to meet the long-term growth and data-driven initiatives of that organization.

Performance optimization

Data engineering encompasses performance optimization wherein the collection of data is efficient, swift, and ready to scale. The increased dependency of organizations on data for decision-making implies that inefficiency in any part of data collection may have far-reaching impacts, from delayed analytics to increased operational costs. Optimizing performance is not just about improving speed, it is also important to minimize resource consumption, ensure the scalability of a system, and provide high reliability.

Understanding performance bottlenecks

Let us understand what may cause performance bottlenecks in data collection systems before we explore optimization strategies. The challenges normally include:

- **Network latency**: Data collection typically involves data transfer over networks and can exhibit a good degree of latency if not treated appropriately. High latency especially affects systems that rely on real-time data.

- **Data volume**: The greater the volume, the more the storage systems and pipelines get overwhelmed, hence slowing them down. This is especially the case in systems that were not designed for such scale.

- **Processing power**: In cases where the collecting or processing systems are not computational enough to handle data, the process of ingestion slows down to a crawl, or even hampers the flow. This is mostly exacerbated by poor computation resource allocation.

- **Concurrency**: Processing several data streams or a huge volume of data simultaneously imposes strains on a platform not designed to handle concurrency.

These sorts of challenges can be resolved by applying some kind of optimization that allows better performance of the whole system, from the data pipeline.

Optimization of network performance

Among the effective ways for handling performance issues in data collection systems is optimizing network performance in cases of distributed or cloud-based systems.

Several strategies will be able to reduce network latency and enhance data throughput in such situations, as follows:

- **Data compression**: Compressing data before transmission can drastically reduce the amount of data that needs to be transmitted over the network. It reduces transfer time and bandwidth consumption. Modern algorithms for compression are rather efficient and generally bring little overhead.

- **Edge computing**: Collecting and processing data closer to the source reduces latency by lessening the distance over which data may travel. It offloads a part of the job from the hub and provides quicker responses with far better load sharing.

- **Efficient protocols**: Using binary protocols like Protocol Buffers or Apache Avro could potentially be many times faster compared to text-based protocols like JSON or XML, especially in volume scenarios.

By focusing on these areas, the time that data takes to traverse across the networks can be brought down dramatically, hence allowing faster and more reliable data collection.

Optimizing storage and access

Once data has been collected, another key to better performance lies in optimizing how it is stored and accessed. In fact, efficient storage strategies can ensure that collection does not get slowed down due to backlogs or storage limitations.

Some key strategies namely partitioning, indexing, and caching can significantly improve data retrieval and processing times in large-scale systems, as follows:

- **Partitioning or sharding**: When data is divided across a multitude of databases or even sharded across a set of different nodes, it allows for the distribution of the load, hence allowing for more efficient access and retrieval of information. This will be useful when huge volumes of data must be processed since parallel processing would reduce contention on any particular resource.

- **Indexing**: Proper indexing of your data can reduce the time taken to retrieve data drastically. By creating indexes on a field that is often queried, the database may access the required data much faster and, therefore, speed up the entire pipeline of data.

- **Caching**: The caching mechanisms can greatly improve performance by in-memory storage of frequently accessed data, hence reducing the need to repeatedly access slower storage systems. It is most effective when repeated access to the same data occurs several times within small intervals.

Combining these techniques helps make sure that data is not only efficiently stored but also accessed and processed as fast as possible.

Load balancing and parallel processing

Systems should be designed for very high load and use parallel processing of data collection and processing wherever possible. Some critical strategies namely, load balancing, parallel processing, and the selection between batch and stream processing play a significant role in optimizing the flow and management of large data workloads, as follows:

- **Load balancing**: It distributes the oncoming load of traffic across multiple servers or nodes to avoid dependency on one node. This keeps the process fast and reliable, avoiding bottlenecks in data collection even when the load increases.

- **Parallel processing**: Unlike the collection and processing of data in serial form, systems can be developed to process it in parallel. Chunks of tasks can be broken down and with parallel processing, it can give the same result, hence reducing overall time taken for data collection and analysis. An example is that frameworks, such as Apache Kafka and Apache Flink provide out-of-the-box parallel data processing to guarantee efficient data collection at scale.

- **Batch vs. stream processing**: Sometimes, performance optimization requires switching between batch and stream processing. It is possible to collect big chunks at a time in batch processing, reducing the need for frequent interactions with storage systems. Stream processing is usually used in cases when data is needed on a continuous real-time basis which makes it generally more efficient while dealing with continuous flows of data. Choosing one of these approaches depends on a concrete data-gathering task.

Horizontal and vertical scaling

As the volume of data is increasing with each passing day, your infrastructure of data collection must be able to scale up without performance degradation. A brief about horizontal scaling and vertical scaling, as follows:

- **Horizontal scaling**: Horizontal scaling refers to the addition of more servers or nodes in a system where data collection work is distributed among multiple machines. It is often far more cost-effective than throttling up an individual machine, and it usually provides load balancing rather effectively. Cloud platforms also allow for elastic scalability of their provided resources, such as AWS, Azure, and Google Cloud.

- **Vertical scaling**: This refers to upgrading your existing machines by adding more RAM or computing power to them. In general, this is simpler to do but often has limits since there is only so much you can upgrade on a single machine before hitting physical or financial constraints.

Accordingly, a great deal of importance should be given to the selection of a correct scaling method that would provide your use case with the best results while developing a scalable data intake system. This would typically involve horizontal scaling for cloud-based architectures, or vertical scaling if you are dealing with on-premises systems and your hardware resources are severely limited.

Figure 2.3 explains how horizontal and vertical scaling happens. On the left, more servers are being added and they communicate. However, on the right, there is a single server but with more added CPU and RAM.

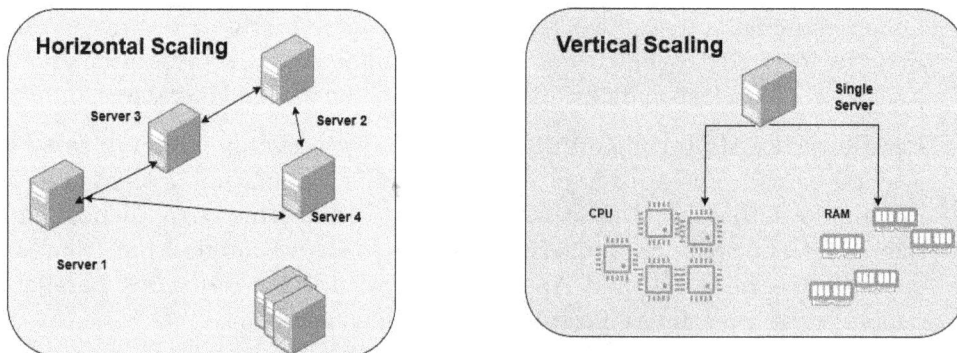

Figure 2.3: Horizontal scaling vs. vertical scaling

Monitoring and metrics

It always pays to be vigilant about the performance of one's data collection system. Tracking your performance with tools such as Prometheus, Grafana, or AWS CloudWatch will provide real-time metrics and insights into the health of your systems. Proactive performance monitoring lets you find performance issues before they reach criticality.

Some essential performance metrics that can help identify bottlenecks, improve load distribution, and ensure balanced resource consumption, as follows:

- **Latency metrics**: Network latency monitoring will provide a way to find the bottlenecks in this pipeline. If latency spikes, then it might be indicative of an issue with your network, your data compression algorithms, or how you balance loads.

- **Throughput metrics**: These deal with the amount of data that your system is collecting and processing within a particular time frame. Consistently benchmarking these metrics will help you see if the system is performing with the expected capacity and tune the system accordingly.

- **Resource utilization**: Monitoring the trend of CPU, memory, and storage helps in knowing how well your infrastructure is utilized. In case some nodes/servers are at a high workload, whereas others are sitting idle, this could indicate the need for better load balancing or horizontal scaling.

Ensuring reliability and data quality

Reliability and quality of data are the bedrock of any data engineering framework. As more organizations become data-driven, their inability to capture reliable and quality data becomes highly critical for informed business decisions, enabling ML models, and creating competitive differentiators in the market. The quality of the data leads directly to faulty insight, misused resources, and even reputational damage. Indeed, reliability and quality could be guaranteed only by an entire set of practices and technologies able to ensure the accuracy, consistency, and trustworthiness of data throughout its life cycle.

Importance of data reliability

Reliability in data ingestion refers to the consistency and dependability of the data being captured. It ensures that whatever data is supposed to be captured gets captured every single time, under changing external conditions or the systems in the back. Unreliable data can cause a ripple effect where even analytics teams create flawed reports due to a single incorrect assumption and machine learning models generate bad predictions. In such industries as healthcare, finance, and autonomous systems, each of these might turn out to have serious, life-threatening consequences.

The system for gathering data reliably has several factors that it needs to take into consideration, including the consistency of the data over a period of time and its availability.

For example, sensor data coming from IoT devices or logs from software applications should reflect coherent results, without fluctuating based on system or network issues. If there are several interruptions in gathering data because of network outages or system crashes, the system should be strong enough to handle such disruptions seamlessly.

Some key considerations for ensuring your system can effectively manage interruptions such as network outages or system crashes are as follows:

- **Completeness**: The missing data often leads to failure or distortions in downstream processes. Therefore, completeness ensures that data for all the requirements is captured, and no record or partial data inputs are missed.

- **Reliability**: It is the basis of data quality. Without reliable systems that ensure that the data is correctly captured, any effort toward maintaining data quality will never pay off.

Role of data quality in decision-making

Data quality entails more than reliability; the data is fit for its purpose. High-quality data fulfills the following factors:

- **Accurate**: It correctly represents real-world phenomena.
- **Timely**: It is available when required.
- **Complete**: All the required data is captured.
- **Consistent**: It is the same across the data sets.
- **Relevant**: It serves the purpose of the use for which it is put to.

Good quality data facilitates more effective decision-making, reduced chances of error, and effectiveness of insights from business data. On the other hand, poor data quality more often results in poorly informed strategies, erroneous resource usage, and high operational risks. Data quality is not a spot effort; it is a continuous process of consistently and recurrently monitoring, validating, and correcting.

The proactive organizational steps taken to reduce the risks posed by inconsistency in data, system downtimes, or network failures create the root for reliability in building data collection.

The following are several ways to build reliability in your data collection process:

- **Redundant systems**: Redundancy is one of the important methods of ensuring system reliability. In this case, an organization may apply multiple systems of data collection or make backups, so that in the event of the failure of one system, the other can support operationalization without disruption. In the context of storage solutions, redundancy refers to the need for backing up data at different locations to minimize the chances of data loss.

- **Failover mechanisms**: The failover systems automatically switch to the backup system in case of failure in the primary operating system, for instance, in the case of a distributed system, in the case of one server going down, the failover mechanisms will automatically redirect all data collection activities to another server for continuity.

- **Fault-tolerant design**: Fault tolerance allows the general system to keep working in case of failure within any constituent part. It can be enabled by the implementation of different error detection and correction techniques, load balancing, and retries as a means of coping with transient errors that could arise from network disruptions.

- **Monitoring and alerts**: Due to this, reliability needs to monitor the data collection systems continuously. This is achieved by using software such as Grafana, Prometheus, and CloudWatch, which can be configured to track KPIs and send notifications of any anomalies in real-time. In case anything was to go wrong, an alert system would trigger along with interventions of the teams concerned well before any data gets lost or corrupted.

- **Data integrity checks**: One best practice includes adding integrity checks at every point in the process of data collection. It would be easy to check using checksum and hash values, for instance, if data had not been changed during transmission. Another example is the application of end-to-end encryption so that data can be kept safe from any alterations while in transport, ensuring that the data is reliable from its creation right through to its delivery.

- **Data quality management frameworks**: The quality of the data demands a proper framework to ensure that all aspects touching on data collection, storage, and usage are properly observed. The key components of a data quality management framework include:

  o **Data profiling**: It involves looking at the incoming data for assessment in terms of quality, structure, and relevance. Through this process, one can normally detect some important problems, such as the presence of missing values, inconsistent formats, or outliers. Profiling usually occurs at the early stages of data ingestion to ensure that only good-quality data goes into the system.

  o **Data validation**: It ensures the data being acquired follows certain pre-set rules and standards. The validation can be performed at various levels-from input to storage for more processing-ensuring correctness, consistency, and usability for the purpose intended.

General checks that may be used for data validation include:

- **Format validation**: Format validation ensures that data adheres to a predefined structure or pattern, such as verifying that dates are in *MM/DD/YYYY* format or that numeric fields contain only valid numbers.

- **Range validation**: It ensures values fall within acceptable ranges, such as temperature being between -30° to 50°C. Others include uniqueness to help avoid duplicates, which distorts analysis and results. Data cleansing is the process of correcting or removing data that is inaccurate, duplicated, or incomplete. Ideally, information should be captured correctly at the source, but no system in this world is perfect, so errors may occur. Data cleansing helps correct those issues before they spread in the system.

Automation can flag or correct issues in real time, thereby ensuring that whatever bad data might be present is rectified before it could ever have an opportunity to disrupt business. Sometimes, higher-order issues require manual intervention, but again, automation greatly expedites the process.

Standardization

Data often originates from different sources and normally possesses different formats, naming conventions, and structures. Standardizing means making the data uniform irrespective of origin. Such an environment pops up in cases when data is fetched from heterogeneous systems, such as IoT, social media, or customer bases.

This, in turn, helps in the easier integration and analysis of data because the consistency of data formats will yield more correct queries and machine learning models. Standardization of date formats or numerical precision ensures that analytics pipelines do not encounter unexpected mismatches in data.

Automation in data quality management

Automation plays an essential role in data quality regarding scaling. Intelligent intake systems can handle hundreds of thousands of volumes, and it cannot be practical to perform quality checks individually. Automated tools and frameworks like Talend, Apache NiFi, and Informatica provide advanced mechanisms for quality at every juncture of the data pipeline. The various types of validation mechanisms for ensuring data quality are as follows:

- **Real-time validation**: Automation facilitates real-time data validation. It flags any anomaly as and when it occurs and automatically initiates responses, such as sending notifications and rejecting faulty data.

- **Self-healing systems**: Some forms of automation are designed to discover issues on their own and auto correct them. For example, when a data stream detects a formatting inconsistency, the system can automatically correct the format before storing the data.

Automating tools enable continuous data quality monitoring and reduce manual work. The tools also create dashboards and reports needed to track time-based data quality metrics, enabling an organization to take timely proactive action before problems worsen.

Building confidence with valid and quality data

Data reliability and quality are much more important than being a mere technical requirement. They relate to earning confidence among an organization and its stakeholders. Teams that make decisions with data, conduct analytics, or build products should be confident in the accuracy and reliability of their data. Thus, with trustworthy and high-quality data in place, some of the benefits are as follows:

- **Better decision-making**: Where leaders can be assured of the reliability of data, they make better decisions. This leads to more accurate forecasts, better strategic planning, and, in turn, improved business outcomes.

- **Customer confidence**: Often, customers and end-users are in a better position to trust organizations that demonstrate a commitment towards data quality. Reliable data improves customer experience, ensuring insights, and predictions are accurate.

- **Regulatory compliance**: Most regulations within industries like healthcare, finance, and telecommunications require strict data governance and standards of quality. Meeting such a need minimizes the risk of legal issues and financial penalties.

Checks on data quality

Data quality checks are fundamentally necessary to ascertain that data from different sources is accurate, complete, and reliable. They can broadly be categorized into two classes, functional and non-functional checks, each serving a purpose that helps maintain the integrity and usability of the data.

Functional data quality checks

Functional data quality checks have to do with the content of the data and its business relevance. They make sure the data collected fits the specific needs for which it is being used, such checks will involve:

- **Accuracy**: It is the verification that data correctly describes things that exist in reality. For example, customer addresses are input accurately and then checked against postal databases for validation.

- **Completeness**: It is the requirement that no required data must be missing. An example is a customer record which must have fields for name, email, and phone, and it is required to fill in all before saving.

- **Consistency**: It is the need for data homogeneity throughout systems and time. For example, the price of a product must be the same across the e-commerce website and its internal database.

- **Uniqueness**: There should be no duplicate entries, such as customer identifiers not being replicated within the data set.

- **Timeliness**: The data is current and remains valid for time-sensitive business requirements. An example could be to ensure that sales data is captured and processed promptly to enable real-time analytics.

Non-functional data quality checks

Non-functional checks address performance and dependability regarding system requirements, in which data collection and processing systems work effectively and perform well in terms of operational standards, these include:

- **Scalability**: When the volume of data starts to grow, data collection and processing systems should not degrade; they have to scale with ease to meet demands.

- **Performance**: This includes checking a system that is supposed to collect and process data within a fixed time for quicker response times in real-time use cases.

- **Availability**: The system shall be always on and gathering data because failure in the system or network failures must be dealt with. That would include redundancy and failover mechanisms.

- **Security and compliance**: Provide for the secure gathering and storage of data behind access, according to relevant regulations, such as the GDPR or **Health Insurance Portability and Accountability Act (HIPAA)**.

- **Resilience**: Whenever an error or failure occurs, a system should spring back to nominal operation with no data loss or corruption. This will enhance the general dependability of the data pipeline.

Integrating functional and non-functional checks

Both types of checks should be introduced into the data pipeline with the automated validation rules at each stage: data ingestion, storage, and transformation. This can be ensured using Apache NiFi, Talend, and custom scripts that are implemented with these checks, ensuring the data coming into the system meets the functional requirements and non-functional requirements of optimum system performance.

This balance of functional versus non-functional checks provides confidence not only in the quality of the data itself but also in the efficiency and reliability of the systems that manage and process such data. This will ensure consistency in the delivery of high-quality data and the ability of the system to scale and perform reliably over time.

Data governance and cost management

Data governance and cost management rank among the two most important constituents of any data-driven organization. Collectively, these allow for well-managed data, compliance with regulations, and efficient usage towards keeping operational costs as low as possible.

Data governance

Data governance refers to the framework, policies, and procedures that can use data based on its availability, usability, integrity, and security. A robust data governance framework will include the following:

- **Policies and standards**: Set rules as to how data is collected, stored, accessed, and shared to ensure that data is consistent and of good quality. Such a policy prevents data silos and ensures that at least procedures for all departments are the same.

- **Ownership and stewardship**: It provides accountability through ownership and stewardship of the data. Data owners are responsible for the accuracy and quality of data integrity, while data stewards are concerned with compliance and governance practices.

- **Governance and compliance**: With the different governance frameworks comes alignment with legal and regulatory standards, such as GDPR, HIPAA, or CCPA for data handling securely and ethically, with minimal risk on legal grounds.

- **Data lineage and auditing**: It shows a record of where data originates, how it changes over time, and where it is consumed to give insight into the use of data. Auditing tools are crucial in tracking access to data and ensuring that policy adherence is followed.

Cost management

Cost management represents planning and monitoring of consequences along financial dimensions while collecting, storing, and processing data. The main objective of cost management in this context is optimization. Costs tend to mushroom rather fast in case organizations scale up their respective operations related to data operations. The key aspects to consider are as follows:

- **Efficient data storage**: AWS, Azure, and Google Cloud have scalable options to store data, but if this is not optimized, then costs will spiral upwards. The implementation of tiered storage-scoped cold, warm, and hot means that the more frequently used data will be stored on more expensive, higher-performance storage, while the older, less-used data is moved to less costly, slower storage.

- **Resource optimization**: By automatically scaling resources up or down to meet demand, over-provisioning is avoided. Serverless technology's **function as a service (FaaS)** like AWS Lambda enable economical processing by charging only for the time that code is running.

- **Data retention policies**: Data retention and deletion policies can be issued to avoid unnecessary storage costs of data. A complete plan for how long the data is to be retained and at what time it must be deleted will avoid storage bloat and extra overhead.

- **Monitoring and notification**: Like AWS CloudWatch, services offered by Azure Monitor enable teams to observe data usage in real-time to identify areas of cost inefficiency and make timely interventions. It helps in eliminating unused resources, reducing the commitment size of data pipelines, or rightsizing them.

This is how companies can give comfort as far as assurance over the integrity and compliance of their data is concerned, while at the same time keeping off useless spending by properly governing and managing data to unlock value out of the operations.

Impact of AI and BI

AI combined with BI has been revolutionizing organizational approaches toward data collection. Integration of AI and BI allows for efficiency and insight into the process. Both AI and BI contribute much value to making data more accessible, actionable, and valuable for decision-making.

Impact of AI on data collection

AI provides automation, intelligence, and prediction capabilities in data collection. In essence, it allows organizations to capture and analyze data at a volume and speed that, earlier, was not even thought of.

The key impacts include the following:

- **Automated data collection**: AI will automate the gathering of data from different sources like IoT devices, social media, and enterprise applications. This reduces manual effort in collecting and preparing data.

- **Improved data quality**: AI-driven systems, which can identify at the time of gathering if any anomaly or inconsistency exists in data, or if there is any missing data point, mean better quality right from the time of origin. AI algorithms can perform real-time validation and correction, reducing extensive post-processing.

- **Predictive insights**: AI-driven tools analyze inbound data streams and convert them into predictive insights that then inform immediate actions. For instance, machine learning models can predict what a customer is most likely to do next or an impending failure in equipment in real-time, thus enabling quick responses.

Impact of BI on data collection

BI amplifies how an organization looks at and presents its data to derive deeper insights that could form the basis of strategic decisions.

When integrated with AI, the BI tools bring about the following effects:

- **Real-time analytics**: The next-generation BI tools like Power BI, Tableau, and Looker are capable of real-time data dashboards to immediately show the performance metrics for any business. Such tools present decision-makers with the ability to see their data as it is collected, thus making the spotting of trends or anomalies all that much easier.

- **Data democratization**: Since the BI tools make it possible for data access by non-technical users, the user-friendly interface and drag-and-drop functionality enable departmental employees to gather, analyze, and report on data without IT or any data engineering support.

- **Smarter decision-making**: BI enables the analysis to be done from a historical, current, and predictive perspective. The organizations will be better positioned to make effective decisions with such precise and timely information as sale trends, customer behavior, or supply chain performance.

Real-world case studies

The case studies in this section, highlight how major companies like *Coca-Cola*, *Tesla*, and *Amazon* have successfully implemented real-time data collection and analysis solutions to solve complex challenges and improve operational efficiency. Each case explains the details of how IoT, machine learning, cloud computing, and data analytics can transform traditional business processes into smarter, more responsive systems.

Case study of Coca-Cola

Coca-Cola, one of the largest beverage companies in the world, had to find a way to capture sales and stock information in real-time from its over six million vending machines worldwide. Conventionally, the majority of machines gave very little if any insights on product sales, restocking requirements, and machine maintenance, all things which caused inefficiency because of not being able to buy the product because it was out of stock or because the machine was broken.

The solution would be that Coca-Cola installed IoT-enabled vending machines that were connected to the cloud to observe data in real-time. Each such machine came with sensors installed to gather essential data regarding product sales, stock levels, and machine health status. The data collected was then transmitted to a central hub for processing and analytics.

The following technologies can be used:

- **IoT sensors**: They are implanted in the vending machines to monitor sales and inventory.

- **AWS IoT and cloud services**: They can be used to collate, store, and process the data in real-time.

- **Big data analytics**: This is used to develop insights on customer preference, sales patterns, and machine performance.

The outcomes include the following:

- **Improved restocking efficiency**: Real-time data helped Coca-Cola optimize restocking schedules and made sure the vending machines were always well stocked with the right product.

- **Less downtime**: Predictive maintenance insights from machine data helped reduce machine downtime by spotting issues before they happened.

- **Increased sales**: By analyzing customer preferences and trends of the geographical location for each product offered, Coca-Cola was able to increase overall sales.

This case proves that with IoT and cloud-based data collection, real-time insights can drive businesses to improve operational efficiency and customer satisfaction while boosting revenue.

Case study of autonomous driving data collection

Tesla wanted to completely develop autonomous vehicles, which require loads of data to train the machine learning models for improvement in the accuracy and safety of the software in autonomous driving. It was also quite challenging to collect data from various vehicles around the world with support for real-time responsiveness.

The solution would be that Tesla designed a highly scalable and distributed data intake framework using edge computing, ML, and big data platforms. Every vehicle manufactured by Tesla is equipped with various sensors, including cameras, radar, and LIDAR, which continuously collect data on road and traffic conditions and driver behavior. The data from each car would be transferred to Tesla's centralized, cloud-based system in real-time for processing.

The following technologies can be used:

- **Edge computing**: Each vehicle processes some data directly at the vehicle level to ensure real-time decision-making for autonomous driving.

- **Cloud storage**: Massive amounts of driving data flow into Tesla's cloud infrastructure for storage and processing.

- **Machine learning**: Training of Tesla AI models is an ongoing process with the ever-building data, to improvise better autonomous driving behavior.

The outcomes include the following:

- **Continuous improvement**: Tesla's continuous update of the autonomous driving algorithms from data collected from millions of miles that Tesla cars worldwide have driven, translates into improved performance and safety over time.

- **Real-time decision-making**: Tesla does the edge processing for some data to make sure all its cars can make split-second decisions independently without going back to the cloud.

- **Safety enhancements**: Due to the volumes of driving data that Tesla can gather and analyze; its vehicles have been enhanced to better avoid accidents in real-time.

Tesla's deployment of edge computing and AI further illustrates how the collection of data can be done globally with PII data yet maintain real-time responsiveness and enable innovative advanced systems to be built, as in Tesla's newest features in autonomous driving.

Case study of inventory management

The challenge, therefore, was how such a massive catalog could be inventoried by one of the largest e-tailers, *Amazon*. It required a system that would predict inventory demand in real-time and allow the stocking of inventory on time at the least cost with no overstocking issues arising.

The solution would be that Amazon leveraged AWS Kinesis to build a real-time streaming data capture platform, allowing it to process voluminous inflows emanating from every part of its supply chain across the world. AWS Kinesis thus helped Amazon to capture continuous streams of data in real-time, everything from order transactions to shipment tracking and warehouse inventory. This provides Amazon with the ability to accurately forecast inventory needs and dynamically control its stock level.

The following technologies can be used:

- **AWS Kinesis**: Ingest and stream data in real-time from Amazon's e-commerce platform and supply chain.

- **Predictive analytics**: This helps to comprehend how to estimate demand for inventory, integrating sales trends, seasonality, and customer preferences.

- **Data warehousing**: Use AWS Redshift for long-term storage and analysis of historical inventory.

The outcomes will include the following:

- **Inventory cost optimization**: Amazon, with more correct demand forecast accuracy, cut issues of overstocking/understocking that consequently reduces holding costs and enhances efficiency.

- **Faster replenishment**: Amazon could stock up its shelves way before it ran out of a certain product because of real-time data capture and analytics, ensure products were timely restocked, and orders were processed fast. It kept customers more satisfied.

- **Data-driven insights**: The system helped to gain insight into customer behavior and sales trends, which helped Amazon develop an efficient product recommendation and inventory management strategy.

This is a case that best describes how intelligent use of real-time data intake using AWS Kinesis enables Amazon to enjoy a very efficient supply chain, keeping costs down while enhancing the overall customer experience.

Conclusion

In this chapter, we explored the critical role of data collection, focusing on gathering data from various sources while ensuring scalability, reliability, and quality. Now that we have learned how to gather data from different places, the next step is to build strong and reliable pipelines to bring that data together.

In the next chapter, we will see how to move data efficiently and securely, ensuring it is ready for analysis and even to power smart AI systems. Think of it as building the essential pathways for your data journey.

Join our book's Discord space

Join the book's Discord Workspace for Latest updates, Offers, Tech happenings around the world, New Release and Sessions with the Authors:

https://discord.bpbonline.com

CHAPTER 3
Data Ingestion in Action

Introduction

Data ingestion is the pivotal process that moves raw data from various sources into target systems for processing, analysis, storage, and usage in AI and BI applications. This chapter will focus on the architecture, strategies, and best practices that make data ingestion efficient, reliable, and scalable.

In the modern data landscape, ingestion pipelines play a crucial role in fueling AI systems, ensuring that data reaches machine learning models in time for real-time analysis and decision-making. Without a robust ingestion strategy, organizations risk falling behind in their AI-driven initiatives. Industries like healthcare rely on seamless data ingestion for real-time patient monitoring and diagnostics, while finance depends on it for fraud detection and risk management. In the upcoming section, we will look at the broad overview of data ingestion, what differentiates it from data collection, and why it is a critical phase in the data lifecycle.

Structure

The chapter covers the following topics:

- Scalability strategies
- Enhancing performance

- Reliability mechanisms

- Data quality assurance

- Data governance practices

- Non-functional error controls

- Cost management

- AI and BI integration

- Real-world examples of technologies in data ingestion

Objectives

By the end of this chapter, readers will have a comprehensive understanding of data ingestion processes, focusing on scalability, performance, and reliability to handle large volumes of data efficiently. It explores strategies for enhancing performance through distributed systems and optimized algorithms, while ensuring data quality through validation and cleansing techniques. Emphasis is placed on implementing robust reliability mechanisms, such as failover strategies and redundancy, to maintain data integrity. The chapter also highlights governance practices to secure and manage data, ensuring compliance and traceability. Cost management techniques are discussed to create efficient yet affordable data pipelines, aligning with business needs. Finally, the integration of AI and BI tools into data ingestion processes is covered, providing real-world examples and case studies to illustrate best practices.

Scalability strategies

Scalability is one of the most critical aspects of designing a robust data ingestion pipeline. As data volumes grow, the pipeline must be able to handle increasing loads without compromising performance, reliability, or availability. This section expands on key strategies that ensure your ingestion pipeline can scale effectively, whether you are handling batch data, streaming data, or hybrid use cases.

A scalable data ingestion system ensures that no matter how much data flows through the system, it can process the data in a timely manner, efficiently utilizing resources. We will explore how different types of horizontal and vertical scaling come into play, discuss advanced partitioning techniques, and examine cloud-native solutions that automatically scale based on the load.

Horizontal vs. vertical scaling

Scalability is typically achieved through either horizontal or vertical scaling. Understanding the distinction between these two methods and when to use each is essential for building flexible, future-proof ingestion systems.

Horizontal scaling

Horizontal scaling, or **scaling out**, involves adding more machines or nodes to the system to handle additional load. This is the most common scaling technique used in distributed systems, as it offers greater flexibility and resilience.

The key advantages are as follows:

- **Increased fault tolerance**: If one node fails, others can take over, preventing downtime and ensuring continuity of data ingestion.

- **Elastic scaling**: Adding more nodes in a cloud environment is relatively straightforward, allowing the system to scale on demand.

- **Better resource distribution**: By distributing the data across multiple nodes, horizontal scaling avoids overloading any single server, balancing the load efficiently.

For example, consider an e-commerce company handling millions of transactions daily. A horizontally scaled ingestion pipeline can use tools like AWS Glue or Google Cloud Dataflow to distribute ingestion across multiple servers. As traffic surges (e.g., during a Black Friday sale), additional nodes are provisioned to handle the extra load without impacting performance.

The challenges are as follows:

- **Increased complexity**: Horizontal scaling introduces complexities in managing distributed systems. Coordination, data partitioning, and network overhead must be carefully managed.

- **Cost**: Adding more nodes, especially in cloud environments, can increase costs. Managing resource utilization efficiently is essential to avoid unexpected expenses.

Vertical scaling

Vertical scaling, or **scaling up**, involves increasing the capacity of existing nodes by adding more CPU, memory, or storage. This can be effective for smaller systems or legacy applications, but has limitations compared to horizontal scaling.

The key advantages are as follows:

- **Simplicity**: Vertical scaling is often easier to implement as it does not require the complexities of managing distributed systems.

- **Application of specialized hardware**: In specific cases, such as **high-performance computing** (HPC) or where particular applications require substantial computational power, vertical scaling can make sense.

For example, financial services companies running on-premise systems may choose to scale vertically by upgrading their existing infrastructure with more powerful servers to handle data ingestion from multiple stock exchanges. This approach reduces the need to re-architect their system for horizontal scaling.

The challenges are as follows:

- **Single point of failure**: Vertical scaling increases dependency on individual nodes, meaning if a node fails, the entire system could be affected.

- **Resource limits**: There is an upper limit to how much you can scale vertically. At a certain point, the hardware will max out, making it unsustainable as a long-term solution for rapidly growing systems.

Figure 3.1 illustrates how EC2 instances are auto-scaled. This means, that as more data streams in, the auto-scaling group automatically provisions additional EC2 instances to process the increased load. When the data load decreases (e.g., outside of peak hours), the system decommissions unnecessary instances to save costs and optimize resource usage.

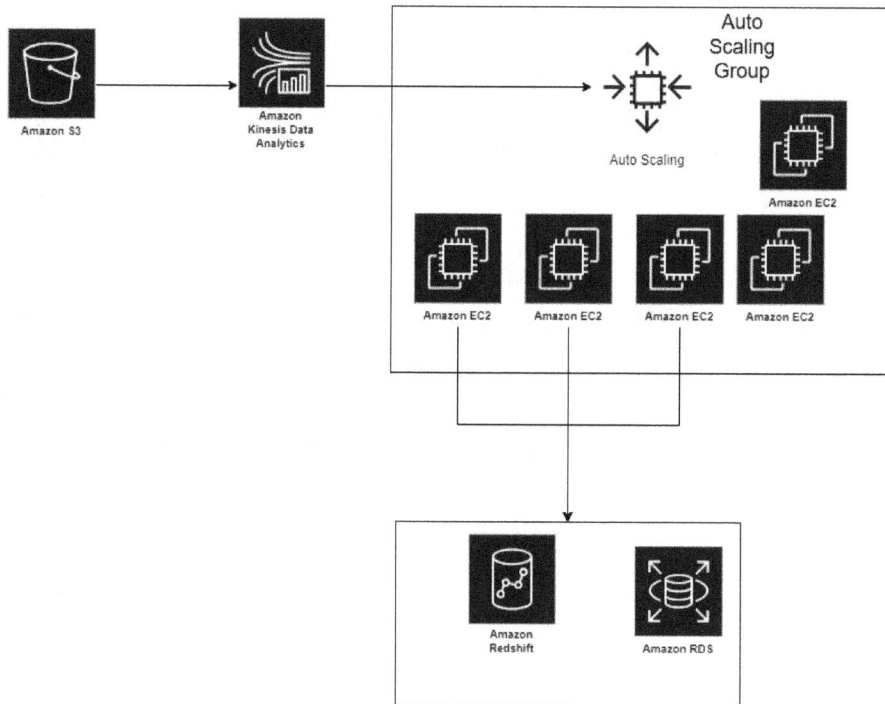

Figure 3.1: *Efficient handling of varying data volumes by the ingestion pipeline*

Partitioning for parallel processing

Partitioning is a crucial technique for optimizing ingestion pipelines, especially for horizontal scaling. It involves dividing large datasets into smaller, more manageable chunks (partitions), allowing parallel processing for a significant boost in throughput.

The following are the types of partitioning:

- **Hash-based partitioning**: In hash-based partitioning, data is distributed across different nodes based on the hash value of a key (e.g., a user ID or transaction ID). Each partition is processed independently, allowing for parallelism in the ingestion process, for example, a social media platform uses hash-based partitioning to distribute user activity data across multiple servers. Each server ingests data from a specific set of users, based on their hashed user IDs, ensuring that the workload is evenly balanced and processed in parallel.

  The advantages are as follows:

  o **Load balancing**: Hash-based partitioning ensures that data is distributed relatively evenly across nodes, preventing bottlenecks.

  o **Scalability**: As the system grows, new nodes can be added, and data can be re-partitioned efficiently.

  The challenges are as follows:

  o **Data skew**: If the hash function is not well-designed or the data is unevenly distributed, some partitions may end up receiving more data than others, leading to imbalances in processing.

  o **Hash collisions**: It can occur when different data values produce the same hash result, causing multiple records to be assigned to the same partition. This can lead to uneven data distribution and potential performance bottlenecks, as certain partitions may become overloaded while others remain underutilized. Managing and mitigating hash collisions requires the use of more sophisticated hash functions or secondary partitioning strategies.

- **Range-based partitioning**: In range-based partitioning, data is divided based on a range of values, such as timestamps or numerical IDs. This technique is particularly useful when ingesting time-series data or ordered data, for example, in a time-series database used for IoT sensor data, range-based partitioning allows the system to store and process data from different time intervals in parallel. For instance, one partition may handle data from 1-2 PM, while the other processes data from 2-3 PM.

  The advantages are as follows:

  o **Optimized for ordered data**: Range partitioning is ideal for scenarios where data is naturally ordered (e.g., time-series or sequential data).

  o **Efficient queries**: Optimizing queries on data ranges can lead to faster retrieval from specific partitions.

The challenges are as follows:

o **Range hotspots**: If certain ranges of data receive disproportionately high traffic (e.g., real-time events during a market crash), it can lead to performance degradation in those partitions.

• **Boundary management**: In range-based partitioning, managing boundary conditions can be challenging, especially when data grows or evolves. As new data falls outside the predefined ranges, partitions may need to be split or rebalanced, which can lead to downtime or performance overhead. Additionally, poorly defined boundaries may cause uneven distribution, requiring constant adjustments to maintain efficiency.

Sharding for scalability in distributed systems

Sharding is a common strategy used to split large databases or datasets into smaller, more manageable pieces (shards) that can be processed or stored independently across multiple nodes. Each shard contains a subset of the entire dataset.

For example, a global SaaS provider divides its customer data into shards based on geographic location. Customers from *North America* are assigned to one shard, while customers from Europe are assigned to another. Each shard operates independently, allowing for region-specific optimizations and faster processing.

The advantages are as follows:

• **Improved performance**: By distributing data across multiple shards, processing workloads can be parallelized, resulting in faster ingestion.

• **Geographical scaling**: Sharding by geographic region allows for data localization, reducing network latency and improving user experiences in specific areas.

The disadvantages are as follows:

• **Shard rebalancing**: As data grows or new regions are added, shards may need to be rebalanced, which can be a complex and resource-intensive process.

• **Data management**: Sharding adds complexity in managing distributed datasets, requiring careful planning to ensure data integrity and consistency across shards.

Auto-scaling in cloud-native environments

Cloud platforms like AWS, Azure, and Google Cloud offer native auto-scaling capabilities that dynamically adjust the ingestion infrastructure based on data load. This allows ingestion pipelines to grow or shrink according to demand without manual intervention.

• **Auto-scaling in AWS Glue**: AWS Glue is a fully managed ETL service that can automatically scale based on the size and complexity of the data ingestion workload. AWS Glue can handle both batch and streaming data, making it an ideal solution for dynamic data environments, for example, during peak traffic periods, such as a holiday sale for an e-commerce platform, AWS Glue can automatically scale its resources to accommodate a sudden influx of user activity data, ensuring that data ingestion remains smooth without manual intervention.

The advantages are as follows:

o **Cost efficiency**: By scaling only when needed, cloud-native auto-scaling minimizes unnecessary costs during low-traffic periods.

o **Flexibility**: Auto-scaling supports both vertical and horizontal scaling, depending on the specific requirements of the ingestion pipeline.

The disadvantages are as follows:

o **Cost management**: Auto-scaling can lead to unexpected cost spikes if not properly managed. Setting thresholds and monitoring usage is crucial to avoiding surprise billing.

o **Resource contention**: In cases of high demand, auto-scaling may lead to resource contention if limits on compute or memory resources are reached in the underlying infrastructure. This can result in delays or failed tasks if adequate quotas are not set.

- **Auto-scaling in Azure Data Factory:** Azure Data Factory provides similar auto-scaling capabilities for ingestion pipelines. It can scale compute resources dynamically for data integration tasks, making it ideal for large-scale ETL processes, for example, a global logistics company uses Azure Data Factory to ingest real-time data from IoT devices attached to its delivery vehicles. When the number of active vehicles increases, Azure Data Factory automatically scales its ingestion pipeline to ensure no data is lost during periods of peak activity.

The advantages are as follows:

o **Cost optimization:** Similar to AWS Glue, scaling resources on demand helps minimize expenses during periods of lower data volume.

o **Adaptability**: Azure Data Factory supports dynamic allocation of compute resources, allowing pipelines to handle varying workloads efficiently.

The disadvantages are as follows:

o **Unforeseen expenses**: Without proper monitoring and defined limits, the automatic scaling of resources can potentially lead to unexpected increases in operational costs.

o **Infrastructure limitations**: In situations of extreme processing demands, the underlying Azure infrastructure might experience resource constraints, potentially impacting pipeline performance if sufficient quotas are not configured.

- **Google Cloud Dataflow's dynamic scaling:** Google Cloud Dataflow offers dynamic scaling, especially suited for streaming pipelines. It automatically adjusts the number of workers based on the rate of incoming data, which is particularly useful for real-time analytics and machine learning pipelines, for example, a financial institution uses Google Cloud Dataflow to ingest real-time stock market data. During high-volume trading periods, such as the opening and closing bells, Cloud Dataflow automatically scales its workers to accommodate the increased volume, ensuring that all data is processed in real-time.

The advantages are as follows:

- o **Real-time responsiveness**: Dynamic scaling enables timely processing of fluctuating streaming data, which is crucial for real-time analytics and ML applications.

- o **Resource efficiency**: By automatically adjusting worker counts based on data flow, Cloud Dataflow optimizes resource utilization and reduces unnecessary costs during low-activity periods.

The disadvantages are as follows:

- o **Potential cost variability**: Just like other auto-scaling services, inadequate monitoring and lack of defined spending limits can result in unexpected cost escalations.

- o **Scaling latency**: While dynamic, the scaling process might introduce a slight delay in resource allocation, potentially causing temporary backlogs during sudden and extreme spikes in data volume.

Hybrid scaling models

In many real-world scenarios, a hybrid approach combining both batch and real-time ingestion can optimize scalability. For instance, a system might use batch processing for less time-sensitive data and real-time ingestion for critical data streams.

Example of hybrid scaling in a real-world scenario

A healthcare organization might use batch processing for historical patient records (ingested overnight in bulk) and real-time ingestion for live patient monitoring data from IoT devices in an emergency room. The combination allows them to efficiently handle large volumes of data while ensuring critical real-time data is available for immediate analysis.

The benefits of hybrid models are as follows:

- **Cost optimization**: By using batch ingestion for non-urgent data, hybrid models reduce the cost of maintaining always-on, real-time ingestion systems.

- **Flexibility**: Hybrid models offer flexibility by allowing organizations to adjust the balance between real-time and batch processing as business requirements evolve.

The challenges are as follows:

- **Complexity**: Managing two ingestion modes (real-time and batch) introduces additional complexity in orchestration and resource allocation.

- **Coordination**: Hybrid models require careful coordination between batch and real-time processes to avoid data duplication and ensure synchronization.

Enhancing performance

Performance optimization is critical in data ingestion pipelines, as it ensures that data flows efficiently from source to target without unnecessary delays. Optimizing the performance of your data ingestion pipeline involves fine-tuning various factors such as latency, throughput, transformation speed, and resource utilization. A well-optimized pipeline guarantees that downstream systems, such as machine learning models, data analytics platforms, and business intelligence tools, can access fresh, high-quality data in real-time or near-real-time, enabling timely decision-making.

This section explores various strategies to enhance the performance of data ingestion pipelines, including buffering, backpressure, efficient data transformation, minimizing latency, and performance monitoring tools.

Buffering for high-performance

Buffering plays a critical role in optimizing the flow of data in an ingestion pipeline. By temporarily holding incoming data in a buffer, the system can balance workload distribution and prevent bottlenecks, especially during spikes in data volume. Buffers smooth out data surges and ensure that downstream processes are not overwhelmed by fluctuating data velocities.

Working of buffering

A buffer is essentially a temporary storage area where data is held before being processed or forwarded to the next stage of the pipeline. Buffers help prevent data from overwhelming downstream systems, ensuring that the entire ingestion process runs smoothly, especially when dealing with high-throughput data or unpredictable traffic patterns.

Consider a stock trading platform where data surges are common during market open and close times. If real-time ingestion pipelines are not equipped with buffers, they may become overwhelmed by the sudden spike in trade volumes. Buffering mechanisms allow the system to temporarily hold data and process it at a manageable rate, ensuring that no data is dropped, and downstream systems continue to operate without delay.

The types of Buffers are as follows:

- **In-memory buffers**: They are typically used in high-performance systems where latency is a critical concern. Since data is stored in memory (RAM), it can be processed rapidly and passed onto the next stage with minimal delay.

  o **Advantages**: In-memory buffers are extremely fast, making them ideal for real-time ingestion pipelines where even small delays could negatively impact decision-making (e.g., in financial trading, fraud detection, or emergency response systems).

  o **Challenges**: Memory is a limited resource, so in-memory buffers can be overwhelmed if data volumes grow too quickly. Additionally, if the system crashes, data held in memory could be lost.

  Streaming platforms like *Netflix* use in-memory buffering to optimize video delivery. The video data is buffered in memory to ensure that it can be delivered to users without stuttering or pauses, even if there are brief network interruptions.

- **Disk-based buffers**: They store data on persistent storage, such as hard drives or **solid-state drive (SSDs)**, offering a more scalable solution for handling large volumes of data over time. While slower than in-memory buffers, disk-based buffers provide a greater capacity for handling data surges.

  o **Advantages**: Disk-based buffers are much more scalable and can store large amounts of data, making them suitable for long-term or batch processing ingestion pipelines.

  o **Challenges**: Disk-based buffers introduce additional latency due to slower read/write operations compared to memory. This makes them less suitable for time-sensitive real-time applications.

  For example, in a data lake architecture, disk-based buffers are used to temporarily store large datasets before they are ingested into a data warehouse. For instance, an IoT system may buffer sensor data on a disk before batching it for ingestion into a cloud storage system like AWS S3 or Google Cloud Storage.

Let us discuss when we should use buffering:

- **High-velocity data streams**: Ingestion systems dealing with high-velocity streams (e.g., sensor data from IoT devices) can benefit from buffering to ensure smooth and consistent data flow.

- **Data surges**: Buffering is crucial in scenarios where data traffic is unpredictable or bursty, such as retail websites during holiday sales or news websites during major breaking events.

- **Batch vs. real-time ingestion**: Buffering is especially useful when integrating batch processing with real-time data streams, helping bridge the gap between the two modes.

The best practices for implementing buffering are as follows:

- **Set buffer limits**: Define clear thresholds for your buffer size to prevent memory overflow or excessive disk I/O.

- **Monitor buffer usage**: Implement monitoring tools to track buffer utilization. Overflows or underflows in buffer size can be indicators of performance bottlenecks or inefficiencies in the pipeline.

- **Dynamic buffer sizing**: In cloud environments, consider using dynamic buffer sizing to automatically scale up or down based on data volume.

Back-pressure and flow control

Backpressure is a technique used in data ingestion pipelines to control the flow of data and prevent overwhelming the system. When a downstream system (e.g., a data processor or storage system) cannot handle the rate at which data is arriving, backpressure mechanisms slow down the upstream flow, ensuring that the ingestion pipeline does not get overloaded.

Let us see back-pressure work. Back-pressure works by applying a feedback loop between different stages of the ingestion pipeline. If a downstream component is experiencing a high load and cannot process data as quickly as it is arriving, the upstream components reduce the rate at which they send data, preventing system overload and potential failures. For example, in a streaming data pipeline using **Apache Kafka**, if a consumer, such as an analytics system, is processing data slower than the producer, such as an IoT sensor network, backpressure mechanisms will slow down the producer. This ensures that the consumer does not become overwhelmed, maintaining system stability.

The benefits of backpressure are as follows:

- **Prevents data loss**: Without backpressure, data could overflow in buffers or be lost entirely if downstream systems cannot keep up with ingestion speeds.

- **Improves system stability**: By regulating data flow, backpressure ensures that the entire ingestion pipeline operates within safe limits, preventing crashes and bottlenecks.

- **Optimizes resource usage**: Backpressure mechanisms help avoid over-provisioning of resources. Instead of always running at maximum capacity, the pipeline can dynamically adjust based on the load.

Backpressure is a critical mechanism in data ingestion systems that ensures the efficient handling of data flow by regulating the pace at which data is processed, preventing system overloads, and maintaining stability. The implementation details of back-pressure in data ingestion systems are outlined to demonstrate how it can effectively regulate data flow and maintain system stability.

Refer to the following:

- **Reactive Streams**: The Reactive Streams API is a specification for handling back-pressure in data streams. It provides standard interfaces for applying backpressure in Java-based systems. Tools like Akka Streams and RxJava follow the Reactive Streams standard.

  For example, in a real-time financial trading platform, backpressure is used to control the flow of stock market data streams. If a trading algorithm starts lagging due to high market activity, the ingestion system reduces the incoming data rate to avoid overloading the algorithm.

- **Message queuing systems**: Tools like Apache Kafka, RabbitMQ, and AWS SQS implement built-in back-pressure mechanisms to regulate data flow between producers and consumers.

  For example, an IoT system that ingests data from thousands of connected devices can use Kafka's backpressure mechanisms to prevent device data from overwhelming the system during a peak load event, such as a large-scale system malfunction where all devices send alerts simultaneously.

Data transformation optimization

Data transformation is often required before ingested data can be used for downstream processing, analytics, or machine learning. However, inefficient transformations can introduce significant performance bottlenecks. Optimizing data transformations during the ingestion process is crucial for maintaining high throughput and minimizing latency.

The types of data transformations are as follows:

- **Filtering**: Removing unnecessary or irrelevant data points to reduce the overall volume of data ingested.

  - **Example**: In a social media monitoring platform, only posts that contain specific keywords might be ingested, while irrelevant posts are filtered out.

- **Aggregation**: Summarizing or combining data points to reduce the complexity and volume of ingested data.

  - **Example**: A weather monitoring system might aggregate hourly sensor readings into daily summaries, reducing the volume of data sent to downstream systems.

- **Normalization**: Standardizing data formats to ensure consistency across different data sources.

  - **Example**: A multi-channel retail platform might normalize transaction data from different e-commerce websites to a single format before ingestion into a central data warehouse.

To ensure smooth and high-performance data ingestion, it is crucial to manage how and when transformations are applied. By strategically handling transformations, organizations can minimize latency, enhance throughput, and reduce the computational burden on ingestion pipelines.

The following techniques outline best practices for optimizing data transformation during the ingestion process:

- **Minimizing on-the-fly transformations**: Transformations applied during data ingestion can introduce latency. To optimize performance, consider performing transformations in the background or as part of post-ingestion processing, especially for non-critical data.

  For example, a retail company might ingest raw transaction data into a data lake first and then apply transformations asynchronously, reducing the time it takes to ingest data into the system.

- **Vectorized operations**: When transforming large datasets, vectorized operations (which process data in batches) are significantly faster than iterative, row-by-row processing. Tools like Apache Spark support vectorized operations, enabling efficient transformation of large-scale data.

  For example, an e-commerce company using Apache Spark for ETL processes can benefit from vectorized transformations, reducing the time to aggregate and normalize product catalog data from millions of transactions.

- **Lazy evaluation**: It is a technique used in tools like Apache Flink and Apache Spark, where transformations are only applied when absolutely necessary, rather than at every stage of the ingestion process. This can lead to significant performance improvements by avoiding redundant computations.

  For example, in a real-time data pipeline using Apache Flink, a series of transformations (e.g., filtering, aggregation) might be defined but not applied until the data is needed by the downstream consumer, optimizing resource usage and reducing latency.

Minimizing latency in data ingestion

Latency is a key performance metric in data ingestion pipelines, particularly for real-time systems where data must be available for analysis or action as soon as possible. Minimizing latency ensures that data is transferred from source to target without unnecessary delays, which is critical for time-sensitive applications.

The factors contributing to latency are as follows:

- **Network delays**: The time it takes for data to travel across networks, especially in geographically distributed systems, can introduce significant delays.

- **Processing delays**: Data transformations, filtering, and validation steps can slow down ingestion if not optimized.

- **Storage delays**: Writing data to disk or cloud storage systems can be a major source of latency, especially if the storage system is not optimized for high-speed data ingestion.

The strategies to minimize latency are as follows:

- **Edge processing**: Performing data processing at the edge (closer to the data source) can significantly reduce latency. In edge processing, basic transformations, filtering, and aggregation are performed before data is sent to the central system, reducing the amount of data that needs to travel over the network.

  For example, in a smart city infrastructure, edge devices (e.g., traffic cameras or environmental sensors) process and filter data locally, sending only relevant events to the central system for further analysis. This reduces latency and network bandwidth requirements.

- **In-memory processing**: In-memory data processing significantly reduces latency compared to disk-based processing. Tools like Apache Spark and Flink offer in-memory processing capabilities, which can be leveraged to speed up real-time data ingestion.

  For example, a financial trading platform might use in-memory data grids to store and process real-time stock market data, ensuring near-zero latency in trading decisions.

- **Using efficient storage solutions**: Leveraging high-performance storage systems such as Amazon S3 (with optimized write operations) or Google Cloud Bigtable for real-time data storage can minimize latency in writing and retrieving ingested data.

Reliability mechanisms

In data ingestion pipelines, reliability is essential to ensure that data is not lost, corrupted, or delayed. Reliability mechanisms help maintain system stability and ensure that data flows smoothly through the pipeline, even in the face of failures such as network issues, system crashes, or data source outages. In this section, we will explore the key strategies and mechanisms that enhance reliability, including retry logic, failover systems, checkpointing, deduplication, and dead letter queues.

Retry logic and failure handling

Retry logic ensures system reliability by reattempting operations after temporary failures, such as an API endpoint being unavailable or network disruptions. This mechanism prevents data loss and ensures smooth recovery by delaying retries appropriately based on the failure type and system requirements, for example, in an IoT-based system ingesting sensor data, network disruptions may temporarily prevent the system from receiving data. Retry logic ensures data is ingested once the network stabilizes, preventing data loss and maintaining system stability.

The techniques for implementing retry logic are as follows:

- **Exponential backoff**: The time between retry attempts increases exponentially (e.g., 1 second, 2 seconds, 4 seconds, etc.), preventing the system from overwhelming the source and allowing time for temporary issues to resolve.

- **Jitter (randomized delay)**: Adding randomness to delays avoids synchronization issues where multiple systems retry simultaneously, reducing the risk of sudden load spikes.

The advantages are as follows:

- **System stability**: Retry logic ensures smooth recovery from transient failures without overloading the system.

- **Reduced downtime**: By reattempting operations intelligently, the system minimizes the impact of temporary disruptions.

The best practices are as follows:

- **Max retry attempts**: Set a limit to prevent infinite retries. If the limit is reached, send failed operations to a **dead letter queue** (**DLQ**) for further investigation.

- **Logging and alerts**: Track retry attempts and configure alerts for persistent failures to enable proactive issue resolution.

Checkpointing for data recovery

Checkpointing is a technique used in streaming ingestion pipelines to ensure that data is not lost in the event of a system failure. It involves saving the state of the system at regular intervals so that if a failure occurs, the system can resume processing from the last successful checkpoint rather than restarting from the beginning.

Working of checkpointing

In a streaming ingestion pipeline, data is often processed in real-time from sources such as sensors, logs, or transactional systems. If the pipeline crashes and we do not have checkpointing, all unprocessed data might be lost. By periodically saving the state of the system (i.e., the last successfully ingested data), checkpointing ensures that the pipeline can recover without reprocessing already ingested data.

For example, a financial services company that processes real-time transaction data from multiple exchanges uses checkpointing in its ingestion pipeline. If the system crashes during a volatile trading session, checkpointing allows it to resume from the last processed transaction rather than restarting from the beginning of the data stream.

The types of checkpointing are as follows:

- **Periodic checkpointing**: The system saves its state at fixed intervals (e.g., every minute). If a failure occurs, the system can recover from the most recent checkpoint.

- **Event-based checkpointing**: The system checkpoints after processing a specific number of events (e.g., every 1,000 records). This is useful in scenarios where the data rate is highly variable.

The advantages are as follows:

- **Minimal data loss**: Checkpointing ensures that only a small amount of data is lost during a failure, depending on the frequency of checkpoints.

- **Efficient recovery**: The system can resume processing from the last checkpoint, reducing downtime and the need for manual intervention.

Deduplication for data integrity

Deduplication ensures that unique data is ingested into the system, preventing duplicates that could skew analysis or lead to incorrect conclusions in downstream applications like business intelligence or machine learning models.

Working of deduplication

Deduplication involves identifying and removing duplicate records from the data stream before they are ingested. This can be done by comparing incoming records against previously ingested data, using unique identifiers such as timestamps, transaction IDs, or hash values.

For example, in a log aggregation system, where logs from multiple servers are ingested, deduplication ensures that the same log entry is not ingested multiple times. This is critical in real-time monitoring systems, where duplicate entries could lead to false alerts or inaccurate reporting.

The techniques for deduplication are as follows:

- **Hash-based deduplication**: A hash function is applied to each incoming record, and if a record with the same hash has already been ingested, it is discarded.

- **Key-based deduplication**: Records are compared based on a unique key (e.g., transaction ID or user ID). If a record with the same key exists, the new record is considered a duplicate and is ignored.

The advantages are as follows:

- **Data accuracy**: Deduplication ensures that unique records are processed, improving the accuracy of downstream systems.

- **Resource efficiency**: By discarding duplicate data, deduplication reduces the load on storage and processing resources.

Dead letter queues

A DLQ is a holding area for problematic data that could not be successfully ingested. If the pipeline encounters data that repeatedly fails ingestion, due to format issues, corruption, or validation errors, the data is sent to a DLQ for later inspection and resolution.

Working of dead letter queues

When the retry logic in the ingestion pipeline reaches its maximum number of attempts, the problematic data is sent to a DLQ instead of being discarded. This ensures that no data is lost and that the problematic data can be analyzed and corrected.

For example, in an e-commerce platform, customer order data is ingested in real-time. Occasionally, an order may fail validation due to missing fields or format mismatches (e.g., incorrect date format in the free text form that the customer has entered). Instead of discarding the data, the pipeline sends it to a DLQ. Engineers can later review the data, correct the errors, and re-ingest the corrected records.

The advantages of DLQs are as follows:

- **Data preservation**: DLQs ensure that even problematic data is retained, allowing it to be fixed and reprocessed.
- **Error resolution**: By isolating problematic records, DLQs make it easier to troubleshoot specific ingestion issues without affecting the rest of the pipeline.

The best practices for DLQs are as follows:

- **Alerting**: Set up alerts to notify engineers when data is sent to the DLQ, allowing for prompt investigation and resolution.
- **Periodic review**: Regularly review DLQ contents to identify recurring issues or patterns in problematic data.

Failover systems for high availability

Failover systems ensure that the ingestion pipeline remains operational, even if one or more components fail. Failover mechanisms allow the system to switch to a backup server, node, or cluster in the event of a failure, maintaining high availability.

Working of failover systems

In a failover setup, multiple ingestion nodes or servers run in parallel. If the primary node fails (e.g., due to hardware failure or software crash), a secondary node takes over automatically, ensuring continuous data flow.

For example, in a streaming analytics platform, data from social media feeds is ingested in real-time. If the primary ingestion node fails due to a server crash, the failover system automatically redirects the data to a secondary node, ensuring no interruptions in the data stream.

The types of failovers are as follows:

- **Active-Passive failover**: A secondary node is kept in standby mode, ready to take over if the primary node fails. This is the most common failover setup.

- **Active-Active failover**: Multiple nodes are actively processing data in parallel. If one node fails, the remaining nodes can handle the load, ensuring uninterrupted service.

The advantages are as follows:

- **High availability**: Failover systems ensure that the ingestion pipeline remains operational, even in the event of component failures.

- **Minimized downtime**: Failover systems reduce downtime, allowing the system to recover quickly from failures.

Data quality assurance

Ensuring high data quality is critical for the success of data ingestion pipelines. Poor-quality data can lead to inaccurate insights, misinformed decision-making, and failures in machine learning models or business intelligence tools. Data quality assurance ensures that the data being ingested is accurate, complete, consistent, and reliable. In this section, we will explore key strategies for ensuring data quality during ingestion, including schema validation, data cleaning, completeness checks, monitoring, and error handling.

Schema validation

Schema validation is one of the first lines of defense against poor-quality data. It involves checking incoming data against a predefined schema, ensuring it adheres to the expected structure, format, and types before being ingested into the system.

Working of schema validation

When data is ingested, the system checks that each data record conforms to a specified schema, which defines the required fields, data types (e.g., string, integer, date), and format. The data is either rejected or flagged for further processing if it does not match the schema.

For example, in a financial services platform ingesting transaction data, schema validation ensures that each transaction record includes necessary fields such as transaction ID, amount, timestamp, and account number. The record is flagged or rejected if a record is missing any of these fields or contains data in the wrong format (e.g., a string where an integer is expected).

The benefits of schema validation are as follows:

- **Prevents invalid data**: By enforcing schema validation, the pipeline ensures that only well-structured data is ingested, preventing malformed or incomplete data from entering the system.

- **Error detection**: Validation errors help identify issues in data sources early in the ingestion process, allowing for timely resolution.

The best practices are as follows:

- **Use flexible schemas**: While rigid schemas enforce strict quality control, more flexible schemas (e.g., allowing null values in non-critical fields) can accommodate variations in data formats without rejecting valid data unnecessarily.

- **Real-time feedback**: Provide real-time feedback to data providers or upstream systems when schema validation fails, allowing them to correct data before reattempting ingestion.

Data cleaning

Data cleaning, or data cleansing, involves identifying and correcting errors or inconsistencies in the data before it is ingested into the system. Cleaning processes may include removing duplicate records, handling missing or null values, and correcting inaccurate or inconsistent data entries.

Common data cleaning techniques are as follows:

- **Deduplication**: Identifying and removing duplicate records from the data stream is a crucial step in ensuring data accuracy. Duplicate data can lead to skewed analysis or inflated results in downstream systems like machine learning models, for example, in an e-commerce platform ingesting customer order data, deduplication ensures that multiple submissions of the same order (e.g., due to accidental double-clicking) are not ingested multiple times, preventing inventory discrepancies.

- **Handling missing data**: Missing or null values can be problematic for downstream processes. Data cleaning involves either imputing missing values with estimated values or removing records with incomplete data, depending on the importance of the missing information, for example, in a healthcare platform ingesting patient record, missing vital signs (e.g., blood pressure, heart rate) might be handled by imputing reasonable default values, while critical fields like patient ID may result in the record being rejected.

- **Outlier detection and removal**: Outliers can significantly impact data analysis and decision-making. Detecting and handling outliers, whether by removing them or flagging them for further investigation, is an essential part of the cleaning process., f or example, in a sales platform ingesting daily sales data, a sudden spike in sales (e.g., 10,000 units sold in a single minute) may be flagged as an outlier and investigated for potential fraud or data entry errors.

The best practices are as follows:

- **Automate cleaning processes**: Automate the data cleaning process where possible to ensure consistency and efficiency in handling large volumes of data.

- **Monitor for recurring issues**: Track recurring data quality issues (e.g., missing fields from specific data sources) to address the root cause, rather than relying on repeated cleaning.

Completeness and accuracy checks

Data completeness ensures that all required data fields are present in each record, while accuracy checks ensure that the data values fall within valid ranges or constraints. These checks are critical for maintaining the quality of ingested data.

Let us look at them in detail:

- **Completeness checks**: It involves ensuring that all required fields are present in each data record. This is particularly important in industries where missing data can have serious consequences, such as healthcare or finance.

  o **Example**: In a real-time payment processing system, completeness checks ensure that each transaction record includes a valid transaction ID, account number, amount, and timestamp. Missing or incomplete data could result in failed or delayed transactions, leading to customer dissatisfaction.

- **Accuracy checks**: It involves validating that the data values fall within expected ranges or constraints. For instance, numeric fields should contain values within a specific range, and categorical fields should only contain predefined values.

  o **Example**: In an IoT-based system for monitoring environmental data, accuracy checks ensure that sensor readings (e.g., temperature, humidity) fall within realistic ranges. If a sensor reports a temperature of 300°C, the data is flagged as inaccurate and removed from the dataset.

The best practices are as follows:

- **Set up rules and thresholds**: Define rules and thresholds for completeness and accuracy checks to ensure that only high-quality data is ingested.

- **Implement alerting**: When data fails completeness or accuracy checks, set up alerting mechanisms to notify engineers or data providers of the issue for prompt resolution.

Monitoring data quality

Monitoring the quality of ingested data in real-time is essential for ensuring long-term reliability and consistency. By tracking key metrics such as data validation errors, missing fields, duplicate records, and failed ingestion attempts, organizations can maintain high data quality standards and quickly address issues as they arise.

The key data quality metrics are as follows:

- **Validation error rates**: The percentage of records that fail schema validation. High error rates may indicate issues with data sources or upstream systems.

- **Duplicate records**: The number of duplicate records identified and removed during ingestion. Sudden increases in duplicate records may signal a problem with data collection or transmission.

- **Missing fields**: Monitoring the frequency of missing or null values in key fields helps identify patterns and recurring data quality issues.

- **Ingestion failures**: Tracking the number of failed ingestion attempts provides insight into the reliability of data sources and the stability of the ingestion pipeline.

Tools for monitoring data quality are as follows:

- **Grafana and Prometheus**: These tools provide real-time dashboards and alerting capabilities for monitoring data quality metrics in ingestion pipelines. They can track validation error rates, missing fields, and other data quality issues.

- **AWS CloudWatch**: For cloud-native environments, AWS CloudWatch can be used to monitor data ingestion pipelines, providing detailed insights into the quality and reliability of ingested data.

The best practices are as follows:

- **Set up real-time dashboards**: Use monitoring tools to visualize data quality metrics in real-time, enabling quick detection of issues.

- **Proactive alerts**: Configure alerts for specific data quality thresholds (e.g., if more than 5% of records fail validation) to prompt immediate action.

Data governance practices

Data governance practices ensure the proper management, security, and compliance of data throughout the ingestion process. These practices involve defining policies for data access, quality, and privacy, ensuring adherence to regulations like the GDPR and the HIPAA. By implementing strong governance, organizations maintain data integrity, consistency, and security across their pipelines.

Functional error controls

Functional errors are critical to the integrity of the data itself. These errors affect the validity, completeness, and accuracy of the ingested data. If not properly handled, functional errors can lead to significant issues downstream, such as incorrect business intelligence reports, inaccurate machine learning model predictions, or failed data analyses.

The types of functional errors are as follows:

- **Schema mismatches**: Schema validation is used to ensure that the data being ingested conforms to a predefined structure. A schema mismatch occurs when the incoming data does not match the expected schema, such as when a field is missing, a data type is incorrect, or the data format is invalid.

  o **Example**: A financial services company receives transaction data from multiple external partners. If the expected schema requires a `transaction_id`, `amount`, and `timestamp`, and one of these fields is missing or in the wrong format, it triggers a schema mismatch error.

- **Missing or invalid fields**: Missing required fields or fields with invalid values are common functional errors. These errors occur when essential data points are not present or are filled with invalid entries, such as null values where actual data is required.

  o **Example**: In a customer feedback system, if the `customer_id` field is missing or filled with invalid values (e.g., null), the data cannot be linked to the correct customer, rendering the feedback useless for analysis.

- **Data type errors**: These occur when the type of the incoming data does not match the expected type. For instance, if an integer is expected but a string is provided, it leads to a functional error.

  o **Example**: In an IoT monitoring system, sensor readings are expected to be in a numeric format. If the sensor sends readings as a string (e.g., 30°C instead of a numeric 30), this leads to a data type error.

Functional error handling techniques are as follows:

- **Schema validation**: One of the most effective ways to handle functional errors is by implementing schema validation. Ingestion systems such as AWS Glue, Azure Data Factory, and Apache NiFi allow users to define schemas for incoming data and automatically validate each record against the schema. Any record that does not conform to the schema can be rejected, logged, or sent to a DLQ for later processing.

  o **Example:** Consider an e-commerce platform ingesting customer order data. The defined schema for each order record specifies fields like `order_id` (integer), `customer_id` (string), `order_date` (date in YYYY-MM-DD format), product_name (string), and quantity (integer). If an incoming order record has the order_date field formatted as May 10, 2025 instead of 2025-05-10, the schema validation process would identify this as a data type mismatch.

- **Error logging and alerts**: When a functional error is detected, it is important to log the error for future review and troubleshooting. This is typically done through monitoring tools like Grafana or AWS CloudWatch. Alerts can also be configured to notify engineers when functional error rates exceed predefined thresholds.

  o **Example:** Imagine a social media platform ingesting user activity data like posts, likes, and shares. The ingestion pipeline is designed to process millions of events per minute. If a sudden change in the upstream data source introduces a new, unexpected data format for user IDs (e.g., switching from integers to alphanumeric strings without prior notice), this could lead to a surge in data type errors during ingestion. The error logging mechanism, integrated with tools like AWS CloudWatch Logs or Elasticsearch, would capture each instance of this data type error, including a timestamp, the specific record that failed, and the nature of the schema violation.

- **Fallback and default values**: In some cases, especially for non-critical fields, pipelines can be designed to handle missing or invalid data by providing fallback values or defaults, for instance, if a field is missing, a default value can be inserted to ensure the data continues to flow.

  o **Example**: In an analytics system for retail sales, if the customer_age field is missing, the system can assign a default age group, such as **unknown**, rather than halting the ingestion process.

Non-functional error controls

Non-functional errors are not directly related to the data itself but to the system's performance, availability, and scalability. These errors can affect the overall efficiency of the pipeline and its ability to meet **service-level agreements** (**SLAs**) for throughput, latency, and uptime.

The types of non-functional errors are as follows:

- **Throughput bottlenecks**: Throughput bottlenecks occur when the ingestion system cannot process data at the required rate, leading to backlogs and delayed data processing. Bottlenecks can arise due to insufficient processing capacity, network constraints, or poorly optimized queries.

  o **Example**: An IoT system that ingests sensor data from hundreds of thousands of devices might experience throughput bottlenecks if the processing infrastructure is not scaled to handle the incoming data rate, leading to data delays and potential losses.

- **High latency**: Latency refers to the time it takes for data to be ingested, processed, and made available for downstream systems. High latency can degrade the performance of real-time systems, such as fraud detection platforms or recommendation engines, which rely on low-latency data.

  o **Example**: In an online retail platform, if product recommendation systems rely on data ingested with high latency, the recommendations may become outdated and irrelevant by the time they are delivered to users, impacting customer satisfaction.

- **Resource exhaustion**: Resource exhaustion occurs when the ingestion pipeline consumes more CPU, memory, or storage than is available, leading to system crashes or severely degraded performance. This is common in systems that handle unpredictable data spikes or poorly managed resource allocation.

  o **Example**: A social media platform ingesting posts, images, and videos may encounter resource exhaustion during major global events (e.g., a sporting event), where the volume of user-generated content spikes significantly, overwhelming the infrastructure.

Non-functional error handling techniques are as follows:

- **Auto-scaling**: Its mechanisms allow the ingestion pipeline to dynamically adjust its resource allocation based on the volume of incoming data. Cloud-native platforms like AWS Glue, Azure Data Factory, and Google Cloud Dataflow offer auto-scaling features that add or remove compute nodes based on real-time data loads.

  o **Example**: In a video streaming platform, the ingestion pipeline scales up its processing nodes during peak traffic (e.g., during the release of a new season of a popular show) and scales down during off-peak times to save costs and optimize resource utilization.

- **Load balancing**: Load balancing ensures that the data load is evenly distributed across multiple processing nodes or servers. This prevents any single node from becoming overwhelmed and ensures that the pipeline can handle large volumes of data efficiently.

  o **Example**: A real-time analytics platform for stock market data uses load balancing to distribute the data ingestion across multiple servers, preventing any one server from being overwhelmed during periods of high market volatility.

- **Monitoring and alerts**: Monitoring tools, such as Prometheus, Grafana, and AWS CloudWatch allow engineers to track the performance of the ingestion pipeline in real-time. These tools provide metrics on throughput, latency, CPU usage, memory consumption, and more. Alerts can be configured to notify the team when KPIs fall below acceptable thresholds, allowing for quick intervention.

○ **Best practice**: Set up thresholds and proactive alerts to notify engineers when system performance begins to degrade (e.g., when latency exceeds a defined limit or when memory usage reaches 80%).

- **Resource throttling**: It allows the system to control the rate at which data is ingested, preventing resource exhaustion during periods of high data volume. By limiting the rate of ingestion, the system can avoid crashes or slowdowns caused by overloading.

  ○ **Example**: In a financial institution's fraud detection system, throttling ensures that during peak transaction times, the system processes critical transaction data first, avoiding resource exhaustion that could lead to missed fraud alerts.

Combined functional and non-functional error handling

In some cases, errors may have both functional and non-functional aspects. For example, a malformed data record (a functional error) could also cause processing delays and resource exhaustion (non-functional errors). Errors can manifest in various forms, impacting both functional correctness and overall system efficiency. Addressing these errors holistically ensures seamless data flow, minimizes downtime, and optimizes resource utilization.

This section outlines the key error categorization strategies and approaches to mitigate both functional and non-functional issues during data ingestion:

- **Immediate failures (functional)**: Errors like schema mismatches or missing fields are often detected early in the ingestion process. These errors can be addressed by rejecting the malformed data, sending it to a dead letter queue, or fixing the issue automatically using data cleaning techniques.

- **Performance degradations (non-functional)**: Errors related to system performance, such as high latency or throughput bottlenecks, are often monitored over time. Continuous monitoring allows for pro-active adjustments to the system, such as scaling resources or throttling data.

- **Hybrid approaches**: In some cases, functional errors may lead to non-functional issues, such as resource exhaustion due to high retry rates for data with missing fields. Hybrid approaches that combine functional error control with performance management techniques are needed to handle these situations, for example, a weather forecasting system that ingests data from thousands of sensors globally. If one of the sensors sends incomplete data (a functional error), the system retries the data ingestion. However, if too many sensors experience the same issue, the retries could overwhelm the system (a non-functional error), leading to performance degradation. A hybrid approach would involve limiting retries (functional control) and scaling up resources (non-functional control) to handle the issue without overwhelming the system.

Cost management

Managing costs is a critical aspect of building and maintaining data ingestion pipelines, especially when handling large-scale data or operating in cloud environments. Data ingestion processes often consume significant computational resources, network bandwidth, and storage, and without proper cost management strategies, expenses can quickly spiral out of control.

In this section, we will explore key strategies for optimizing cost in data ingestion pipelines, focusing on areas such as resource allocation, auto-scaling, storage optimization, and data retention policies.

Cloud cost optimization

Cloud platforms like AWS, Azure, and Google Cloud offer flexible, scalable infrastructure for data ingestion, but they also come with varying pricing models based on factors like storage, compute power, and data transfer. Optimizing costs in a cloud environment requires careful planning and resource management.

Auto-scaling and dynamic resource allocation

One of the main advantages of cloud-native ingestion systems is the ability to auto-scale resources based on the current load. For example, services like AWS Glue and Azure Data Factory allow pipelines to automatically adjust their resource usage like CPU, memory, and bandwidth, depending on the data volume at any given time.

For example, a company running an ingestion pipeline that processes website clickstream data can configure auto-scaling to scale up resources during peak hours and scale down during off-peak hours. This ensures that resources are only being paid for when they are needed.

Reserved instances and savings plans

Cloud providers offer options like reserved instances (AWS, Azure) or committed use discounts (Google Cloud) that allow companies to pay a lower rate for compute resources in exchange for committing to use a certain amount over time.

For example, if an organization knows that its ingestion pipeline will run consistently at a base load for the next year, it can reserve instances to lock in lower costs compared to using on-demand instances.

Cost-aware data storage

Data storage can quickly become one of the largest cost drivers in cloud environments. By using cost-efficient storage options and tiering storage, organizations can significantly reduce expenses.

With S3 Lifecycle policies in AWS, organizations can establish rules to automatically relocate older, less frequently accessed data to more cost-effective storage tiers, such as Amazon S3 Glacier. This helps reduce overall storage costs while maintaining data availability.

For example, a company that ingests real-time log data can store recent data in fast-access storage and archive older logs in a lower-cost tier, optimizing costs based on access frequency.

Efficient data processing and transfer

Data processing and transfer costs are another key consideration when managing ingestion pipelines, particularly when dealing with large volumes of data.

Batch vs. real-time processing

Real-time ingestion pipelines tend to be more resource-intensive than batch processing pipelines, given the need to handle data streams continuously and with low latency. For use cases where real-time processing is not essential, using **batch processing** can reduce costs significantly, for example, a retail company might use real-time ingestion to monitor website traffic but rely on batch processing for less time-sensitive data, such as daily sales reports or inventory updates. This hybrid approach allows the company to optimize costs for different types of data processing.

Optimizing data transfer costs

In cloud environments, transferring data between different geographic regions or moving data out of the cloud (known as **egress**) incurs additional fees, which can substantially increase costs. To manage expenses, it is crucial to design data ingestion pipelines that avoid or reduce unnecessary data transfers across regions or out of the cloud. By processing data close to its source (within the same cloud region) and minimizing cross-region transfers, organizations can keep costs lower and improve efficiency.

Refer to the following points for a better understanding:

- **Use localized data processing**: Processing data close to its source (e.g., within the same cloud region) can help avoid high data transfer fees. Tools like Google Cloud Dataflow allow for localized data processing to reduce network costs.
- **Example**: A company that operates in multiple regions can deploy ingestion pipelines regionally to process data locally and only transfer aggregated results to a central location, thereby reducing cross-region data transfer fees.

Managing long-term data retention

Not all ingested data needs to be retained indefinitely, and managing data retention policies is essential for controlling costs. Long-term data storage, especially for compliance or backup purposes, can become expensive if not properly managed.

Data retention policies

Setting clear data retention policies ensures that only data that is necessary for long-term use is stored indefinitely, while other data is archived or deleted after a certain period.

For example, a healthcare organization might set a retention policy to keep patient data for ten years due to compliance regulations, while log data from IoT devices can be deleted after six months.

Data compression and deduplication

Using data compression and deduplication techniques can also help reduce storage costs. Compression reduces the amount of storage required for data, while deduplication ensures that redundant copies of data are not stored multiple times, for example, an IoT platform that collects sensor data might compress readings before storage, reducing the total volume of data stored over time and cutting storage costs by a significant margin.

Monitoring and controlling costs

Tracking costs in real-time and setting up alerts are essential for ensuring that ingestion pipelines remain within budget. Cloud providers offer built-in cost-monitoring tools to help organizations stay on top of their expenses.

The cost monitoring tools are as follows:

- **AWS Cost Explorer** and **Azure Cost Management** allow teams to visualize their spending trends, identify areas of inefficiency, and adjust usage to optimize costs. These tools provide granular insights into how much each component of the pipeline costs, from computing to storage to data transfer.

  For example, a company using **Google Cloud** can set up **budgets and alerts** to notify administrators when their spending exceeds a certain threshold, allowing them to take corrective actions before costs get out of control.

The best practices for cost management are as follows:

- **Right-sizing resources**: Continuously monitor resource usage to ensure that the pipeline is using the appropriate amount of computing power and storage. This avoids over-provisioning and unnecessary costs.

- **Leverage spot instances**: Use spot instances (e.g., **AWS Spot Instances**) for non-critical workloads, such as batch processing, where interruptions can be tolerated. These instances are much cheaper than on-demand instances.

- **Evaluate and review regularly**: Regularly review the performance and cost of the ingestion pipeline, identifying opportunities to optimize or reduce costs based on changing data volumes or business requirements.

Cost management in data ingestion pipelines is a balancing act between performance, scalability, and budget. By optimizing resource allocation, leveraging cloud-native tools for auto-scaling and cost monitoring, and implementing efficient data storage and transfer strategies, organizations can significantly reduce their expenses while maintaining high performance and reliability in their ingestion pipelines. Continuous monitoring and regular reviews of cost drivers are crucial to ensuring that the pipeline remains cost-effective as data volumes and business needs evolve.

AI and BI integration

The integration of AI and BI with data ingestion pipelines is essential for enabling data-driven decision-making and automating analytics at scale. AI systems require high-quality, real-time data to train models, make predictions, and generate insights, while BI platforms rely on clean, structured data to provide accurate reports and dashboards for business stakeholders. In this section, we will explore how ingestion pipelines support AI and BI integration, the challenges involved, and best practices for building pipelines that enable seamless data flow into these systems.

Role of data ingestion in AI systems

AI systems, such as ML models and NLP applications, rely heavily on data ingestion pipelines to continuously feed data for training, validation, and inference. In many cases, AI models need access to both historical and real-time data streams to make predictions, detect patterns, and drive decision-making processes.

Feeding data to AI models

For AI systems to function effectively, they require a steady stream of high-quality, labeled data. This data must be ingested from various sources, cleaned, transformed, and delivered to the AI system in a structured format that is ready for model training or real-time inference, or example, a recommendation engine for an e-commerce platform relies on real-time ingestion of customer behavior data (clicks, searches, purchases) to continuously update its recommendation models. Without an efficient ingestion pipeline, the AI model would operate on outdated data, leading to irrelevant recommendations.

Handling real-time and historical data

AI systems often combine real-time data with historical datasets to improve accuracy and relevance in predictions. Ingestion pipelines must therefore support both real-time streaming data and batch processing of historical data.

For example, in a predictive maintenance system for industrial equipment, the AI model ingests real-time sensor data from machines to detect anomalies. However, it also requires access to historical data about past failures and maintenance schedules to make accurate predictions about when a machine might need servicing.

Data quality for AI

Data quality is a key concern for AI systems. Poor-quality data can lead to inaccurate predictions and unreliable models. Ingestion pipelines must therefore include processes for data validation, deduplication, and cleaning before feeding data to AI systems.

For example, a fraud detection system that uses machine learning must ensure that all financial transaction data is accurate and free of duplicates or missing fields. If fraudulent transactions are incorrectly labeled or missed due to poor data quality, the model's performance will degrade.

Role of data ingestion in BI systems

BI platforms provide organizations with the ability to generate reports, dashboards, and visualizations based on ingested data. These insights allow businesses to make informed decisions, track KPIs, and identify trends. Data ingestion pipelines play a vital role in ensuring that BI systems receive timely, accurate, and structured data for analysis.

Enabling real-time analytics in BI

Real-time data ingestion is crucial for BI systems that provide live dashboards and reporting. Business stakeholders often rely on these systems to make quick decisions based on up-to-date information, for example, a retail company uses a BI dashboard to monitor sales data in real-time across different regions. The data ingestion pipeline collects sales transactions from POS systems and pushes them into the BI platform, enabling managers to track sales performance by product, store, and region throughout the day.

Supporting historical reporting and trend analysis

In addition to real-time insights, BI platforms also support historical reporting and trend analysis. This requires ingestion pipelines to handle batch processing of large historical datasets and store them in data warehouses or lakes for long-term access, for example, a financial services company uses BI dashboards to analyze quarterly revenue performance. The ingestion pipeline collects financial data from various accounting systems, processes it in batches, and stores it in a centralized data warehouse. BI analysts can then generate reports that compare performance across different quarters and years.

Figure 3.2 illustrates how AI and BI models are the downstream consumers of ingested and processed data:

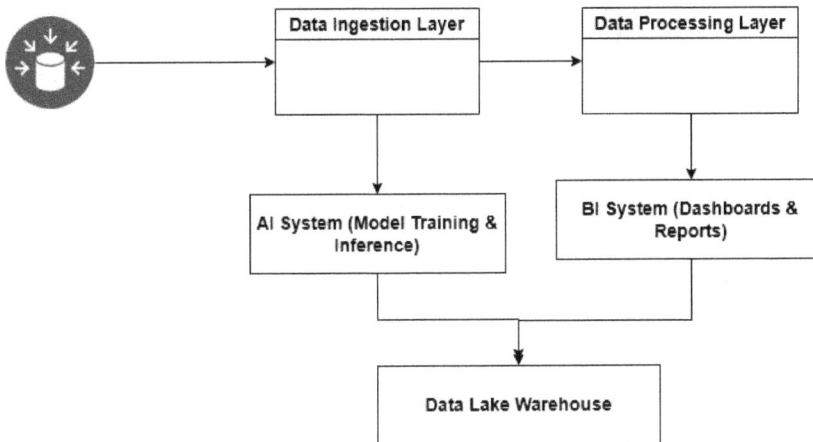

Figure 3.2: *AI and BI models are the downstream consumers of ingested and processed data*

Challenges of AI and BI integration

While AI and BI systems depend on recommendation ingestion pipelines for data, integrating these systems comes with several challenges, particularly around data volume, quality, and latency.

Data volume and scalability

AI and BI systems often ingest data from numerous sources, including IoT devices, social media feeds, enterprise systems, and transactional databases. The volume of data can be overwhelming, requiring ingestion pipelines to scale dynamically to handle fluctuating loads.

A challenge you might face is that a large media company ingests billions of events per day from its streaming services, including user activity, playback history, and content preferences. The ingestion pipeline must be able to scale horizontally to accommodate this high volume while ensuring that data is processed in near-real-time for BI dashboards and AI-powered recommendation engines.

Data quality and consistency

Data inconsistency, missing values, and errors can severely impact the performance of AI and BI systems. Ingestion pipelines need to incorporate mechanisms for ensuring data quality, such as schema validation, error handling, and deduplication.

A challenge you might face is that an AI system for customer churn prediction may fail to make accurate predictions if the data being ingested contains inconsistent customer interaction histories or missing attributes. Ensuring that the data is complete and validated is critical for the model's performance.

Latency and real-time requirements

For AI systems that rely on real-time predictions and BI systems that deliver live dashboards, data latency is a critical factor. Ingestion pipelines must minimize latency to ensure that data is available to downstream systems with minimal delay.

A challenge you might face is that a logistics company relies on real-time data from delivery vehicles to monitor the progress of shipments. High latency in the ingestion pipeline could delay updates to the BI dashboard, leading to poor decision-making and delayed responses to customer inquiries.

Best practices for integrating AI and BI

To successfully integrate AI and BI systems with data ingestion pipelines, organizations must follow best practices that ensure data is delivered in a timely, accurate, and scalable manner. The following are the best practices that help achieve the integration:

- **Unified data model**: Building a unified data model that both AI and BI systems can use helps standardize data ingestion and ensure consistency across the organization. A unified data model ensures that different data sources are ingested in a format that can be used for both analytics and AI-driven predictions.

  o **Example**: A healthcare organization creates a unified data model that standardizes patient records across hospitals, clinics, and IoT devices. This enables both AI models for diagnosis predictions and BI systems for operational reporting to use the same data set.

- **Data transformation and enrichment**: Before data reaches AI or BI systems, it often needs to be transformed or enriched. Ingestion pipelines should be designed to handle transformations (e.g., normalizing data, converting formats) and enrichment (e.g., adding contextual data) before feeding them into downstream systems.

  o **Example**: A telecom company enriches real-time call data with customer demographic information before feeding it to both AI-powered marketing recommendation systems and BI platforms for sales reporting.

- **Low-latency data processing**: For real-time AI and BI systems, minimizing latency in data ingestion is crucial. Organizations should implement real-time data processing frameworks, such as Apache Kafka, Apache Flink, or AWS Kinesis, to ensure low-latency data flow.

  o **Example**: A fraud detection system for a bank requires sub-second data latency to flag fraudulent transactions in real-time. The data ingestion pipeline uses AWS Kinesis to stream transaction data with minimal delay to the AI system for real-time analysis.

- **Monitoring and performance tuning**: Monitoring the performance of the data ingestion pipeline is key to ensuring that AI and BI systems receive data in a timely and reliable manner. Using tools like Grafana, Prometheus, or AWS CloudWatch, organizations can track key performance metrics such as data throughput, error rates, and latency.

  o **Example**: A BI team monitors the ingestion pipeline for a global retailer to ensure that sales data is processed within the agreed SLA (e.g., data must be ingested and available in the dashboard within five minutes of a sale). Alerts are triggered if performance degrades or if data latency increases.

Real-time AI use cases

Real-time data ingestion pipelines enable AI systems to deliver immediate predictions and insights across a variety of industries.

The following are some common use cases:

- **Predictive maintenance**: AI systems ingest real-time sensor data from industrial machines to predict when maintenance is needed, preventing costly downtime.

- **Real-time personalization**: E-commerce platforms use AI models that ingest real-time customer behavior data to personalize recommendations and improve the shopping experience.

- **Fraud detection**: Financial institutions use AI to detect fraudulent transactions in real-time by ingesting payment data as it occurs and flagging suspicious activity.

The integration of AI and BI systems with data ingestion pipelines is crucial for enabling real-time decision-making, predictive analytics, and operational insights. By following best practices such as building unified data models, optimizing for low latency, and ensuring data quality, organizations can create robust ingestion pipelines that power both AI models and BI platforms. These pipelines are foundational to scaling AI and BI initiatives, ensuring that both systems are always working with the most accurate and up-to-date data.

Real-world examples of technologies in data ingestion

Real-world data ingestion systems rely on a variety of technologies to collect, process, and transport data from diverse sources to target systems such as data lakes, warehouses, or analytics platforms. In this section, we will explore the leading technologies used in data ingestion pipelines, including Apache Kafka, AWS Glue, Azure Data Factory, and Google Cloud Dataflow, and discuss how they are applied in real-world scenarios.

Apache Kafka

Apache Kafka is one of the most widely used platforms for building real-time data streaming pipelines. Originally developed by *LinkedIn*, Kafka allows organizations to ingest large volumes of streaming data from multiple sources and distribute it to various consumers in near-real-time.

LinkedIn

LinkedIn originally developed Kafka to handle real-time tracking of user activity, including page views, likes, and posts. Kafka now processes billions of events per day, allowing LinkedIn to track user behavior and deliver personalized content and recommendations in real-time.

Kafka is built around the concept of producers and consumers. Producers generate data and send it to Kafka topics, while consumers subscribe to those topics and receive data in real-time. Kafka's high throughput, low latency, and horizontal scalability make it ideal for large-scale streaming data ingestion.

The key features of Kafka are as follows:

- **Fault tolerance**: Kafka replicates data across multiple brokers to ensure high availability.

- **Scalability**: Kafka can scale horizontally by adding more brokers to handle higher data volumes.

- **Low latency**: Kafka supports sub-second latency, making it suitable for real-time applications like fraud detection, recommendation engines, and IoT monitoring.

AWS Glue

AWS Glue is a fully managed ETL service designed for building scalable data ingestion pipelines. AWS Glue automates much of the data processing required to move data from various sources into data lakes and warehouses, making it a popular choice for cloud-based data ingestion.

FINRA

The **Financial Industry Regulatory Authority (FINRA)** uses AWS Glue to process and store over 75 billion financial market events every day. The ingestion pipeline built on Glue enables FINRA to analyze this data for regulatory compliance, fraud detection, and market surveillance in near real-time.

AWS Glue automates many tasks related to data ingestion, such as schema discovery, transformations, and loading. It integrates seamlessly with services like Amazon S3, Redshift, and RDS for efficient data storage and analytics.

The key features of AWS Glue are as follows:

- **Serverless**: No need to manage infrastructure, as Glue automatically provisions and scales resources as needed.

- **Data catalog**: Automatically discovers and catalogs metadata from ingested data, making it easier to query and analyze.

- **Flexible ETL**: Supports both batch and real-time data ingestion, allowing organizations to handle a wide range of use cases.

  Azure Data Factory is a cloud-based data integration service that allows organizations to build complex data ingestion pipelines for collecting, transforming, and moving data between various on-premises and cloud sources. It supports a wide range of data connectors, making it highly versatile for integrating disparate systems.

Toyota

Toyota uses Azure Data Factory to ingest and process data from its global network of manufacturing plants, connected vehicles, and customer service systems. This data is then used to optimize production processes, improve vehicle performance, and deliver personalized customer experiences.

Azure Data Factory enables users to build data ingestion workflows, known as **data pipelines**, which orchestrate the movement and transformation of data. These pipelines can be triggered on a schedule or in response to specific events, enabling both batch and real-time data ingestion.

The key features of Azure Data Factory are as follows:

- **Integration with Azure services**: Seamlessly integrates with other Azure services like Azure Data Lake, Azure Blob Storage, and Azure Synapse Analytics.

- **Hybrid data support**: Can ingest data from both cloud-based and on-premises systems, making it ideal for hybrid environments.

- **Visual workflow designer**: Provides a drag-and-drop interface for building data pipelines, making it accessible for users without deep technical expertise.

Google Cloud Dataflow

Google Cloud Dataflow is a fully managed service for building data pipelines that support both stream and batch processing. It is built on Apache Beam, an open-source model for defining and executing parallel data processing jobs, making dataflow highly flexible and scalable.

Spotify

Spotify uses Google Cloud Dataflow to ingest and process real-time data from millions of listeners worldwide. Dataflow allows Spotify to stream user activity data, such as song plays, skips, and playlist updates, in real-time to its analytics and recommendation systems, ensuring personalized experiences for its users.

Dataflow enables developers to write data processing jobs using Apache Beam, which can then be executed as either batch or streaming pipelines. Dataflow automatically scales resources based on the data volume, ensuring high availability and performance.

The key features of Google Cloud Dataflow are as follows:

- **Unified programming model**: Supports both stream and batch data processing in the same pipeline, reducing complexity.

- **Auto-scaling**: Automatically scales resources up or down depending on the workload, ensuring cost-efficiency and performance.

- **Integration with Google Cloud services**: Integrates seamlessly with other Google Cloud services like BigQuery, Cloud Storage, and pub/sub, enabling powerful analytics and machine learning workflows.

Conclusion

In this chapter, we learned that effective data ingestion plays a pivotal role in ensuring that modern data ecosystems remain scalable, reliable, and efficient. By leveraging scalable architectures, robust error handling mechanisms, and optimized transformation techniques, organizations can prevent bottlenecks and ensure the smooth flow of data from diverse sources into storage and processing systems. Addressing both functional and non-functional errors not only enhances data quality but also protects system performance, allowing ingestion pipelines to handle varying loads and maintain stability even under high traffic conditions. This resilience is critical for supporting downstream applications that rely on consistent, timely data delivery.

Furthermore, incorporating AI and BI tools into the data ingestion process unlocks new opportunities for real-time analytics and predictive modeling. These integrations empower organizations to extract valuable insights from ingested data, fostering more informed decision-making and strategic growth. Effective data ingestion also enables the implementation of governance practices, ensuring that data is secure, compliant, and traceable across its lifecycle.

As data ingestion forms the cornerstone of the broader data pipeline, the next chapter will discuss **data storage architectures** that ensure ingested data is not only preserved but also optimized for long-term accessibility and performance. The focus will shift to exploring distributed storage solutions, data lakes, and warehouses that provide the infrastructure necessary to manage large datasets, support real-time querying, and enable seamless integration with advanced analytics and AI workflows.

CHAPTER 4
Data Storage in Real-time

Introduction

In the previous chapter, we discussed the intricacies of **data ingestion**, covering its significance in the data pipeline, scalability strategies, performance enhancements, and how real-time and batch data ingestion methods differ in terms of business use cases. As we transition from ingestion, the next critical phase in the data engineering lifecycle is **data storage**, particularly focusing on how data is stored and managed in real-time environments. The flow from data ingestion into storage is vital because it determines how the data can be accessed, processed, and used in AI models, BI dashboards, and real-time analytics.

In this chapter, we explore the various architectures, strategies, and technologies associated with **real-time data storage**. This chapter will discuss the challenges of maintaining scalability, consistency, and performance while storing real-time data. It will also prepare us for the next chapter, *Chapter 5, Data Processing Techniques and Best Practices*, where we will move into **scalable data processing**, showing how stored data is processed in real-time for further analysis and use in business-critical applications.

Structure

This chapter covers the following topics:

- Connecting data ingestion and storage

- Scalable storage architectures

- Data consistency, availability, and partitioning

- Balancing CAP theorem in real-time systems

- Key technologies for real-time data storage

- Storage solutions optimized for AI workloads

Objectives

By the end of this chapter, readers will have a comprehensive understanding of real-time data storage and its critical role in maintaining the flow and accessibility of ingested data. Readers will explore the architectural patterns, technologies, and strategies that enable low-latency, high-availability storage solutions essential for supporting AI models, BI applications, and real-time analytics. Key topics include the Lambda and Kappa architectures, data partitioning, and balancing **consistency, availability, and partition tolerance (CAP)** in distributed systems.

Readers will have a solid grasp of how to design scalable and resilient storage solutions that ensure data remains accessible for downstream processing. This sets the foundation for the next chapter, scalable data processing techniques and best practices, which will focus on transforming and analyzing stored data to drive actionable insights. The seamless integration of storage and processing is essential for businesses seeking to leverage real-time data for decision-making, ensuring that data pipelines are not only efficient but also capable of handling growing workloads and complex analytics.

Connecting data ingestion and storage

Once the data has been ingested, whether in real-time via streaming services or in batch mode, it needs to be stored efficiently for downstream processes, like analytics, AI modeling, and business intelligence. Ingested data can come from various sources, including transactional databases, IoT devices, social media platforms, and enterprise systems. Efficient real-time storage ensures that this data is readily available for querying, processing, and analysis with minimal latency.

Real-time storage

In today's fast-paced world, businesses depend on quick insights derived from data. Real-time storage systems are essential for applications that require up-to-the-minute data for operational decision-making, such as:

- Financial trading platforms that need real-time market data to execute trades instantly.

- IoT-driven monitoring systems that collect sensor data to predict equipment failures.

- Customer behavior tracking for personalized experiences in e-commerce.

The transition from ingestion to storage must be seamless to avoid bottlenecks, data loss, or delayed access to the data. As we have seen above, financial trading platforms depend on instantaneous market data to execute trades, while IoT systems leverage real-time storage to monitor and predict equipment performance. These examples highlight how robust, low-latency storage underpins operational efficiency in dynamic environments.

Key components of real-time data storage

Before discussing the specific architectures and solutions, it is essential to break down the key components of any real-time data storage system, as follows:

- **Data consistency**: Ensuring that data remains consistent across distributed systems.

- **Scalability**: Ability to handle increasing amounts of data as business operations grow.

- **Low latency**: Data must be stored in such a way that it can be accessed instantly when needed.

- **Availability and fault tolerance**: The storage system should be resilient to failures and capable of recovering without data loss.

- **Data partitioning**: Distributing data across multiple storage units for parallel processing and quick access.

Each of these components will be explored in detail, providing a foundation for the advanced topics to come, including the choice of storage systems and architectural patterns.

Scalable storage architectures

Real-time data storage demands an architecture that is optimized for low-latency access, high throughput, and horizontal scalability. This section discusses a few common architectural patterns used in modern real-time storage solutions.

Lambda architecture

The Lambda architecture is a design pattern developed to handle massive quantities of data by leveraging both real-time and batch processing. This architecture is particularly effective for systems where low-latency responses are required, but accuracy over time is also critical. It operates by dividing incoming data into two distinct processing streams, a batch layer and a speed layer. These two layers serve complementary purposes, ensuring that the system can provide fast, real-time data insights while also generating accurate, comprehensive data results through batch processing.

At the core of the batch layer, the system focuses on processing vast amounts of historical data. This layer ingests data in large volumes over longer intervals, allowing for the generation of accurate, comprehensive views of the data. The processing in this layer typically uses distributed systems like Apache Hadoop or Apache Spark, which can handle massive datasets across many nodes. The results from the batch layer are stored in a durable and scalable data storage system like Amazon S3 or HDFS, where they can be queried later. The main drawback of the batch layer is that the results are delayed, as processing large datasets takes time.

The speed layer, on the other hand, is designed for real-time data processing. It ingests data as soon as it arrives and immediately processes it to generate fast, albeit less accurate, insights. Technologies like Apache Kafka, Apache Flink, or AWS Kinesis are often used in the speed layer to handle the continuous flow of data. This layer provides near-instantaneous feedback, which is essential for applications like real-time fraud detection, recommendation engines, or live monitoring dashboards. The insights from the speed layer may be less thorough than those from the batch layer, but they provide immediate value in situations where time is critical.

The serving layer in the Lambda architecture plays a vital role by merging the results from both the batch and speed layers. This layer stores the processed data and allows users to query it, ensuring that they receive both real-time and historical insights. Initially, queries may return real-time data from the speed layer, but as more accurate batch data becomes available, the serving layer updates its results to reflect the full dataset. This dual-path system ensures that businesses can make decisions quickly based on real-time data, while also benefiting from the comprehensive, error-free insights generated by the batch process. This balance between real-time responsiveness and long-term accuracy makes the Lambda architecture ideal for applications requiring both immediacy and reliability in data processing.

Figure 4.1 represents Lambda architecture, showcasing data flow from sources into a batch layer for historical processing and a speed layer for real-time insights. Both layers feed the serving layer, providing unified query results and enabling immediate actions.

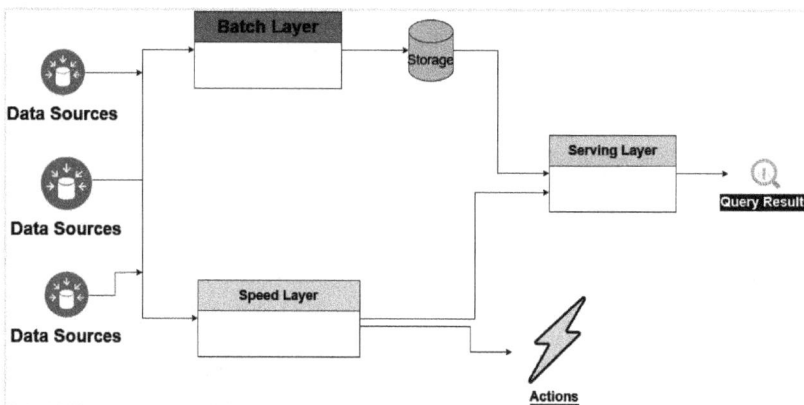

Figure 4.1: *Lambda architecture*

The combination of these two layers provides a balance between immediate data availability and historical data analysis, for example, in an e-commerce system, real-time user data (clicks, page views, and purchases) flows through the speed layer, providing immediate insights for marketing campaigns, while batch processing provides long-term analytics on sales performance.

Kappa architecture

Unlike Lambda, which requires both a batch and a real-time (speed) layer, the Kappa architecture processes all data as streams, ensuring real-time analytics and insights as the data flows through the system. This eliminates the need to maintain a batch layer, reducing complexity and operational overhead. The idea behind Kappa is that in a world where data is constantly arriving at high velocity, processing data as a stream not only provides quicker insights but can also meet most long-term storage and analytics needs without the need for separate batch processing. Systems that rely on real-time event processing, such as IoT platforms, stock trading applications, and online recommendation systems, benefit significantly from this architecture due to its simplicity and immediacy.

The following figure illustrates the Kappa architecture, where data from multiple sources flows through a single speed layer for real-time processing. The processed data is then sent to the serving layer to deliver insights and enable immediate actions.

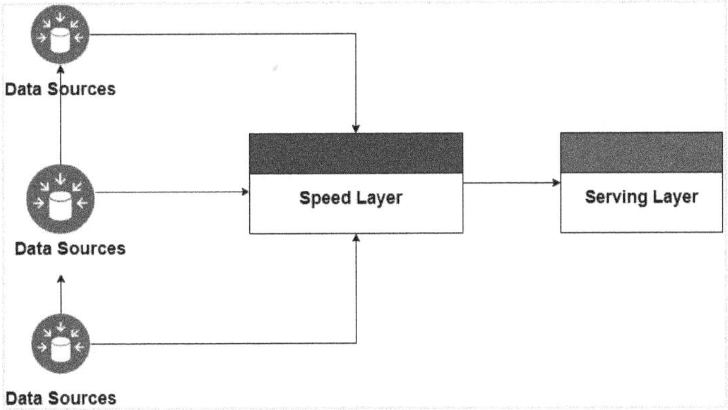

Figure 4.2: *Kappa architecture*

The power of Kappa architecture lies in its flexibility and efficiency. With all data being processed as a stream, you can reprocess historical data as if it were live, using the same code and infrastructure. This means that the architecture supports not only real-time processing but also retrospective analysis by replaying streams. This single framework is capable of handling both historical and current data, making it an ideal choice for use cases that require low-latency insights and the ability to easily scale horizontally to handle increasing data loads. For organizations focused on minimizing complexity and maximizing the value of real-time data, Kappa is a compelling alternative to Lambda.

Data lake architecture

The data lake architecture is a modern approach to storing large volumes of data in its raw, native format, offering flexibility and scalability that traditional storage systems cannot provide. Unlike structured databases or data warehouses, which require data to be pre-processed and structured before storage, a data lake allows for the ingestion of data as is, whether it is structured, semi-structured, or unstructured. This approach is highly beneficial for organizations dealing with diverse types of data such as IoT sensor data, logs, videos, images, and more. By storing everything in a centralized repository, businesses can access their raw data at any time for further processing, analysis, or application in various use cases.

One of the main advantages of a data lake is its ability to support a wide range of data processing frameworks and analytics tools. Raw data stored in a data lake can later be processed using technologies like Apache Hadoop, Apache Spark, or Presto to extract insights. This enables organizations to cater to multiple use cases, from real-time data analytics to long-term data archiving. Data lakes are often built on scalable cloud infrastructure, such as Amazon S3, Google Cloud Storage, or Azure Data Lake, allowing them to grow with the data without incurring the performance limitations of traditional systems. The elasticity of data lakes makes them ideal for businesses that expect rapid data growth and need a storage solution that scales cost-effectively.

The following figure represents a data lake architecture, where raw data from multiple sources flows into the ingestion layer for processing and storage:

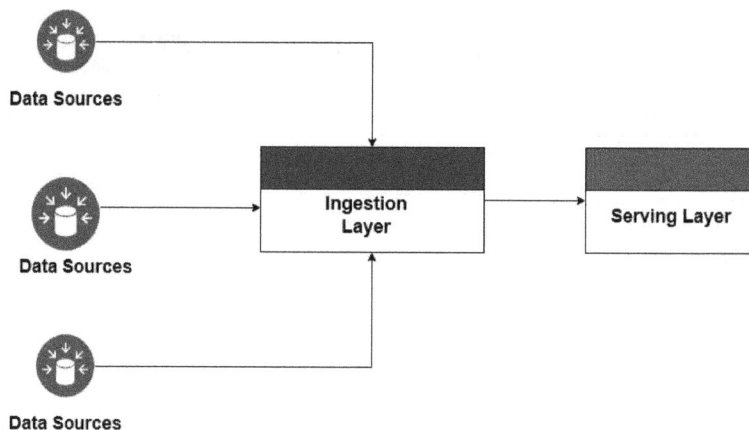

Figure 4.3: Data lake architecture

In addition to scalability, the data lake architecture also empowers businesses to future-proof their data strategy. By keeping raw data in its original format, organizations maintain the flexibility to reprocess it as new technologies, business questions, or use cases emerge. For example, a machine learning team can revisit older datasets stored in the lake to apply newer models or algorithms, while data scientists may extract different insights using advanced analytics techniques. This flexibility ensures that the organization gets long-term value from its data, regardless of how the use cases evolve over time. As a result, data lakes have become a key architecture for enterprises focused on harnessing the full potential of big data and AI-driven innovation.

Data consistency, availability, and partitioning

In distributed data systems, achieving the right balance between data consistency, availability, and partitioning is crucial to ensure that real-time data storage systems can scale effectively, provide low-latency access to data, and remain resilient in the face of failures. These three aspects are often discussed in relation to the CAP theorem, which states that in a distributed system, you can only achieve two of the three guarantees: consistency, availability, and partition tolerance. In real-time data storage, this balance becomes even more critical as systems must not only handle large volumes of data but also deliver accurate and timely results across geographically distributed environments. In this section, we will explore the interplay between these three factors and discuss best practices for implementing them in real-time architectures.

Consistency ensures data accuracy

Consistency in a distributed system means that every read operation returns the most recent write for a given piece of data. In other words, all nodes in a distributed database should agree on the current state of the data. Achieving strong consistency ensures that users always receive accurate and up-to-date information, which is essential in certain use cases like financial transactions, online banking, and e-commerce platforms, where even minor discrepancies can lead to significant issues.

However, strong consistency can be challenging to maintain in distributed environments because of the need for all nodes to coordinate with each other before acknowledging a write operation. This coordination introduces latency, which can be problematic in real-time systems that require fast, low-latency access to data, for instance, if multiple copies of data exist across different geographic regions, ensuring that each copy is updated before allowing reads can slow down the system, especially in environments with high write throughput.

In order to address this, many real-time systems opt for eventual consistency instead of strong consistency. Eventual consistency guarantees that all nodes will eventually converge to the same state, but it allows for temporary inconsistencies. This is often a good trade-off for applications that prioritize availability and low latency over absolute correctness, such as social media platforms or real-time analytics systems, where minor discrepancies in data may be tolerable for short periods. Systems like Apache Cassandra and Amazon DynamoDB offer tunable consistency levels, allowing developers to choose between strong consistency, eventual consistency, or something in between, depending on the application's requirements.

Availability ensures uptime and accessibility

Availability refers to the system's ability to ensure that every request receives a response, whether it is successful or failed. In highly available systems, data is always accessible, even in the event of hardware or network failures. This is particularly important in real-time data storage systems, where downtime or inaccessibility of data can have significant consequences. For instance, in a stock trading platform, a few seconds of downtime could result in missed trades or inaccurate market data, while in IoT systems, a delay in accessing sensor data might prevent critical actions from being taken in real time.

Achieving high availability often involves replicating data across multiple nodes or geographic regions so that if one node or region becomes unavailable, the data can still be accessed from another. This replication ensures that the system can continue to operate, even if individual components fail. In real-time systems, replication strategies must also consider how quickly changes made in one region can propagate to other regions, as this affects both consistency and latency.

The challenge with ensuring availability in distributed systems is that it often conflicts with consistency. For example, to achieve high availability, a system might allow reads and writes to occur on different replicas without waiting for all replicas to be updated. This improves availability because the system can always serve requests, but it also increases the risk of users seeing outdated or inconsistent data. This is why some real-time storage technologies, such as Redis, emphasize availability by providing data from memory caches, but may sacrifice strong consistency in the process to ensure low-latency access.

Partition tolerance ensuring network failure resilience

Partition tolerance refers to the system's ability to continue operating correctly even when communication between nodes is temporarily lost, such as during network failures. In distributed systems, network partitions, where nodes in different regions or data centers become temporarily unable to communicate with each other, are inevitable, especially in large-scale systems that span multiple geographic regions. A partition-tolerant system ensures that it can continue to operate and serve requests, even if some nodes become unreachable or network communication is disrupted.

Partition tolerance is especially important in real-time data storage systems because these systems often operate across multiple data centers or cloud regions. In the event of a partition, the system must decide how to handle the loss of communication between nodes. This decision often involves making trade-offs between availability and consistency. For example, some systems might prioritize availability and continue serving requests from the remaining nodes, even if it means serving stale data, while others might prioritize consistency and refuse to serve data until the partition is resolved and all nodes are synchronized.

Technologies like Apache Kafka and Cassandra are designed to handle partition tolerance effectively. They use replication strategies that ensure that even if some nodes or regions become unavailable, data can still be accessed from other nodes. However, this comes with the trade-off that data may not be fully consistent until the partition is resolved. For real-time systems, partition tolerance is critical for maintaining uptime and ensuring that services remain operational even in the face of network failures.

Balancing CAP theorem in real-time systems

The CAP theorem highlights the trade-offs that must be made in distributed data storage systems. Since, a distributed system cannot simultaneously guarantee all three properties, real-time data systems often prioritize different aspects depending on the use case, for instance, financial systems might prioritize consistency to ensure that transactions are always accurate, even if that means sacrificing some availability during network partitions. On the other hand, social media platforms might prioritize availability, ensuring that users can always access the platform, even if it means temporarily showing slightly outdated information.

In real-time systems, the focus is often on balancing availability and partition tolerance, as these systems need to ensure that data remains accessible, even in the face of network failures or high data loads. Technologies like DynamoDB and Cassandra provide tunable consistency levels that allow developers to adjust the system's behavior based on their specific requirements, for example, a system could prioritize availability during normal operations but switch to eventual consistency when network partitions occur, ensuring that the system remains operational while sacrificing some consistency temporarily.

Ultimately, the best way to balance these factors is to design the system based on the specific needs of the application. For systems that require low-latency, real-time access to data, such as IoT platforms, online gaming systems, or real-time analytics dashboards, availability and partition tolerance are often prioritized, with consistency being relaxed to ensure fast, uninterrupted access to data. For other systems, such as, e-commerce platforms or financial systems, consistency might be more important, even if that means introducing some delays during network partitions.

Data partitioning for scalability

Data partitioning plays a crucial role in ensuring scalability and performance in real-time data storage systems. Partitioning involves splitting data into smaller subsets (partitions) that can be distributed across multiple nodes or servers. This allows the system to handle larger datasets and higher read or write throughput by distributing the workload across multiple machines. By partitioning data, real-time systems can achieve horizontal scalability, where additional servers can be added to the system to handle increasing amounts of data and traffic.

In real-time systems, partitioning is often combined with sharding, where data is distributed across different partitions based on a key (e.g., user ID, timestamp, or geographic location). This ensures that related data is stored together in the same partition, allowing for faster queries and more efficient data processing. For example, in a real-time analytics system, data might be partitioned based on the time it was ingested, ensuring that recent data can be accessed quickly without having to search through older partitions.

Partitioning also helps improve fault tolerance and availability. By distributing data across multiple partitions, the system can continue to operate even if some partitions become unavailable. This is especially important in real-time systems that need to maintain uptime and performance even in the face of hardware failures or network outages. Technologies like Cassandra, DynamoDB, and Google Bigtable all leverage partitioning to ensure that their systems can scale horizontally and remain highly available in real-time environments.

Key technologies for real-time data storage

In real-time data storage, choosing the right technologies is crucial to ensure low-latency, high-throughput data access. With the rapid expansion of data-driven applications, ranging from IoT devices and real-time analytics to AI model training, businesses require storage solutions that are both scalable and responsive. These technologies must provide robust mechanisms for data availability, fault tolerance, and real-time querying. In this section, we will explore seven key technologies that are widely used for real-time data storage, detailing their strengths, use cases, and how they integrate into modern data architectures.

Amazon DynamoDB

Amazon DynamoDB is a fully managed NoSQL database service provided by AWS, designed for applications that require consistent, low-latency access to data. One of the key features of DynamoDB is its ability to scale automatically, ensuring that the database can handle any increase in data volume or read or write operations without the need for manual intervention. It is particularly well-suited for real-time applications like gaming leaderboards, recommendation engines, and real-time monitoring systems, where data needs to be available instantaneously.

DynamoDB employs a partition-based architecture, distributing data across multiple servers to ensure high availability and fault tolerance. Each partition is replicated to ensure that even in the event of a failure, data remains accessible. The system also supports in-memory caching with **DynamoDB Accelerator (DAX)**, which improves read performance by up to ten times, making it ideal for applications requiring ultra-low-latency data retrieval.

One of DynamoDB's strengths is its event-driven architecture, which can trigger actions when data is modified. This makes it useful for real-time applications that require immediate actions based on changes in data, such as sending alerts or notifications when certain thresholds are exceeded. DynamoDB's seamless integration with other AWS services, such as Lambda for serverless computing and Kinesis for real-time streaming, makes it a popular choice for building scalable, real-time data systems.

Apache Cassandra

Apache Cassandra is a highly scalable, distributed NoSQL database designed to handle large amounts of data across many servers without a single point of failure. Initially developed by *Facebook*, Cassandra has since become a widely adopted open-source solution for real-time data storage, especially in use cases where data must be available 24/7 with no downtime, such as in financial services, telecommunications, and e-commerce.

Cassandra's architecture is based on a peer-to-peer model, meaning that every node in the cluster is identical and can handle read and write requests. This decentralized approach ensures high availability, even in the face of hardware failures, making it an excellent choice for geographically distributed systems that need real-time access to data. Additionally, Cassandra's eventual consistency model allows for highly efficient write operations, enabling it to handle high-velocity data streams in real time.

For businesses focused on real-time analytics and operational intelligence, Cassandra is often integrated with Apache Kafka or Apache Spark, where data can be ingested in real time and stored in Cassandra for fast querying. The combination of write-anywhere capabilities and real-time data retrieval makes Cassandra an optimal solution for applications that demand both scalability and high availability.

Google Bigtable

Google Bigtable is a fully managed, distributed NoSQL database service provided by Google Cloud, specifically designed for high-throughput, low-latency workloads. It powers several of Google's own applications, such as *Gmail*, *Google Maps*, and *YouTube*, making it one of the most battle-tested data storage technologies available. Bigtable is highly scalable, allowing organizations to store petabytes of data across thousands of nodes while maintaining millisecond-level response times.

Bigtable is ideal for time-series data, where data points are captured over time and require fast access for real-time analysis. This makes it a popular choice for IoT applications, financial market analysis, and operational monitoring systems. Bigtable's ability to handle both structured and semi-structured data allows businesses to build highly flexible real-time data architectures, where data from multiple sources is ingested, stored, and processed in near real-time.

One of Bigtable's strengths is its seamless integration with Google Cloud BigQuery and Google Cloud Dataflow, enabling businesses to perform real-time queries and data processing with ease. Whether it is for real-time dashboarding, ML model training, or dynamic data analysis, Bigtable provides the scalability and performance needed for high-velocity data environments. Its simplicity and flexibility also allow businesses to focus more on data processing and insights, rather than infrastructure management.

Apache HBase

Apache HBase is an open-source, distributed NoSQL database that runs on top of the **Hadoop Distributed File System** (**HDFS**). Originally modeled after *Google's Bigtable*, HBase is designed for real-time read and write access to large datasets. It is particularly useful for real-time analytics where massive amounts of unstructured or semi-structured data need to be stored and retrieved quickly. One of the key strengths of HBase is its ability to store billions of rows of data with very low latency, making it suitable for applications like fraud detection, clickstream analysis, and social media analytics.

HBase is built for **horizontal scalability**, allowing businesses to add more servers to the system as their data grows. This makes it a reliable solution for large-scale, real-time applications where data growth is exponential. HBase integrates well with the broader Hadoop ecosystem, enabling businesses to perform complex data processing and analytics on top of the data stored in HBase using tools like Apache Spark or Hive.

Additionally, HBase supports **time-series data** storage, allowing businesses to store and query data over time, which is particularly valuable for real-time monitoring systems. For example, companies in the telecommunications industry use HBase to monitor network traffic in real time, allowing them to detect anomalies and respond to issues as they arise.

Redis

Redis is an open-source, in-memory data structure store used as a database, cache, and message broker. Known for its blazing-fast performance, Redis is widely used in applications where low-latency access to data is critical, such as gaming leaderboards, real-time analytics, and recommendation engines. By storing data in-memory rather than on disk, Redis can provide millisecond response times, making it ideal for real-time data storage and retrieval.

One of Redis's key features is its support for a variety of data structures, such as strings, hashes, lists, sets, and sorted sets, which enables developers to implement a wide range of use cases with minimal effort. Additionally, Redis supports **pub/sub messaging**, which allows for real-time data broadcasting, making it a popular choice for chat applications, live feeds, and real-time event tracking.

Redis can also be used as a **cache** to complement other real-time databases. By caching frequently accessed data, Redis helps reduce the load on backend databases and speeds up response times for end-users. For applications that require both fast, transient data storage and long-term persistence, Redis can be configured to periodically write data to disk, combining the benefits of in-memory speed with durable storage.

Amazon Redshift

While primarily known as a data warehouse, Amazon Redshift has evolved to support near real-time data analytics through its Redshift Streaming Ingestion capabilities. Redshift allows businesses to ingest streaming data from services like Amazon Kinesis or Apache Kafka and perform real-time queries and analytics on that data. This makes it a powerful tool for organizations that need to combine both historical data analysis and real-time insights within a single platform.

Redshift's distributed architecture enables it to scale horizontally, allowing businesses to process petabytes of data while maintaining low-latency query performance. This makes it ideal for real-time business intelligence, where users can interact with dashboards that display both historical data and real-time metrics. By integrating with AWS services like S3 for storage, Lambda for serverless processing, and QuickSight for visualizations, Redshift offers a complete ecosystem for real-time data storage and analytics.

Another feature of Redshift that supports real-time use cases is materialized views. These views can be refreshed in real-time, allowing businesses to maintain up-to-date results without having to re-run complex queries. For organizations that require both real-time data processing and the ability to query historical data, Redshift provides a seamless way to manage both workloads in a unified architecture.

Azure Cosmos DB

Azure Cosmos DB is a globally distributed, multi-model database service provided by Microsoft Azure, designed to handle real-time data ingestion and querying at a massive scale. One of the most unique features of Cosmos DB is its global distribution model, which allows data to be replicated across multiple regions with low latency read and write capabilities. This makes Cosmos DB an excellent choice for businesses operating across multiple geographies that need real-time data synchronization, such as e-commerce platforms, social media networks, and financial applications.

Cosmos DB supports multiple data models, including key-value, document, graph, and column family, making it highly flexible for a variety of real-time use cases. The database is designed to deliver single-digit millisecond response times, ensuring that applications can provide fast, real-time access to data. Additionally, Cosmos DB offers tunable consistency levels, allowing businesses to choose the trade-off between consistency, availability, and latency based on their specific needs.

By integrating with Azure's broader suite of services, including Azure Stream Analytics and Azure Machine Learning, Cosmos DB enables organizations to build end-to-end real-time data pipelines that can ingest, process, and analyze data in near real-time. Its ability to support both operational and analytical workloads in a globally distributed environment makes it a key technology for businesses that require real-time data storage at scale.

Storage solutions optimized for AI workloads

As AI and ML continue to revolutionize industries, the demands on data storage systems have grown immensely. AI workloads, especially machine learning training and inference processes, require the storage and retrieval of large datasets, including structured, semi-structured, and unstructured data such as text, images, videos, and sensor readings. Efficient storage solutions optimized for AI workloads must be designed not only for scale but also for speed, reliability, and integration with high-performance computing environments. In this section, we will discuss some of the key storage technologies and approaches that are tailored for AI workloads, focusing on their ability to handle vast amounts of data while minimizing latency and maximizing throughput.

Object storage for AI workloads

One of the most popular storage solutions for AI workloads is object storage, which provides a scalable, flexible, and cost-efficient method of storing large datasets. Unlike traditional file systems or block storage, object storage organizes data as discrete objects that can be easily indexed and retrieved using unique identifiers. This structure is ideal for AI applications because object storage can scale horizontally, allowing for the storage of vast amounts of unstructured data, including images, audio, video, and other large data types commonly used in AI model training.

Leading cloud providers offer object storage solutions, such as Amazon S3, Google Cloud Storage, and Azure Blob Storage, all of which are optimized for AI and machine learning workloads. These services provide near-infinite scalability, allowing organizations to store petabytes of data without performance degradation. Additionally, object storage solutions typically offer seamless integration with compute services like AWS EC2 or Google Cloud AI Platform, enabling AI workloads to easily access the data they need for training models or running inference.

One of the key benefits of object storage is its cost-efficiency. AI workloads often involve storing massive datasets for long periods, and object storage solutions use tiered storage models that allow organizations to store frequently accessed data in high-performance tiers and move less critical data to cheaper, slower storage tiers over time. For instance, Amazon S3 offers S3 Intelligent Tiering, which automatically moves data between storage tiers based on access patterns. This feature helps organizations optimize storage costs while maintaining performance for active datasets.

Parallel file systems

AI workloads, especially when training deep learning models, require not only vast amounts of data but also extremely fast access to that data. Large-scale models, such as those used in computer vision or **natural language processing** (**NLP**), often rely on high-throughput and low-latency access to datasets to ensure that training can proceed efficiently. This is where parallel file systems come into play, as they are designed to provide high-performance storage solutions that can keep up with the demands of AI model training.

A parallel file system distributes data across multiple servers and storage devices, allowing multiple compute nodes to access the same dataset simultaneously. This setup dramatically improves the throughput of read/write operations, enabling faster data loading during model training. One popular example of a parallel file system is Lustre, which is widely used in **high-performance computing** (HPC) environments, including AI and machine learning. Lustre is known for its ability to handle petabytes of data and provide extremely high I/O speeds, making it an excellent choice for AI workloads that require frequent access to large datasets.

Another example is the IBM Spectrum Scale (formerly GPFS), which also provides high-throughput, low-latency access to large-scale datasets and is commonly used in AI training environments. These systems are optimized for distributed computing environments, where multiple GPUs or CPUs are used to train AI models. By enabling simultaneous access to data from multiple compute nodes, parallel file systems ensure that the training process is not bottlenecked by slow data retrieval, leading to faster time-to-results for AI models.

For organizations running AI workloads in the cloud, services like Amazon FSx for Lustre or Azure NetApp Files provide managed parallel file systems that integrate with cloud computing services. These solutions enable data scientists and AI engineers to leverage high-performance storage without having to manage the underlying infrastructure, allowing them to focus on model development and training.

Combining object and block storage

AI workloads often require a combination of storage types to optimize both performance and cost. Hybrid storage solutions that combine object storage and block storage are frequently used in AI environments to achieve this balance. Object storage, as discussed earlier, is highly scalable and cost-efficient, making it ideal for storing raw, unstructured data like videos or large image datasets. However, for AI models in production or high-frequency access patterns, block storage can provide the low-latency, high-performance characteristics necessary for real-time inference.

Block storage operates at a lower level than object storage and is more akin to traditional disk storage. It allows for faster data access times and is better suited for applications that require rapid I/O operations, such as databases or real-time analytics. AI applications that require near-instantaneous access to small datasets, such as autonomous vehicles or financial trading systems, often rely on block storage to store models and critical real-time data. Cloud-based block storage solutions, such as Amazon EBS or Azure Managed Disks, can be used alongside object storage to ensure that AI applications have both the capacity and the speed they need.

One example of how hybrid storage solutions can optimize AI workloads is in the development and deployment of deep learning models. During the training phase, object storage is used to store large amounts of training data (e.g., images or text). Once the model is trained, it can be stored on block storage for faster access during the inference phase, where predictions must be made in real time. This approach maximizes cost-efficiency during the training phase and ensures high performance when the model is deployed in production.

Moreover, hybrid storage architectures are particularly useful for AI-driven industries like healthcare and autonomous systems, where both long-term data storage (for research and historical analysis) and real-time data access (for diagnostics or autonomous navigation) are essential. By combining object and block storage, AI workloads can meet diverse performance and storage requirements without sacrificing scalability or efficiency.

Conclusion

In this chapter, we explored the critical aspects of real-time data storage, connecting it to the previous chapter on *Data Ingestion* and laying the groundwork for the next chapter on *Scalable Data Processing*. Efficient real-time storage ensures that ingested data is immediately available for processing, querying, and analysis in AI and BI systems. By integrating real-time storage solutions with a solid data ingestion pipeline, organizations can ensure that their data is always available for immediate analysis, powering decisions that drive business success.

In the next chapter, we will explore how this stored data is processed and transformed into actionable insights, enabling businesses to remain agile and competitive.

Join our book's Discord space

Join the book's Discord Workspace for Latest updates, Offers, Tech happenings around the world, New Release and Sessions with the Authors:

https://discord.bpbonline.com

## CHAPTER 5

Data Processing Techniques and Best Practices

Introduction

As our journey through data engineering continues, we have covered the essential steps of data collection, ingestion, and storage, as well as processes that ensure raw data is gathered, moved, and organized into accessible storage systems. Now, we arrive at the critical phase of data processing, where raw data is transformed into structured, actionable insights ready for analytics and AI applications. This chapter will walk you through the techniques and best practices for scalable data processing, focusing on the choices, tools, and frameworks that allow data engineers to handle massive data volumes efficiently.

In data processing, we make decisions that directly impact how data flows through the pipeline: ETL vs. ELT workflows, SQL vs. NoSQL processing, and batch vs. streaming systems, each tailored to fit different data requirements. By exploring each of these techniques, along with best practices for data quality, governance, and cost management, we will see how scalable processing forms the backbone of a successful data pipeline. This chapter will introduce specific technologies, from Apache Spark to AWS Glue, and focus on how these tools prepare data to feed into AI and BI applications effectively.

As we go forward, this chapter will set the stage for understanding *Chapter 6, Data Integration and Interoperability,* where the goal is to ensure that all data sources work together seamlessly within the broader data ecosystem. Together, these steps create a streamlined, comprehensive approach to managing and utilizing data at scale.

Structure

The chapter covers the following topics:

- Best practices for choosing between ETL and ELT
- Introduction to SQL and NoSQL
- Batch and streaming data systems
- Data quality assurance
- AI and BI applications
- Real-world examples and technologies

Objectives

By the end of this chapter, readers will explore the critical techniques and best practices for efficient data processing, a cornerstone of modern data pipelines. It explores the importance of structuring data for optimal performance, highlighting the role of ETL and ELT in transforming raw data into actionable insights. Key topics include the use of SQL and NoSQL for managing structured and unstructured data, as well as batch and streaming systems for handling large-scale datasets. The chapter also emphasizes the significance of data quality assurance, governance, and cost-effective processing. By mastering these practices, organizations can ensure that their data pipelines are robust, scalable, and primed for AI and BI applications. The next chapter will build on this foundation by focusing on data quality assurance, reinforcing the importance of accuracy and consistency in driving reliable analytics.

Best practices for choosing between ETL and ELT

In data engineering, two primary workflows, ETL and ELT, represent essential approaches for preparing raw data from various sources for analytics, machine learning, and reporting. Although they share a common goal of transforming data into a usable form, the order of operations, storage environments, and data handling requirements vary significantly between the two.

ETL is a traditional approach in which data is extracted from its source, transformed to fit the schema and requirements of the target, and then loaded into a data warehouse or structured environment. This method is favored when data quality and consistency are top priorities, as the transformation step ensures data integrity before it enters storage. Conversely, **ELT** represents a more flexible, modern approach where data is loaded directly into a storage environment in raw form, and transformations are applied later within the target system itself. ELT's structure is highly scalable, especially when dealing with vast amounts of semi-structured or unstructured data, and it suits environments that benefit from a schema-on-read model.

This section will discuss the fundamental differences between ETL and ELT, exploring the benefits and challenges of each approach and examining optimal use cases and best practices. A strong understanding of these two methods helps data engineers choose the right approach based on their data needs, ensuring efficient and reliable data pipelines.

Key differences between ETL and ELT

The workflows of ETL and ELT differ significantly in sequence, structure, and storage requirements. In ETL, the sequence follows a traditional order: data is extracted from source systems, transformed for consistency and quality, and then loaded into a target system. This process ensures that only structured, clean data enters storage, making ETL ideal for systems where consistency is important. In contrast, ELT shifts this sequence by loading data directly into storage after extraction, delaying transformations until after the data has been ingested. This difference allows ELT to handle high volumes of raw, diverse data that is commonly found in data lakes.

Regarding storage, ETL is frequently implemented in environments that rely on predefined schemas, like data warehouses. Structured data that adheres to a known schema allows for efficient querying, which aligns with the goals of ETL, however, it is better suited to data lakes or similar storage systems capable of handling unstructured or semi-structured data in raw form. Data lakes are highly flexible and scalable, making them ideal for scenarios involving high-volume or IoT data where rapid ingestion is necessary.

Processing time and data handling vary significantly between the two methods as well. ETL can be resource-intensive upfront, as data transforms loading, which ensures structured and high-quality data is ready for immediate use. ELT, in contrast, allows for faster initial loading by deferring transformations. This approach benefits applications that need to handle high-velocity data streams, where rapid ingestion is prioritized, and schema adjustments can occur later based on specific use cases.

Figure 5.1 shows the differences between the ETL and ELT processes:

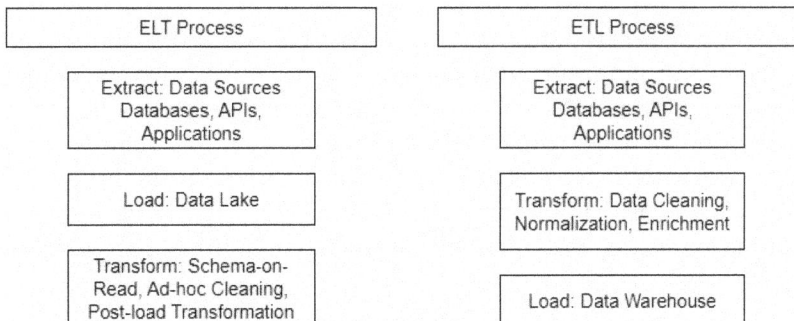

Figure 5.1: ETL vs. ELT process

Extract, transform, load

The ETL process begins by extracting data from various sources, such as relational databases, APIs, and external applications. The extracted data is then subjected to transformation, a stage where it is formatted, cleaned, and enriched to meet the quality and consistency standards required by the target system. Finally, the transformed data is loaded into a target environment, often a structured data warehouse, ready for analysis. ETL is particularly effective for organizations that handle structured data and prioritize high data quality and consistency.

ETL offers several distinct advantages. First, ETL's transformation phase ensures a high level of data quality and consistency before loading. This quality control step produces a clean dataset for downstream analytics, which is crucial for data-driven organizations relying on accurate insights. Additionally, ETL provides a strong framework for compliance and control, making it ideal for regulated industries, such as finance and healthcare, where data integrity is paramount. ETL also allows for schema enforcement during the transformation stage, which means that the data is fully compatible with relational data models upon entering storage.

However, ETL does present challenges. Transforming data before loading can introduce processing overhead, particularly with large datasets, as transformation tasks demand significant computational resources. ETL also faces scalability limitations in big data contexts, where traditional ETL architectures may struggle to keep up with increasing volumes. Furthermore, ETL workflows are generally better suited to structured data, meaning that flexibility may be constrained when dealing with unstructured or semi-structured data types.

Popular tools and technologies support ETL processes. Informatica PowerCenter is widely used in enterprise environments, offering robust data integration features for structured and unstructured sources. Apache NiFi supports ETL with real-time data flow capabilities, making it suitable for streaming data workflows. Cloud-based solutions, such as AWS Glue provide managed ETL within the AWS ecosystem, while Azure Data Factory offers orchestration capabilities for ETL across cloud and on-premises sources.

When implementing ETL, several best practices can improve efficiency and ensure quality. Optimizing extraction performance is essential, as efficient extraction reduces the load on source systems and improves overall speed. Techniques, such as incremental loads and parallel processing can enhance extraction performance, especially for high-volume data. Transformation best practices include data cleansing to remove duplicates and handle missing values and error handling mechanisms to address issues as they arise. For loading data, batch processing helps maintain performance by minimizing overhead, while partitioning and using bulk APIs enable efficient handling of large datasets in target systems.

Extract, load, transform

The ELT process, by contrast, starts with the extraction and immediate loading of data in raw form into a storage environment, typically a data lake or cloud storage solution. Transformations are then applied post-load within the storage environment, allowing the flexibility needed for large-scale, unstructured data processing. ELT's adaptability and scalability make it ideal for big data environments, IoT applications, and scenarios that benefit from schema-on-read capabilities.

ELT's primary advantage lies in the speed of loading, as raw data can be ingested quickly without initial transformations. This workflow is particularly beneficial when handling large volumes of data that require rapid ingestion, as transformations are delayed until specific analyses are needed. ELT also offers enhanced adaptability, as it can manage a wide variety of data formats, including unstructured and semi-structured data, making it well-suited for heterogeneous data sources. Furthermore, scalability is a core strength of ELT, especially in cloud environments where data lakes, such as Amazon S3 and Azure Blob Storage allow for vast data capacity with dynamic compute resources.

While ELT provides notable flexibility, it also introduces unique challenges. Transforming data within the storage environment can add complexity to queries and require additional resources, especially when dealing with complex transformations. The lack of immediate data validation during loading can also impact data quality, as raw data is stored without initial cleansing. Additionally, post-load transformations are resource-intensive, and storage dependencies may increase costs in environments with high data volume.

Several tools are well-suited to ELT. Apache Spark is a leading framework for ELT, offering large-scale processing and transformations directly within data lakes. Google BigQuery supports SQL-based transformations within storage, enabling rapid data analysis without data movement. Snowflake provides a scalable, cloud-native ELT platform with efficient compute and storage separation, while Databricks, built on Apache Spark, allows for advanced data processing and machine learning within the ELT framework.

ELT's best practices include efficient loading into data lakes by leveraging optimized data formats, like Parquet or **optimized row columnar (ORC)**, which reduce storage costs and improve query performance. Partitioning and compression also play key roles in managing storage efficiency. For transformations, schema-on-read enables flexible handling of semi-structured data, and Spark can perform transformations at scale within storage. Post-load data quality management is essential, with data quality audits and monitoring systems needed to ensure data reliability over time.

Choosing between ETL and ELT

Deciding between ETL and ELT hinges on factors, such as data volume, structure, and the intended application. ETL is generally best suited for structured data environments, particularly where data quality and governance are priorities, as seen in traditional data warehousing and financial analytics. ELT, on the other hand, excels in high-volume big data applications, especially where flexibility is required to handle raw or semi-structured data.

For structured environments, ETL offers predictable data quality and is well-suited for highly regulated settings or traditional analytics, such as financial transaction analysis. ELT, however, is optimal for high-velocity, unstructured data use cases, such as machine learning and real-time applications where rapid ingestion and scalability are critical.

Combining ETL and ELT in hybrid pipelines

In many cases, hybrid pipelines combining ETL and ELT offer greater flexibility. Hybrid pipelines can handle diverse data formats, allowing structured, transformed data from ETL workflows alongside raw data from ELT processes. This dual approach supports varied use cases within the same data system, accommodating both high-quality structured data and scalable, schema-on-read data, for example, e-commerce analytics may involve ETL for customer profile data while applying ELT to clickstream data for real-time insights. In healthcare, ETL can manage structured patient records, while ELT processes IoT sensor data, supporting both compliance and predictive analysis.

Introduction to SQL and NoSQL

In the data engineering landscape, **structured query language** (SQL) and **not only SQL** (**NoSQL**) databases offer distinct approaches to data processing, each tailored to different data models, scalability requirements, and types of workloads. SQL databases operate on a structured, relational model that is highly effective for processing structured data with fixed schemas. These databases have been the backbone of transactional systems and analytical workloads due to their strong **atomicity, consistency, isolation, durability** (**ACID**) properties, which ensure data reliability and consistency.

On the other hand, NoSQL databases emerged to address the limitations of traditional relational databases, particularly when handling large-scale, unstructured, or semi-structured data. Designed with a flexible schema approach, NoSQL databases support a variety of data models, key-value, document, column-family, and graphs, allowing for greater scalability and performance in distributed systems. This flexibility makes NoSQL a preferred choice for high-velocity data environments, such as IoT applications and real-time analytics, where schema constraints would otherwise hinder performance.

In this section, we will explore the strengths, weaknesses, and best practices of both SQL and NoSQL processing, providing data engineers with a clear understanding of when to use each to maximize data pipeline efficiency.

SQL processing

SQL processing revolves around structured, relational data models that rely on tables with predefined schemas. Each table has columns representing specific attributes, and rows correspond to records. This structure is conducive to relational operations, such as joins, aggregations, and filtering, enabling SQL databases to provide powerful querying capabilities that support complex analytical and transactional workloads.

The ACID compliance of SQL databases is one of their most significant advantages. Ensuring atomicity, consistency, isolation, and durability makes SQL databases ideal for scenarios where data accuracy and integrity are crucial, such as financial systems, inventory management, and **customer relationship management** (**CRM**). SQL databases are also equipped with indexing, partitioning, and advanced query optimization, allowing for high performance with structured data, even as datasets grow.

SQL use cases

SQL databases excel in applications where data structure and consistency are paramount. Common use cases include financial data processing, where data integrity is critical, and inventory management systems that rely on consistent, relational data structures. **Business intelligence** (**BI**) applications also benefit from SQL databases, as they allow for powerful analytical querying and aggregations, making them ideal for generating insights and reporting.

SQL tools and technologies

MySQL and PostgreSQL are widely used open-source relational databases, providing robust SQL support for transactional and analytical processing. Oracle Database offers a highly scalable commercial SQL database for enterprise applications, while Microsoft SQL Server serves similar functions in enterprise environments. In the cloud, Amazon RDS and Azure SQL Database offers managed SQL database services with built-in support for high availability, backups, and scaling, making them suitable for applications that require minimal database administration.

Best practices for SQL processing

Effective SQL processing relies on optimizing performance and ensuring data integrity. Indexing is a key technique that improves query speed by reducing the amount of data searched. Data engineers should carefully select columns for indexing based on query patterns to avoid excessive storage use. Partitioning large tables by date or category helps improve query performance and manageability, especially in analytical workloads. Finally, query optimization through techniques like avoiding unnecessary joins, minimizing subqueries, and selecting appropriate aggregation functions is essential for reducing processing times and resource consumption.

NoSQL processing

NoSQL databases are designed for flexibility and scalability, supporting a range of data models that cater to different types of unstructured and semi-structured data. Unlike SQL databases, which enforce a fixed schema, NoSQL databases adopt a schema-less approach that accommodates data with evolving structures. This adaptability makes NoSQL highly suitable for applications dealing with dynamic or high-volume data, as it allows data engineers to store data without the need to redefine schemas continually.

NoSQL databases are divided into four primary categories: key-value stores, document databases, column-family stores, and graph databases. Key-value stores provide simple data storage and retrieval, ideal for caching and session storage. Document databases, such as MongoDB and Couchbase, store data in JSON-like documents, making them highly compatible with applications that require a flexible schema. Column-family stores, like Apache Cassandra, allow for distributed storage of large datasets across multiple nodes, providing high availability and fault tolerance. Lastly, graph databases, such as Neo4j, are optimized for managing data relationships and supporting applications like social networks or recommendation engines.

NoSQL use cases

NoSQL databases are particularly effective in handling high-velocity data from applications that generate large volumes of unstructured or semi-structured data. Common use cases include IoT data ingestion, where data is rapidly streamed from devices with minimal structure, and user-generated content platforms, such as social media or e-commerce, where schemas are constantly evolving. NoSQL is also a preferred choice for real-time applications that prioritize availability and low latency over strict consistency, such as recommendation engines, chat applications, and analytics for live dashboards.

NoSQL tools and technologies

MongoDB and Couchbase are widely adopted document-oriented NoSQL databases, providing flexible storage solutions that support a range of application needs. Apache Cassandra and HBase are column-family databases that excel in distributed environments, where high availability and low latency are essential. Redis is a popular key-value store, frequently used for caching and session management. In graph databases, Neo4j supports complex relationship modeling, ideal for applications that require network analysis or recommendation engines.

Best practices for NoSQL processing

NoSQL databases benefit from a flexible approach to data modeling and processing, but they require specific practices to maintain performance and reliability. Data partitioning is essential in distributed NoSQL databases to balance load and ensure fault tolerance. Selecting appropriate partition keys that evenly distribute data across nodes prevents hotspots, which can degrade performance. Indexing in NoSQL databases, particularly in document stores like MongoDB, improves read performance but requires careful management to avoid unnecessary overhead. In real-time applications, write optimization is crucial; techniques such as batching writes and setting up asynchronous data pipelines can significantly enhance throughput.

Choosing between SQL and NoSQL

The choice between SQL and NoSQL databases depends on factors such as data structure, consistency requirements, scalability needs, and intended use cases. SQL databases excel when data integrity, consistency, and relational modeling are priorities, as seen in financial and transactional applications. The fixed schema of SQL databases is advantageous when the data structure is known and stable, making SQL an ideal choice for business intelligence and reporting applications where precise querying is required.

NoSQL databases, however, are highly effective for applications that handle unstructured or rapidly evolving data, such as social media platforms, real-time analytics, and IoT systems. The flexibility of NoSQL allows data engineers to adapt to changing data schemas without disruption, and its horizontal scalability supports large volumes of data. When low latency and high availability are critical, such as in recommendation systems or real-time dashboards, NoSQL databases offer the responsiveness and partition tolerance that SQL databases may struggle to provide in high-scale environments.

Combining SQL and NoSQL in hybrid architectures

In many modern data architectures, both SQL and NoSQL databases are used in tandem to leverage the strengths of each. Hybrid architectures allow organizations to use SQL databases for structured, transactional data while simultaneously handling unstructured or semi-structured data in NoSQL environments. This approach provides flexibility in managing different data types and allows data engineers to address diverse application needs, for example, in an e-commerce platform, an SQL database might manage customer information, order histories, and payment processing, ensuring data consistency and reliability. Meanwhile, a NoSQL database can store user activity data, product catalog metadata, and clickstream information, enabling rapid updates and real-time analysis without strict schema constraints. In this hybrid setup, each database type plays a specific role, optimizing both transactional and real-time analytical capabilities.

Best practices for hybrid architectures include establishing clear data governance to manage the flow of data between SQL and NoSQL systems. Data integration tools, such as Apache Kafka or AWS Glue, help synchronize data, enabling seamless interaction between structured and unstructured data sources. Schema mapping and data lineage tracking are essential to maintain consistency and transparency across both systems, especially when combining data for analysis or machine learning.

Batch and streaming data systems

Data processing lies at the heart of data engineering, where data is transformed, cleaned, and organized for analytical and operational uses. Two primary modes of processing, batch processing, and streaming processing, define how data flows through systems and how quickly insights can be derived. Batch processing involves processing large volumes of data in chunks at scheduled intervals, while streaming processing focuses on real-time processing of data as it arrives, enabling immediate analysis and action.

Both batch and streaming systems serve different purposes and address unique data engineering challenges. Batch processing is well-suited for large datasets where immediacy is not essential, such as end-of-day reporting or historical data analysis. Streaming processing, on the other hand, is designed for time-sensitive applications where data needs to be processed and analyzed on the fly, making it invaluable for use cases like fraud detection, real-time monitoring, and personalized recommendations.

This section explores the characteristics, advantages, and best practices of batch and streaming systems, along with popular tools and technologies that support each mode. By understanding how these systems operate, data engineers can create responsive and efficient data pipelines that support both analytical and real-time applications.

Figure 5.2 explains the key difference in batch vs. stream data processing:

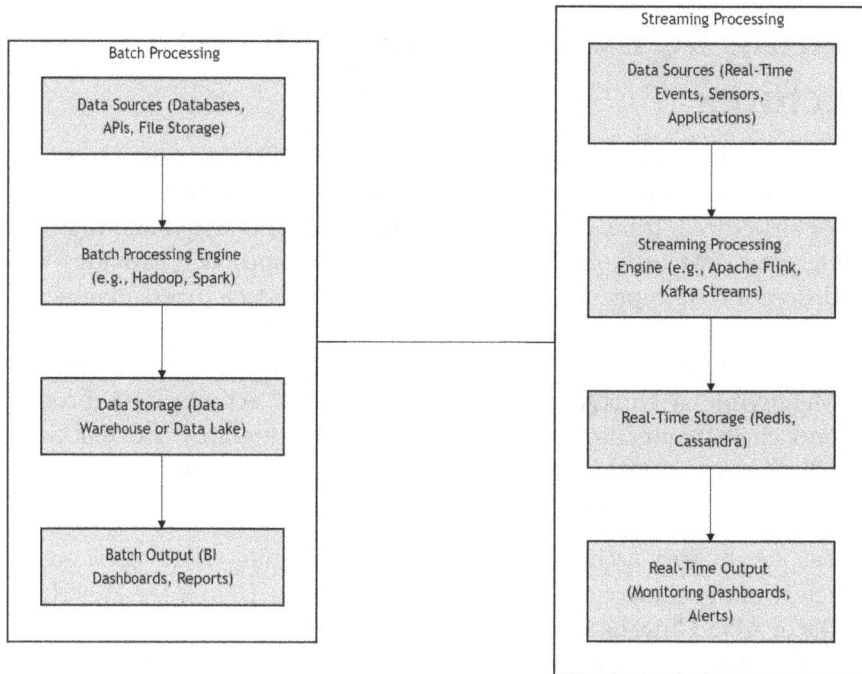

Figure 5.2: Batch vs. stream data processing

Batch data processing

Batch processing is a data processing approach that handles large volumes of data at specified intervals, typically processing the entire dataset in one operation or batch. This method is effective for scenarios where data does not need to be processed immediately, such as financial reporting, aggregating sales data, or performing complex computations on historical datasets. Batch processing is ideal for workloads where data can accumulate over time, and computational efficiency can be achieved by processing data in large chunks.

In batch processing, data is first collected from various sources and stored in a staging area or data lake. The data is then processed according to predefined rules, such as aggregating, filtering, or transforming it before loading it into the target system. Batch jobs are often scheduled during non-peak hours to optimize resource utilization, as they may require substantial computational resources, especially when dealing with large datasets.

Advantages of batch processing

Batch processing offers several advantages for organizations with data-intensive workloads. First, it is cost-effective, as processing data in large volumes minimizes the need for continuous, high-cost computational resources. By scheduling batch jobs during off-hours, organizations can also avoid peak demand charges, which is especially beneficial in cloud-based environments. Additionally, batch processing provides consistency and reliability; once data is processed, it is ready for analysis, ensuring that all data adheres to a consistent state and is complete, making it ideal for use cases requiring historical analysis and reporting.

Challenges of batch processing

Despite its benefits, batch processing has certain limitations. One primary challenge is **latency**. Since data is processed in intervals, there is a delay between data generation and data availability, making batch processing unsuitable for real-time applications where immediacy is critical. Batch processing can also be resource-intensive during job runs, especially with large datasets that require substantial memory and processing power, which may impact other system operations if resources are not managed effectively. Additionally, error handling can be challenging, as batch jobs often process large volumes of data at once; errors discovered post-processing may require re-running the entire batch job, leading to increased processing time and resource usage.

Batch processing tools and technologies

Several tools and platforms support batch processing, each suited to different data processing needs. The following list shows the most widely used technologies and their key capabilities in enabling efficient batch data processing:

- **Apache Hadoop**: One of the foundational big data processing platforms, Hadoop provides a robust framework for distributed storage and processing of large datasets across clusters.

- **Apache Spark**: Known for its in-memory processing capabilities, Spark supports both batch and stream processing, making it versatile for data engineering workflows. Spark's fast, parallel processing capabilities make it an efficient tool for large-scale batch jobs.

- **AWS Glue**: A managed ETL service that integrates with the AWS ecosystem, AWS Glue is designed for large-scale batch processing, particularly in cloud-based environments where scalability and integration are key.

- **Azure Data Factory**: Microsoft's data integration service offers batch processing capabilities across cloud and on-premises environments, with features for data transformation and scheduling.

Best practices for batch processing

In order to optimize batch processing performance; several best practices can be applied. Efficient resource allocation is essential, using parallelism and distributed processing can significantly improve job completion times, especially for large datasets. Data engineers should also schedule jobs strategically, running them during non-peak hours to reduce competition for system resources. Another key practice is error handling and logging, incorporating robust logging mechanisms enables engineers to quickly identify and address issues, minimizing the need for re-running entire jobs. Finally, data partitioning, organizing data by date or other relevant categories improves query performance and simplifies data management, especially when working with large datasets in analytical workflows.

Streaming data processing

Streaming data processing, also known as **real-time** or **stream processing**, is designed for applications that require immediate insights from data as it arrives. Unlike batch processing, which works with large data chunks, streaming processes data continuously, enabling rapid analysis and action. Streaming data processing is especially useful for time-sensitive applications, such as fraud detection, sensor monitoring, and personalized recommendations, where insights are needed as soon as data is generated.

In streaming, data is ingested, processed, and often stored in a matter of milliseconds or seconds, making it suitable for applications where even slight delays can impact outcomes. This processing model is powered by distributed systems that support low-latency data processing, ensuring that each data event is processed as close to real time as possible. Streaming processing is typically implemented using frameworks and tools that support distributed and fault-tolerant data processing, as these features are crucial for managing the high-speed, high-volume data that streaming environments require.

Advantages of streaming processing

The primary advantage of streaming processing is low latency, as data is processed as it arrives, enabling real-time insights. This immediacy is invaluable in applications that rely on quick decision-making, such as automated stock trading or live dashboard monitoring.

Streaming processing also offers scalability, as modern streaming frameworks can handle vast amounts of data from multiple sources, distributing workloads across clusters to ensure rapid processing speeds. Additionally, streaming processing supports continuous data flow, allowing for continuous monitoring, which is particularly useful in applications like IoT, where sensor data is constantly generated.

Challenges of streaming processing

Streaming processing presents unique challenges, including complexity. Real-time data processing requires sophisticated infrastructure and configuration to ensure low latency, fault tolerance, and data integrity. This complexity can lead to resource intensity, as streaming applications often need considerable computational resources to handle high data velocities and ensure resilience. Data ordering is another challenge, as data events may not always arrive in sequence; managing event ordering and ensuring data consistency requires careful handling within the streaming architecture.

Streaming processing tools and technologies

Several tools and technologies support streaming processing, each providing distinct capabilities for handling real-time data, as follows:

- **Apache Kafka**: As an open-source distributed streaming platform, Kafka is widely used for real-time data pipelines and streaming applications, with high throughput and fault tolerance.

- **Apache Flink**: Known for its low-latency processing and support for stateful computations, Flink is ideal for complex streaming applications that require continuous processing with minimal delay.

- **Google Cloud Dataflow**: As a fully managed streaming data processing service built on Apache Beam, Google Cloud Dataflow supports real-time analytics and integrates well with other Google Cloud services.

- **Azure Stream Analytics**: As a real-time analytics service from Microsoft, Azure Stream Analytics enables the processing of large amounts of data with low latency, offering integration with various Azure services.

Best practices for streaming processing

In order to maximize the efficiency and reliability of streaming processing; several best practices should be followed. Low-latency configuration is crucial, data engineers should configure buffering and event batch sizes carefully to minimize delays while ensuring fault tolerance. State management is another critical aspect, using stateful processing frameworks like Apache Flink allows the system to track event states accurately, essential for applications that require continuous data monitoring. Additionally, scalability and fault tolerance are key to managing high-velocity data, autoscaling and partitioning strategies can help ensure the system adapts to varying data loads without compromising performance. Lastly, backpressure handling is important in preventing system overloads by managing data flow rates and ensuring that streaming applications remain responsive and efficient under load.

Choosing between batch and streaming processing

The choice between batch and streaming processing depends on the specific requirements of the application, data velocity, and desired processing speed. Batch processing is ideal for scenarios where data does not need to be processed immediately and where high data volumes are handled efficiently in periodic chunks. This makes it suitable for applications like end-of-day reports, historical data analysis, and data warehousing.

Streaming processing, however, is essential for time-sensitive applications where real-time insights are critical. In fields like fraud detection, IoT monitoring, and dynamic pricing, streaming processing offers the responsiveness needed to make decisions based on live data. While streaming may require more complex and resource-intensive infrastructure, the low-latency insights it provides make it indispensable for scenarios where immediacy is crucial.

Combining batch and streaming in hybrid architectures

In modern data engineering, it is increasingly common to use both batch and streaming processing within a single architecture. This hybrid approach allows organizations to take advantage of the strengths of each mode, creating a flexible data pipeline that meets diverse processing needs. For example, an e-commerce platform might use batch processing to aggregate and analyze customer purchase data, while using streaming processing to track real-time user activity and deliver personalized recommendations.

In hybrid architectures, data orchestration is essential to manage the flow of data between batch and streaming components. Tools like Apache Kafka can act as a central data hub, facilitating data movement between batch processing systems, like Hadoop, and streaming frameworks, like *Flink*. By establishing clear data processing rules, organizations can ensure that batch and streaming pipelines work together cohesively, providing both historical insights and real-time intelligence.

Data quality assurance

Data quality assurance is essential in data engineering, as it ensures the accuracy, reliability, and usefulness of data in downstream applications, such as analytics, AI, and business intelligence. High-quality data minimizes errors, supports informed decision-making, and increases the overall value derived from data assets. With the growing complexity of data environments, incorporating diverse sources, formats, and volumes, data quality management has become more challenging. This section highlights the main dimensions of data quality and presents best practices to maintain high standards of quality across scalable data pipelines.

Key dimensions of data quality

Effective data quality management is built on a few core dimensions, each representing an important aspect of data integrity and usability, as follows:

- **Accuracy**: Ensuring data correctly represents real-world values is fundamental to accurate analysis. Accuracy checks validate data against known standards or reference sources to prevent errors that could lead to incorrect insights.

- **Completeness**: Data completeness ensures that all necessary information is present, avoiding gaps that can skew analyses. Completeness checks include identifying and filling in missing values or flagging incomplete records for review.

- **Consistency**: It ensures uniformity across data sources, making data integration easier and more reliable. For instance, consistent date formats or standard categorizations prevent misinterpretation and simplify analysis.

- **Timeliness**: It measures data relevance based on its freshness and availability, which is crucial in real-time applications. Streaming systems rely on timely data to produce actionable insights, such as for fraud detection.

- **Validity**: It verifies that data conforms to expected formats or ranges. Validation rules check for logical constraints, such as valid email formats or non-negative prices, ensuring data adheres to business rules.

- **Uniqueness**: Ensuring that data records are unique prevents redundancy and maintains data accuracy. Deduplication techniques and unique constraint enforcement help manage uniqueness in batch and streaming environments.

Best practices for data quality assurance

In order to manage data quality across large-scale data systems, data engineers apply several key practices, some are as follows:

- **Automated data validation**: Automation helps ensure that quality checks are consistent and scalable. Automated validation, using tools like Great Expectations and Deequ, allows engineers to set custom rules to assess accuracy, completeness, and validity as data enters the pipeline.

- **Schema management and versioning**: Managing schemas provides structure and enforces standards as data evolves. Schema versioning is critical in complex pipelines, where even small changes can disrupt compatibility. Using tools, like Avro and ProtoBuf for schema definitions allows data teams to track and manage schema versions easily.

- **Data deduplication**: Uniqueness checks are necessary for removing duplicate records, especially when consolidating data from multiple sources. Deduplication techniques can be implemented in batch processing systems or managed in real-time by tracking identifiers to ensure each entry is unique.

- **Monitoring and alerts**: Continuous monitoring and alerts notify data engineers when anomalies arise, enabling quick resolution. Tools such as AWS CloudWatch or Kafka monitoring extensions allow teams to track key metrics, like data arrival rates and latency, and respond to issues immediately.

- **Real-time quality assurance for streaming data**: In streaming systems, lightweight quality checks validate data on arrival without interrupting the flow. Techniques like stateful processing in Apache Flink allow for low-latency checks on format, range, and completeness, ensuring that streaming data maintains quality standards.

Tools for data quality assurance

Several tools and technologies provide structured support for data quality in scalable data engineering environments. Some of the tools are as follows:

- **Great Expectations**: An open-source tool for automated data validation, providing flexibility with custom quality checks across multiple data sources.

- **Deequ**: A data quality library developed by Amazon for large-scale environments, particularly suited for big data and Spark-based workflows, with built-in functions for validation and anomaly detection.

- **Apache Griffin**: This solution focuses on data profiling and validation, is particularly useful for batch environments, and helps manage quality in data lakes.

Each tool offers unique capabilities for managing data quality, enabling data teams to scale quality assurance across diverse data environments.

Governance and cost management

In large-scale data engineering environments, data governance and cost management are essential components that ensure the data pipeline operates efficiently, securely, and within budget constraints. Governance refers to the policies, standards, and processes implemented to control data access, quality, and compliance with regulatory requirements. Effective governance provides a framework for managing data assets responsibly, ensuring data integrity, and fostering trust among data stakeholders. Cost management, on the other hand, focuses on optimizing resources and expenses, particularly as data volumes and processing demands grow in cloud and on-premises environments.

With cloud adoption increasing, cost management has become central to sustainable data operations, as organizations face variable costs tied to storage, compute, and network usage. This section outlines best practices for governance and cost management, supporting scalable, compliant, and cost-effective data ecosystems.

The best practices for data governance are as follows:

- **RBAC**: It assigns data access based on user roles, ensuring that only authorized personnel can access sensitive data. This level of control is crucial for maintaining data security and compliance with privacy regulations, such as GDPR and HIPAA. Implementing RBAC through platforms like AWS IAM or Azure Active Directory provides fine-grained control over data access in cloud environments.

- **Data lineage tracking**: Data lineage provides transparency into data transformations, showing how data flows from sources to its final form. Lineage tracking ensures accountability, as it allows teams to trace errors back to the source, facilitating troubleshooting and quality assurance. Tools like Apache Atlas and DataHub offer data lineage tracking, making it easier to manage and verify data transformations.

- **Metadata management**: It involves cataloging data assets and defining their attributes, making it easier for users to understand data sources, types, and usage. Platforms like AWS Glue Data Catalog and Azure Data Catalog provide automated metadata management, enabling efficient data discovery and governance.

- **Data quality audits**: Regular data quality audits verify that data complies with governance standards, identifying any deviations that could affect data integrity. These audits help maintain consistency and reliability, particularly when data feeds into AI and BI applications.

- **Compliance monitoring**: Implementing continuous monitoring for compliance with industry regulations ensures that the organization meets legal and ethical standards. Many cloud providers, such as AWS and Azure, offer compliance tools to track adherence to regulatory frameworks and mitigate risks associated with non-compliance.

Cost management in data engineering

In order to control expenses in data engineering environments, organizations employ several cost management practices, as follows:

- **Autoscaling and resource allocation**: Cloud-based platforms provide autoscaling, which adjusts compute and storage resources based on workload demand. Autoscaling minimizes costs by reducing idle resources during low demand while supporting high workloads during peak periods. In AWS, tools like Auto Scaling and Amazon EMR offer scalable solutions for data processing tasks.

- **Storage optimization**: Effective cost management includes optimizing storage through data lifecycle policies and tiered storage solutions. Archiving infrequently accessed data to lower-cost storage options, such as Amazon S3 Glacier or Azure Blob Storage Archive, reduces overall storage costs without sacrificing data availability.

- **Code optimization:** Optimizing code efficiency reduces computational overhead, leading to lower processing costs. Techniques like vectorized operations, algorithmic improvements, and efficient memory management help minimize resource consumption. This ensures cost-effective data processing without compromising performance.

- **Cost monitoring and alerts**: Monitoring tools track usage and set alerts for cost thresholds, helping organizations manage expenses proactively. AWS Cost Explorer, Azure Cost Management, and Google Cloud's cost analysis tools provide insights into usage patterns, enabling data teams to optimize resource allocation.

- **Data compression and partitioning**: Compressing data files and using partitioned storage reduces storage costs and improves processing performance. Data engineers can implement compression formats like Parquet or ORC, which save storage space and allow more efficient data retrieval.

AI and BI applications

Data preparation for AI involves creating high-quality training datasets that accurately represent the real-world scenarios in which the AI model will operate. Quality data ensures models are robust, accurate, and free from bias.

The following are specific techniques for processing data for AI model training:

- **Data cleaning**: It involves removing noise, handling missing values, and ensuring consistency. Data inconsistencies or outliers can introduce biases in AI models, so data cleaning is a vital step in model training.

- **Feature engineering**: It creates additional features that capture patterns in the data. Common techniques include normalization, scaling, and encoding categorical variables, which are essential for models that rely on numerical data. In text-based AI models, data engineers apply text vectorization, converting text data into numerical representations using methods like TF-IDF or word embeddings.

- **Data balancing**: AI models trained on imbalanced data may become biased. Data balancing techniques, such as oversampling minority classes or under sampling majority classes, create a balanced dataset, ensuring models perform accurately across different data groups.

- **Data partitioning for model training and validation**: Data is often partitioned into training, validation, and test sets, with each partition serving a different role in model development. The training set is used to train the model, the validation set helps tune parameters, and the test set evaluates model performance, ensuring it generalizes well to new data.

Data preparation for BI applications

BI applications focus on generating insights through data aggregation, visualization, and reporting. Data engineers prepare data for BI applications by structuring it for efficient querying and visual analysis.

The following outlines key techniques and best practices that enhance the performance and efficiency of BI applications:

- **Data aggregation and summarization**: Aggregation techniques combine data across dimensions, enabling summary reports and trend analysis. Common aggregations include summing values, calculating averages, and grouping data by relevant categories.

- **Data indexing and partitioning**: They enhance query performance by organizing data based on frequently accessed columns or categories. Partitioning data by time periods, for instance, allows BI applications to retrieve recent data efficiently without scanning the entire dataset.

- **BI-friendly data modeling**: BI applications benefit from organized data models, such as the star schema or snowflake schema, which optimize data for querying. The star schema includes a central fact table linked to dimension tables, making it efficient for OLAP operations.

Real-world examples and technologies

Data engineering relies on a variety of tools to support batch and streaming data systems, facilitate AI and BI applications, and manage data governance and quality.

The following are real-world examples of how popular tools and frameworks are applied:

- **Apache Spark**: It is a powerful open-source processing engine known for its in-memory processing and flexibility across batch and streaming data workflows. Spark is commonly used in ETL tasks, machine learning model training, and real-time data processing. By providing high-speed data processing, Spark allows data engineers to manage large datasets efficiently and train AI models on distributed clusters, for example, a financial institution may use Spark to process transaction data for real-time fraud detection. Using Spark streaming, the bank processes incoming data streams to identify potentially fraudulent patterns immediately, enhancing security.

- **Apache Flink**: It is designed for low latency, stateful stream processing, making it suitable for applications requiring continuous data monitoring. Flink's advanced features enable real-time processing of data streams, making it popular for complex event processing in IoT and financial sectors, for example, in an IoT application, Flink ingests sensor data from manufacturing equipment, allowing engineers to detect and address anomalies as they occur, preventing equipment failure and reducing downtime.

- **SQL and NoSQL databases**: SQL databases, such as PostgreSQL and MySQL, are ideal for structured data and transactional workloads, while NoSQL databases, like MongoDB and Cassandra, offer flexibility for unstructured data and scalability for high-velocity applications, for example, an e-commerce platform may use SQL databases to manage inventory and transactions while utilizing a NoSQL database to handle unstructured data from customer reviews and user interactions, providing a holistic view of customer activity.

- **AWS Glue and Azure Synapse**: They provide managed data integration services for ETL, supporting data ingestion, transformation, and loading into cloud data lakes and warehouses. AWS Glue is commonly used for data preparation and cleansing tasks, while Synapse combines data integration and analytics, making it versatile for end-to-end data workflows, for example, a retail company may use AWS Glue to integrate sales and inventory data from various sources, while Azure Synapse helps generate insights through BI dashboards that inform business decisions on product stock levels.

- **Google Dataflow**: Based on Apache Beam, it is a unified stream and batch data processing service optimized for the Google Cloud environment. It enables real-time analytics, integrating easily with BigQuery for complex queries, for example, a media company uses Google Dataflow to process and analyze streaming data from user activity across its platforms. By combining real-time insights from Dataflow with historical analysis in BigQuery, the company can optimize content recommendations and improve user engagement.

Conclusion

In this chapter, we explored the essentials of scalable data processing, building on the structured storage frameworks we discussed earlier and setting the stage for effective AI and BI applications. By comparing ETL and ELT, discussing the differences between SQL and NoSQL processing, and exploring batch versus streaming systems, we have laid out the key choices that data engineers face when designing robust data pipelines. These decisions determine how efficiently raw data is transformed into high-quality, actionable insights.

Data processing is the critical stage where raw data is refined, ensuring consistency, accuracy, and speed, qualities that empower both AI model training and advanced BI applications. With the implementation of data quality checks, governance measures, and cost management strategies, we now have a reliable and scalable processing layer that prepares data for real-world applications.

In the next chapter, we will discuss all the components we have built so far. By unifying data sources and ensuring seamless data flow across platforms, we will complete our data pipeline foundation, making it ready to support complex analytics, AI, and business intelligence needs. Together, these chapters build the groundwork for a cohesive and high-performing data ecosystem, capable of driving intelligent decision-making across any organization.

CHAPTER 6

Data Integration and Interoperability

Introduction

In today's data-driven world, the ability to integrate data from multiple sources is fundamental to effective data engineering. Data integration unifies data across different applications and systems, making it accessible and usable throughout an organization. This chapter delves into essential techniques for integrating data effectively, explores tools designed to facilitate integration, and discusses achieving interoperability across AI and non-AI systems. We will also examine the growing importance of data integration in multi-cloud and hybrid environments and review key tools, such as Talend, MuleSoft, and Apache NiFi.

Structure

The chapter covers the following topics:

- Data integration techniques
- Tools for data integration
- Apache NiFi
- Case studies and real-world applications
- Integrating data across AI and non-AI systems
- Real-world applications of AI and non-AI data integration

Objectives

By the end of this chapter, readers will be equipped with a clear and practical understanding of how to manage data integration and ensure interoperability in modern data ecosystems. As organizations grow and operate across diverse platforms, integrating data from multiple sources becomes a foundational requirement. This chapter begins by explaining the fundamental role of data integration in supporting analytics, AI, and daily business operations. Readers will gain familiarity with the various data integration techniques that organizations commonly use ranging from traditional batch processing to real-time streaming, and from ETL to ELT. Each method is discussed in context, with an emphasis on when and why each technique might be appropriate.

The chapter also addresses the increasingly important need to integrate AI-driven systems with traditional enterprise platforms. As AI becomes embedded in more business processes, the ability to bridge insights from machine learning models with operational systems like CRMs or ERPs is essential. Readers will learn the challenges involved, such as aligning data formats, maintaining consistency, and ensuring security, as well as best practices to overcome these hurdles. Finally, the discussion extends to multi-cloud and hybrid architectures.

Data integration techniques

In the modern data ecosystem, data integration serves as a critical backbone for combining disparate data sources into a cohesive and accessible format. As data volumes and sources grow, integrating data effectively is increasingly complex and essential for supporting analytics, artificial intelligence, and operational decision-making. This section explores a range of integration techniques, each tailored to different use cases, system architectures, and organizational goals. Understanding these techniques helps data engineers select the most efficient methods for ensuring data accessibility, consistency, and reliability.

Figure 6.1 represents how data is integrated from various source systems into target systems through an integration platform. It provides a high-level overview of the architecture for centralizing data flows, ensuring consistency and accessibility.

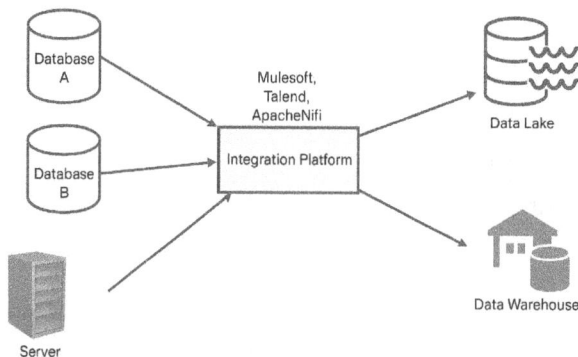

Figure 6.1: *Data integration architecture*

Batch integration

Batch integration, one of the earliest data integration methods, involves processing large volumes of data at scheduled intervals, such as daily, weekly, or monthly. Batch processing efficiently handles high volumes of data that do not require real-time updates. Many organizations rely on batch integration to generate reports, aggregate historical data, and perform bulk updates.

The benefits of batch integration include its cost-effectiveness, as it can be performed during off-peak hours to reduce system load. However, batch integration may not be ideal for time-sensitive applications, as data remains static between batch cycles. Despite this limitation, batch integration remains a powerful technique for applications prioritizing historical analysis over real-time data access. A retail company, for instance, may use batch integration to consolidate sales data from all store locations once a day, allowing analysts to review performance trends without requiring continuous updates.

Real-time integration

Real-time integration is a dynamic approach that enables data to be accessed and updated immediately, supporting applications that demand up-to-the-minute accuracy. Real-time integration is essential for industries where timely data is critical, such as finance, healthcare, and e-commerce. Unlike batch processing, real-time integration continuously streams data, allowing organizations to monitor activity and respond instantly.

For instance, in e-commerce, real-time integration helps track inventory levels across multiple sales channels, ensuring that stock quantities are accurately reflected to prevent overselling. Real-time integration is powered by data streaming tools, such as Apache Kafka and Apache Pulsar, which capture data as it is generated, making it available for immediate processing. This technique is ideal for applications requiring instant feedback, such as fraud detection systems or recommendation engines that tailor content based on user behavior.

Extract, transform, load

ETL is a traditional data integration process involving three key steps, as follows:

- **Extract**: Data is extracted from its source, which could be a database, file, or another storage system.

- **Transform**: The extracted data undergoes transformation, where it is cleaned, standardized, and converted to a format compatible with the target system.

- **Load**: The transformed data is then loaded into a destination, typically a data warehouse or data lake.

ETL is particularly effective for complex transformations that require data to be processed before it reaches the target system. It enables data engineers to ensure that data is clean, consistent, and ready for analysis. A financial institution, for example, may use ETL to consolidate transactional data from various branches, converting it into a unified schema for regulatory reporting.

Although ETL is robust, its transformation-heavy approach can be resource-intensive and time-consuming. This makes it more suitable for structured data and use cases where data does not require real-time access, such as historical data analysis and compliance reporting.

Extract, load, transform

ELT reverses the traditional ETL process by loading data into the target storage first and transforming it as needed. ELT has gained popularity with the rise of cloud-based data warehouses and data lakes, which offer scalable storage and processing power. By loading data immediately, ELT allows for greater flexibility and quicker data availability.

This approach is particularly advantageous for unstructured or semi-structured data, where transformations may vary depending on the analysis required. ELT's flexibility is ideal for large datasets that require different transformations over time, for example, a media company collecting data from multiple social media platforms can use ELT to load raw data into a data lake and apply transformations based on specific campaign analyses.

ELT is highly suited for cloud environments due to the computational power needed for post-loading transformations. It allows for on-demand transformation, which reduces the time to insight and provides more agility in data processing.

Data federation and virtualization

Data federation and virtualization provide organizations with the ability to query data across multiple sources without physically moving it. This technique is particularly useful for scenarios where data resides in multiple locations but must be accessed as a unified dataset.

Data federation consolidates data from different sources into a single, virtual view, enabling users to access and analyze data without physically transferring it. Virtualization, on the other hand, creates an abstract layer over data sources, allowing data to be queried seamlessly as if it resided in one location. These techniques are highly efficient for applications that require data access across systems without redundancy or delays, for example, a multinational corporation may use data federation to create a global view of sales data, integrating data from regional databases into a single dashboard. Data virtualization often used in scenarios where data needs to remain in its original system for regulatory reasons, is particularly beneficial in sectors such as finance and healthcare, where data security and compliance are critical.

API-based integration

Application programming interfaces (**API**) based integration has become a cornerstone of modern data integration, providing real-time data flow and interoperability across diverse systems. APIs allow applications to communicate directly, enabling continuous data synchronization without complex data transfer procedures.

RESTful APIs and GraphQL are common frameworks used in API-based integration. This technique is especially valuable for integrating web applications, mobile applications, and cloud services, as it allows systems to share data and services efficiently. For example, a logistics company can use API-based integration to connect its delivery tracking system with external carrier systems, providing customers with real-time shipping updates.

API-based integration is a versatile approach, supporting both real-time and near-real-time data exchange, and fostering compatibility across both AI-driven applications and traditional systems. With the rise of microservices architectures, API integration has become essential for maintaining agile and responsive data ecosystems.

Data replication

Data replication involves duplicating data from one location to another, ensuring data consistency across systems. This technique is particularly valuable for disaster recovery, where an organization maintains a secondary copy of data to prevent loss in the event of a system failure.

Data replication also supports applications that require fast, local access to data, as it allows frequently used data to be stored in multiple locations. For instance, an organization with distributed offices might replicate customer data to regional servers, ensuring fast access for employees regardless of location.

Data replication can be managed in real-time or as a scheduled process, depending on the organization's requirements. While it ensures data availability and consistency, replication requires careful management to avoid data conflicts and storage inefficiencies.

Change data capture

Change data capture (**CDC**) is a technique that identifies and captures changes made to data in real-time, enabling incremental data updates. CDC is especially useful for applications requiring high data freshness, such as real-time analytics and data synchronization between operational and analytical systems.

By tracking changes in source data, CDC minimizes the need for full data extraction, reducing processing load and improving data timeliness. For example, an e-commerce company might use CDC to capture updates in inventory levels, automatically synchronizing them across all sales channels. This technique ensures that the latest data is available for analysis without redundant processing.

CDC can be implemented using various methods, including database triggers and log-based CDC tools, making it versatile for different system architectures. It is ideal for applications where data accuracy and speed are important.

Tools for data integration

In a data-rich environment, selecting the right tools for data integration is essential for building a scalable and reliable data architecture. Integration tools streamline the process of unifying data from various sources, ensuring it is accessible, consistent, and ready for analysis. This section delves into three widely used integration tools, Talend, MuleSoft, and Apache NiFi, each offering distinct features that support a variety of integration needs, from batch and real-time processing to API-based integrations and data flow automation.

Talend

Talend is a powerful ETL, and data integration tool designed to simplify complex data integration tasks. Known for its user-friendly interface and extensive capabilities, Talend is available in both open-source and enterprise versions, making it accessible to organizations of different sizes. The tool provides a drag-and-drop interface that allows data engineers to build integration workflows quickly, with pre-built connectors to numerous data sources, including databases, cloud platforms, and applications. This flexibility makes Talend an ideal choice for enterprises that manage large volumes of data and require reliable, scalable integration solutions.

Talend supports both batch and real-time processing, allowing data engineers to perform data transformations and ensure that data is clean, consistent, and ready for analysis. For example, in a retail setting, Talend can be used to aggregate and standardize sales data from multiple locations and load it into a centralized data warehouse, enabling analysts to review performance trends without redundant data processing. Talend's compatibility with cloud services, including AWS, Azure, and Google Cloud, adds further flexibility, making it suitable for hybrid and multi-cloud environments where data needs to flow between cloud and on-premises systems seamlessly.

Talend also offers robust data governance features, helping organizations comply with data regulations, such as the GDPR and the HIPAA. By enabling comprehensive monitoring, auditing, and data lineage tracking, Talend helps ensure data integrity and security across all integration workflows. This is particularly valuable in sectors like finance and healthcare, where regulatory compliance is critical. The tool's emphasis on data quality management further enhances its value, allowing organizations to establish quality checks and validation rules that help maintain data accuracy and reliability throughout the integration process.

MuleSoft

MuleSoft is a leading integration platform designed for API-led connectivity, providing organizations with a flexible framework to connect applications, data, and devices across both on-premises and cloud environments. MuleSoft's architecture is particularly well-suited for enterprises with complex integration needs, as it allows them to design, build, and manage API-based workflows. MuleSoft's modular design and scalability make it ideal for large-scale integrations that require robust data flow management and security.

The platform's API-led connectivity approach enables organizations to create and manage APIs efficiently, facilitating data exchange between different systems in a secure and controlled manner. MuleSoft's Anypoint Platform provides a comprehensive suite of tools for API development, deployment, and monitoring, making it a unified platform for managing complex data integrations. For instance, a financial services company might use MuleSoft to connect its CRM system with external financial data providers, allowing real-time access to market data and customer information. This setup not only enhances decision-making but also ensures that customer data remains secure and compliant with regulatory standards.

MuleSoft's extensive library of connectors further simplifies integration, reducing the need for custom development and enabling organizations to integrate legacy systems with modern applications. These connectors facilitate data flow between ERP, CRM, and cloud-based applications, enhancing interoperability across different environments. MuleSoft's support for hybrid and multi-cloud integrations is a valuable feature, allowing organizations to bridge on-premises systems with cloud services while maintaining data consistency. This flexibility is especially beneficial in industries that rely on multi-cloud strategies, such as healthcare, manufacturing, and retail, where data must be accessed across diverse platforms.

One of MuleSoft's key strengths is its API management capabilities, which include built-in security features such as authentication, authorization, and data encryption. These features help protect sensitive data during integration, making MuleSoft an attractive choice for enterprises that prioritize data privacy and security. The platform also offers advanced monitoring and analytics, providing data engineers with insights into API performance and helping to identify potential issues before they impact operations.

Apache NiFi

Apache NiFi is a data integration tool focused on automating and managing data flows between systems. Known for its real-time streaming capabilities and ease of use, NiFi is widely used in applications that require large-scale data ingestion, processing, and transfer. The tool features a visual interface that allows data engineers to design and monitor data flows without extensive coding, making it accessible to both technical and non-technical users.

One ofNiFi's primary strengths is its ability to handle high-volume streaming data, making it ideal for IoT applications and real-time analytics, for instance, an energy company might use Apache NiFi to capture and process sensor data from renewable energy sources, such as wind turbines and solar panels. This data can be transferred to a cloud platform in real-time, where it is analyzed to optimize energy production and monitor equipment health. NiFi's drag-and-drop interface simplifies the process of building complex data flows, enabling organizations to capture and process data continuously without interrupting ongoing operations.

Apache NiFi supports a wide range of data sources, including traditional databases, cloud storage, and IoT devices, allowing organizations to collect and process data from multiple systems in real-time.NiFi also offers data routing, transformation, and enrichment capabilities, providing a comprehensive solution for managing data flows. This is particularly valuable for organizations that operate in distributed environments, as it allows data to be processed close to its source, reducing latency and improving data timeliness.

Another important feature ofNiFi is its data provenance capability, which allows organizations to track data as it moves through different stages of the pipeline. This feature is crucial for ensuring data integrity and compliance, as it provides a complete record of data origins, transformations, and destinations.NiFi's ability to maintain a detailed audit trail is especially beneficial for industries with strict data governance requirements, such as healthcare and finance, where regulatory standards demand accurate and transparent data tracking.

Apache NiFi's support for real-time data streaming makes it highly suitable for organizations that need to monitor and analyze data continuously. Its compatibility with cloud environments enhances its flexibility, allowing data engineers to deploy it as part of a hybrid or multi-cloud strategy.NiFi's seamless integration with data storage and processing systems, including Hadoop, Kafka, and cloud-based analytics platforms, makes it an invaluable tool for building scalable, real-time data architectures.

Choosing the right tool

Each of these integration tools, Talend, MuleSoft, and Apache NiFi offers distinct advantages, catering to different integration needs and technical requirements. Talend's strength lies in its ETL and data transformation capabilities, making it ideal for batch processing and data warehousing. MuleSoft excels in API-based integration, providing a robust platform for enterprise-scale applications that require secure and controlled data flows. Apache NiFi's focus on real-time data streaming and flow automation makes it a valuable choice for organizations handling continuous data flows, especially in IoT and cloud environments.

When selecting an integration tool, data engineers should consider the specific requirements of their organization, including data volume, processing needs, security concerns, and regulatory obligations. By leveraging the right tools, organizations can build resilient data architectures that support seamless data exchange, enabling them to unlock the full value of their data assets.

Ensuring interoperability

In a data-driven organization, interoperability is essential for enabling seamless data exchange between different systems, platforms, and applications. Interoperability ensures that data flows freely across systems, allowing it to be accessed, processed, and analyzed in consistent ways, regardless of the source or destination. Achieving interoperability involves establishing standards, managing data formats, and addressing the unique challenges posed by multi-cloud and hybrid environments. This section explores key strategies and best practices for ensuring interoperability in data engineering, including data standardization, data mapping, multi-cloud integration, and governance.

Data standardization

Data standardization is the process of ensuring that data adheres to a consistent format across different systems. Standardized data is essential for interoperability, as it allows data to be exchanged and understood consistently. Common data standards, such as JSON, XML, and Parquet, facilitate data exchange by providing a uniform structure. By using these standardized formats, organizations can ensure that data is compatible across various systems and applications.

In industries like healthcare and finance, domain-specific standards further enhance interoperability, for instance, the healthcare industry often uses the HL7 standard to enable the exchange of patient data between healthcare providers and applications. By adhering to HL7, healthcare organizations can ensure that patient data remains accessible and consistent, supporting care coordination and data sharing across different systems. Similarly, in the finance industry, the **eXtensible Business Reporting Language** (**XBRL**) standard enables the seamless exchange of financial data between institutions, enhancing regulatory reporting and compliance.

Data standardization also involves adopting consistent naming conventions, units of measurement, and data types. Establishing these conventions across an organization reduces data silos and makes it easier to integrate new systems. For example, standardizing date formats to a universally recognized structure, such as YYYY-MM-DD, ensures that dates are consistently interpreted across different systems. Similarly, using consistent naming conventions for fields like `customer_id` or `transaction_amount` helps prevent confusion and reduces the need for manual data mapping.

Data mapping and transformation

Data mapping and transformation are critical for ensuring that data can be used effectively across multiple systems. Data mapping involves defining relationships between data elements in different systems and ensuring that fields are aligned correctly, for example, mapping **first_name** in one system to **given_name** in another ensures that both systems understand the data in the same way. By establishing clear mappings between fields, data engineers can create compatibility across diverse data schemas.

Data transformation involves converting data from one format or structure to another, allowing it to be used effectively in different systems. Transformation can include processes such as data type conversion, normalization, and aggregation. For instance, transforming temperature readings from Celsius to Fahrenheit or normalizing product names across different systems ensures that data is consistent and accurate.

Data mapping and transformation are especially critical in multi-cloud and hybrid environments, where data may need to be integrated across cloud platforms with varying structures. For example, a company using both AWS and Azure may need to map and transform data to ensure consistency across platforms. By implementing effective data mapping and transformation practices, organizations can enhance interoperability, reduce data discrepancies, and improve the accuracy of data-driven insights.

Multi-cloud and hybrid integration

As organizations increasingly adopt multi-cloud and hybrid environments, achieving interoperability across different platforms becomes more complex. Multi-cloud and hybrid integration allow organizations to leverage the benefits of multiple cloud providers while maintaining data consistency and accessibility across environments. However, these integrations pose unique challenges, including latency, data duplication, and compatibility issues.

Figure 6.2 illustrates how data moves seamlessly across AWS, Azure, and on-premises environments, secured by a central firewall. Data from AWS (e.g., S3 Bucket, EC2) and Azure (e.g., Blob Storage, Virtual Machines) flows through a firewall for validation and security before reaching on-premises systems, such as a local database or internal application. It highlights a multi-cloud integration strategy, ensuring data consistency, governance, and secure access. This setup is ideal for hybrid environments requiring real-time data sharing across platforms.

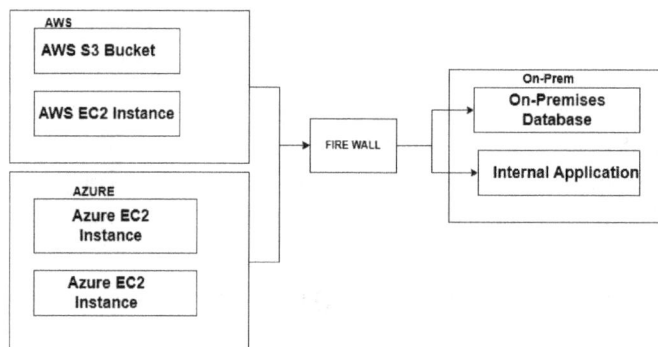

Figure 6.2: *Movement of data across multi-cloud environments to on-prem databases and applications*

One of the primary challenges in multi-cloud integration is managing data latency, as data may need to be synchronized across geographically distributed cloud regions. Latency management techniques, such as data caching and distributed databases, help reduce the time it takes for data to move between platforms, for example, an organization with applications running on both AWS and Google Cloud may use caching to store frequently accessed data locally, minimizing latency and improving performance.

Data duplication is another common issue in multi-cloud and hybrid environments. To address this, organizations can implement deduplication techniques, ensuring that data remains consistent and up-to-date across platforms. Deduplication can be achieved through database replication and conflict resolution strategies, which help maintain data accuracy across distributed systems. By establishing deduplication policies, organizations can prevent data conflicts and ensure that insights are based on accurate information.

Compatibility challenges often arise when integrating different cloud providers, as each platform may use different protocols and data formats. Tools such as MuleSoft and Talend offer pre-built connectors that facilitate interoperability across multiple platforms, enabling data to flow seamlessly between AWS, Azure, and on-premises systems. Apache NiFi further supports hybrid integrations with its ability to automate data flows across cloud environments, making it easier for organizations to manage data across complex infrastructures.

Governance and compliance

Data governance and compliance play a critical role in ensuring interoperability, especially in regulated industries where data privacy and security are paramount. A robust governance framework defines the policies, roles, and responsibilities associated with data management, ensuring that data practices align with regulatory requirements and business objectives. Governance frameworks provide guidelines for data access, quality, and security, enabling organizations to manage data consistently across platforms.

Compliance with data regulations, such as GDPR and HIPAA, is essential for organizations that handle sensitive data. By implementing governance policies, organizations can ensure that data sharing and integration practices align with regulatory standards, protecting customer privacy and minimizing the risk of data breaches, for example, GDPR requires organizations to implement data protection measures and provide customers with control over their personal data. By adhering to these regulations, organizations can build trust with customers and avoid costly penalties.

Governance also encompasses data quality and metadata management, which are essential for maintaining data integrity across systems. Data quality measures, such as validation rules and error detection, ensure that data is accurate and consistent. Metadata management provides context for data, making it easier to understand and integrate. By establishing metadata standards, organizations can ensure that data is easily searchable and accessible, improving interoperability across systems.

In a multi-cloud environment, governance frameworks must account for data stored across different platforms. This may involve defining access controls, encryption standards, and audit trails to ensure data remains secure and compliant with regulations. For instance, an organization using both AWS and Azure might implement role-based access controls to limit data access to authorized personnel, protecting sensitive information and maintaining compliance with industry standards.

Best practices for ensuring interoperability

Achieving interoperability requires a combination of technical strategies and organizational best practices. By implementing these practices, organizations can enhance data accessibility, consistency, and usability across diverse systems, enabling them to derive maximum value from their data assets.

One key best practice is to prioritize data standardization from the outset. By establishing common data formats and naming conventions, organizations can reduce the need for data transformation and simplify integration. This includes adopting industry standards where applicable, such as using **health level seven** (HL7) in healthcare or XBRL in finance, which helps ensure compatibility with external systems and regulatory requirements.

Another best practice is to implement a centralized data integration platform that supports diverse integration needs, such as batch processing, real-time streaming, and API-based integration. Platforms like Talend, MuleSoft, and Apache NiFi provide a unified solution for managing data flows, reducing the complexity of integration and ensuring consistency across systems. By using a centralized platform, organizations can monitor and manage data flows more effectively, enhancing data visibility and control.

Data engineers should also establish clear data governance policies that define roles, responsibilities, and data access controls. Governance policies help ensure that data is used responsibly and in compliance with regulations, reducing the risk of data breaches and improving data quality. Additionally, regular audits and data quality checks can help identify and address data inconsistencies, ensuring that data remains accurate and reliable across systems.

Finally, organizations should prioritize scalability and flexibility in their interoperability efforts. As data volumes and sources continue to grow, scalable integration solutions enable organizations to adapt to changing demands without compromising data quality. Flexible architectures, such as microservices and cloud-native designs, allow organizations to integrate new data sources and applications more easily, supporting long-term interoperability and agility.

Case studies and real-world applications

The impact of data integration and interoperability is best understood through real-world applications. Organizations across industries leverage data integration to streamline operations, improve decision-making, and enhance customer experiences. This section explores several case studies that illustrate the practical applications of data integration and interoperability, highlighting the tools, techniques, and benefits achieved in each scenario.

Cross-functional integration in retail

Retail organizations manage vast amounts of data from both online and offline channels, including customer transactions, inventory levels, and marketing campaigns. Integrating this data allows retailers to gain a comprehensive view of their operations and make data-driven decisions. A leading retail chain implemented a cross-functional data integration strategy to unify data from e-commerce platforms, POS systems, and CRM software.

Using Talend as their integration tool, the retail chain established ETL workflows to aggregate sales data from various sources into a centralized data warehouse. This integration enabled the retailer to track customer purchasing trends in real time, monitor inventory levels across stores, and personalize marketing campaigns. For example, by analyzing customer behavior data from both online and in-store purchases, the retailer identified popular product combinations, allowing them to create targeted product bundles and promotions.

The data integration solution also enhanced inventory management by providing real-time insights into stock levels and demand patterns. When certain products were low in stock, the system automatically generated alerts for the supply chain team, ensuring that inventory was replenished efficiently. As a result, the retailer reduced stockouts by 15% and increased customer satisfaction through improved product availability.

Multi-cloud integration in healthcare

Healthcare organizations handle sensitive patient data, often stored in separate systems, such as **electronic health records (EHR)**, laboratory systems, and billing platforms. Integrating these systems is essential for providing holistic patient care, yet interoperability challenges often arise due to regulatory constraints and data security concerns. A regional healthcare provider implemented a multi-cloud data integration solution to address these challenges and unify patient data across different systems and locations.

The healthcare provider used MuleSoft to connect data from AWS, Azure, and on-premises EHR systems, creating a unified patient profile accessible by healthcare providers across the network. MuleSoft's API-led connectivity allowed the healthcare provider to secure patient data while ensuring it was accessible across multiple applications. This integration enabled the seamless sharing of patient data between hospitals, clinics, and pharmacies, improving care coordination and reducing redundancy in diagnostic tests.

For instance, a physician in one location could access recent lab results and medication histories from another location, providing a more comprehensive understanding of the patient's health status. This integrated view helped physicians make informed treatment decisions, ultimately leading to better patient outcomes. Additionally, MuleSoft's built-in security features ensured that sensitive patient data remained encrypted and compliant with healthcare regulations such as HIPAA. By implementing a multi-cloud integration solution, the healthcare provider achieved a 20% improvement in care coordination and a 30% reduction in duplicate testing costs.

IoT data integration in manufacturing

Manufacturers rely on data from **Internet of Things** (**IoT**) devices to monitor equipment performance, optimize production processes, and perform predictive maintenance. A global manufacturing company implemented an IoT data integration solution to capture and analyze data from sensors embedded in factory equipment. Using Apache NiFi, the company developed an automated data pipeline to collect, process, and analyze sensor data in real-time.

The data integration pipeline enabled the company to monitor key performance indicators, such as temperature, pressure, and vibration levels, which are critical for detecting early signs of equipment failure. When sensors detected abnormal readings, the system triggered alerts for the maintenance team, allowing them to address potential issues before they led to costly breakdowns.

In addition to predictive maintenance, the IoT data integration solution allowed the manufacturing company to optimize its production process. By analyzing sensor data across production lines, the company identified areas where energy consumption was high and adjusted machine settings to reduce energy usage. This optimization resulted in a 15% reduction in energy costs and a 25% decrease in unplanned equipment downtime. NiFi's real-time streaming capabilities were essential for capturing and analyzing large volumes of IoT data, enabling the manufacturer to maintain operational efficiency and reduce maintenance costs.

Financial data integration for regulatory compliance

Financial institutions must comply with strict regulatory standards that require accurate, up-to-date reporting of financial data. A multinational bank used data integration to streamline its reporting processes, ensuring compliance with regulatory requirements, such as the Basel III framework and the European Union's MiFID II regulations. The bank integrated data from multiple sources, including trading systems, risk management platforms, and customer databases, to create a unified view of its financial activities.

Talend was selected as the integration tool for this project, as it provided the data transformation and governance features necessary to meet regulatory requirements. The bank established ETL workflows that extracted transaction data from various systems, transformed it into a standardized format, and loaded it into a centralized data repository for analysis and reporting. By standardizing data formats, Talend allowed the bank to create consistent reports that met regulatory standards and minimized the risk of data discrepancies.

The data integration solution improved the bank's reporting accuracy and reduced the time required to prepare compliance reports. For example, the bank was able to automate the generation of daily risk exposure reports, reducing manual effort and ensuring that reports were submitted on time. This automation improved compliance accuracy and helped the bank avoid costly penalties associated with late or inaccurate reporting. By integrating financial data and automating reporting workflows, the bank achieved a 30% reduction in compliance-related costs and strengthened its regulatory posture.

Real-time customer insights in e-commerce

E-commerce companies rely on real-time insights to personalize customer experiences and optimize marketing strategies. A global e-commerce platform implemented a data integration solution to consolidate customer data from website interactions, mobile app activity, and purchase history. Using MuleSoft, the company integrated data from various sources to create a 360-degree view of each customer, enabling personalized recommendations and targeted marketing campaigns.

MuleSoft's API-based integration allowed the e-commerce platform to capture data from multiple touchpoints and deliver it to a centralized analytics engine in real-time. This integration enabled the company to analyze customer behavior, identify purchasing patterns, and make personalized product recommendations based on browsing history and past purchases. For instance, if a customer viewed a specific product multiple times without purchasing, the platform could automatically send a promotional email with a discount code for that item, increasing the likelihood of conversion.

In addition to enhancing personalization, the data integration solution improved inventory management by providing real-time insights into demand trends. When demand for a particular product spiked, the system alerted the inventory team to replenish stock, reducing the risk of stockouts. By implementing real-time customer insights, the e-commerce platform achieved a 20% increase in customer engagement and a 15% boost in sales conversions. MuleSoft's ability to handle real-time data streams and facilitate API-based integration was essential for delivering timely, personalized experiences that enhanced customer satisfaction and loyalty.

Integrating data across AI and non-AI systems

As organizations adopt AI technologies to drive insights and predictions, integrating AI data with non-AI systems has become essential for creating a comprehensive, cohesive view of data across the enterprise. Integrating data from both AI-driven and traditional (non-AI) systems allows organizations to enhance decision-making, streamline processes, and personalize customer experiences. This section explores the importance of integrating AI and non-AI data, examines the challenges associated with such integrations, and presents real-world applications demonstrating the value of cohesive data ecosystems.

Importance of integrating AI and non-AI data

The integration of AI and non-AI data enables organizations to leverage the predictive power of AI within the broader context of business operations, creating a unified data ecosystem. AI-driven data, often encompassing insights generated through machine learning models, natural language processing, and computer vision, provides advanced analytics and predictions. Meanwhile, non-AI systems such as ERP, CRM, and supply chain management systems store critical transactional and operational data that support day-to-day activities.

When AI and non-AI data are integrated, organizations can enhance the relevance and applicability of AI insights by grounding them in real-world operational data. For instance, an AI model predicting customer churn can provide more accurate insights when integrated with CRM data that includes customer interaction history, recent purchases, and support requests. This integration allows companies to implement proactive retention strategies based on both predictive insights and transactional history, creating a data-driven approach to customer management.

The integration also improves operational efficiency by enabling AI to automate tasks within traditional systems. AI models integrated with ERP data, for example, can forecast inventory needs based on historical sales and seasonal trends, informing procurement decisions and reducing stockouts. This alignment of AI insights with business operations promotes seamless data flows across the organization, empowering teams to make informed, timely decisions.

Challenges in integrating AI and non-AI systems

While the benefits of integrating AI and non-AI data are clear, this integration often presents significant challenges. One primary challenge is data compatibility, as AI and non-AI systems often use different data structures, formats, and protocols. AI models typically process unstructured data, such as text, images, and video, while traditional systems rely on structured or semi-structured data stored in relational databases. Data engineers must bridge these structural differences through data mapping, transformation, and standardization to ensure compatibility.

Another challenge is maintaining data consistency across systems. As AI models generate new insights and update records, these updates must be synchronized with the source data in non-AI systems. For instance, if an AI model identifies a high-risk transaction in real-time, this information should be immediately reflected in the ERP system for review by the finance team. Real-time data streaming and event-driven architectures are often necessary to facilitate such updates, ensuring that AI insights are actionable and aligned with the latest operational data.

Data security and compliance also pose challenges, particularly in regulated industries where sensitive data such as customer records and financial transactions must be protected. Integrating AI and non-AI data requires careful governance to ensure that data privacy standards are maintained. This includes implementing role-based access controls, data encryption, and audit trails to track data usage across systems.

Real-world applications of AI and non-AI data integration

Integrating AI with non-AI systems has transformative potential across a variety of industries. This section discusses examples of how organizations leverage this integration to enhance business outcomes:

Customer experience enhancement in e-commerce

E-commerce companies often use AI-driven personalization engines to recommend products, target advertisements, and tailor customer experiences. By integrating AI models with CRM and transactional data, e-commerce platforms can provide more relevant recommendations based on a customer's complete purchasing history, browsing behavior, and demographic information. For example, an AI model might predict a customer's likelihood of purchasing a product based on past browsing patterns and combine this prediction with CRM data to create personalized offers.

This integration also enables more effective retargeting campaigns, as the system can track customer interactions across both AI-powered recommendation engines and traditional CRM systems. When an abandoned cart is detected in the CRM, the AI system can automatically generate a targeted email campaign with personalized recommendations and discounts, encouraging the customer to complete the purchase. By blending AI insights with CRM data, e-commerce companies achieve a 20% increase in conversion rates and a 15% boost in customer engagement.

Predictive maintenance in manufacturing

Manufacturers rely on IoT sensors to monitor equipment health and detect early signs of wear and tear. By integrating AI-driven predictive maintenance models with ERP systems, manufacturers can automate maintenance scheduling based on real-time sensor data and historical maintenance records. For example, an AI model analyzing temperature and vibration data from machinery may predict an impending failure. This prediction can be sent to the ERP system, which generates a work order for the maintenance team to address the issue before it impacts production.

Integrating AI insights with ERP data ensures that maintenance activities align with production schedules, minimizing disruptions and optimizing resource allocation. This approach also enables manufacturers to manage spare parts inventory more effectively, as predictive maintenance alerts can trigger automated reordering based on forecasted equipment needs. By reducing downtime and improving maintenance accuracy, manufacturers see up to a 25% decrease in maintenance costs and a 30% reduction in unplanned equipment failures.

Fraud detection in financial services

Financial institutions use AI models to detect suspicious patterns and flag potentially fraudulent transactions. By integrating these AI models with non-AI systems such as transaction monitoring platforms and customer service tools, banks and financial institutions can respond to threats more effectively. When an AI model identifies a high-risk transaction, it can immediately notify the fraud prevention team through the CRM, creating a unified view of the customer's transaction history and risk profile.

The integration also allows for real-time customer alerts, as non-AI systems can trigger notifications based on AI-generated fraud scores. For instance, if a customer's account is flagged for unusual activity, the CRM can automatically notify the customer and provide instructions for verifying the transaction. This integrated approach not only improves the accuracy of fraud detection but also enhances customer trust by providing timely communication and support. Financial institutions that adopt this approach reduce fraud losses by 20% and improve their response time to potential threats.

Personalized healthcare in clinical settings

Healthcare providers use AI models to predict patient risks, diagnose conditions, and recommend treatments. Integrating AI-driven insights with EHR systems provide healthcare professionals with a more comprehensive view of a patient's health status. For example, an AI model may analyze medical images to identify signs of disease, and then send the results to the EHR, where they are combined with the patient's medical history, lab results, and medication records.

This integration enables doctors to make more informed decisions by considering both AI-generated insights and clinical data from non-AI systems. If an AI model identifies a high risk of complications for a patient, the EHR system can trigger alerts for the care team to schedule follow-up appointments or adjust treatment plans. By integrating AI with EHR data, healthcare providers improve diagnostic accuracy, reduce the likelihood of complications, and enhance patient outcomes.

Supply chain optimization in retail

Retail companies use AI models to forecast demand and optimize inventory levels. By integrating AI predictions with **supply chain management** (**SCM**) systems, retailers can adjust procurement and distribution based on anticipated demand patterns. For example, an AI model might predict an increase in demand for certain products during the holiday season, allowing the SCM system to adjust stock levels and distribution plans accordingly.

This integration enables retailers to reduce excess inventory, avoid stockouts, and improve order fulfillment accuracy. Additionally, the AI model can analyze data from past sales and external factors, such as weather forecasts or economic indicators, to refine demand predictions. When AI-driven demand forecasts are integrated with SCM systems, retailers can achieve a 15% reduction in inventory holding costs and a 20% improvement in order fulfillment rates.

Best practices for integrating AI and non-AI data

Successfully integrating AI and non-AI data requires a thoughtful approach that considers data compatibility, security, and governance.

The following are some best practices to guide the integration process:

- **Use a centralized integration platform**: Platforms, such as MuleSoft, Talend, and Apache NiFi offer pre-built connectors and integration tools that support both AI and non-AI systems. These platforms simplify the process of unifying data from diverse sources and ensure data consistency.

- **Implement real-time data streaming**: Event-driven architectures and real-time data streaming tools, such as Apache Kafka, facilitate continuous updates between AI and non-AI systems. Real-time streaming is essential for applications that require immediate responses, such as fraud detection and predictive maintenance.

- **Establish data governance policies**: Robust data governance ensures that sensitive data remains secure and compliant with regulatory standards. Implement role-based access controls, encryption, and data tracking to protect data across AI and non-AI systems.

- **Maintain data quality**: Data quality is crucial for the accuracy of AI models and operational systems. Establish data validation, transformation, and monitoring practices to ensure that data remains accurate and consistent across systems.

Integrating data across AI and non-AI systems unlocks the full potential of data, enabling organizations to combine predictive insights with real-time operational data for a holistic approach to decision-making. By implementing best practices and leveraging integration tools, organizations can build cohesive data ecosystems that enhance agility, improve customer satisfaction, and drive business success.

Data integration in multi-cloud and hybrid environments

As organizations increasingly adopt multi-cloud and hybrid cloud environments, the need for seamless data integration across these platforms becomes essential. Multi-cloud environments involve the use of multiple cloud service providers (e.g., AWS, Azure, Google Cloud), while hybrid cloud environments combine on-premises infrastructure with cloud services. Both environments offer flexibility and scalability, but they also present unique challenges for data integration. Effective integration in these environments ensures data accessibility, consistency, and security across systems, enabling organizations to maximize the value of their cloud investments.

Data integration benefits

One of the primary benefits of data integration in multi-cloud and hybrid environments is increased flexibility. Organizations can choose the best cloud provider for each application, leveraging the unique features and strengths of each platform, for instance, a company might use AWS for data storage, Google Cloud for machine learning, and an on-premises solution for sensitive data processing. Data integration allows these platforms to function cohesively, enabling seamless data flows across applications and reducing the risk of data silos.

Data integration also enhances operational resilience. By distributing data across multiple cloud providers, organizations can ensure continuity even if one provider experiences downtime. This setup provides redundancy, allowing data to remain accessible from alternative sources, which is particularly valuable for business-critical applications. For example, a financial institution with operations on both AWS and Azure can switch to one provider if the other experiences service disruptions, minimizing the impact on customer transactions and operations.

Another benefit is optimized cost management. In a multi-cloud setup, organizations can balance costs by using different clouds based on pricing structures and service requirements. For example, a company may use a cost-effective provider for data storage and a premium provider for high-performance computing. Effective data integration enables data to flow freely between these providers, allowing organizations to maximize cost savings without compromising performance.

Finally, data integration supports regulatory compliance in hybrid environments by enabling data to remain on-premises while still benefiting from cloud-based processing capabilities. For industries such as healthcare and finance, where regulations may mandate on-premises storage for sensitive data, hybrid environments offer a compliant yet scalable solution. Data integration allows organizations to retain control over sensitive information on-premises while using cloud services for analytics and machine learning.

Challenges in data integration across cloud environments

Despite its advantages, data integration in multi-cloud and hybrid environments presents significant challenges. Data compatibility is one of the primary obstacles, as different cloud providers often use distinct data formats, protocols, and storage structures. For instance, AWS uses its own storage protocols (e.g., S3), while Azure has its unique storage solutions (e.g., Blob Storage). Bridging these differences requires data engineers to employ data transformation and mapping techniques to ensure compatibility across platforms.

Data latency is another challenge in multi-cloud environments, where data needs to be synchronized across geographically distributed regions and providers. This issue is especially problematic for real-time applications that require up-to-the-minute data accuracy, such as financial trading platforms or IoT monitoring systems. Organizations often mitigate latency issues by implementing caching and using distributed databases, which reduces the time required for data to travel between cloud providers. For example, a global retailer might cache frequently accessed inventory data locally on each cloud platform to ensure quick access, reducing delays and enhancing performance.

Data duplication poses additional challenges, as data may be stored across multiple platforms for accessibility and redundancy. Without effective data deduplication strategies, organizations risk storing redundant data, which leads to increased storage costs and potential data inconsistencies. Data deduplication involves consolidating duplicate data entries and maintaining a single source of truth, ensuring data remains accurate and manageable across systems. By implementing deduplication policies, companies can prevent discrepancies and reduce the risk of conflicting data records.

Security and compliance are important concerns in multi-cloud and hybrid environments, particularly for organizations handling sensitive or regulated data. Integrating data across different providers requires strict adherence to data privacy standards, including encryption, access controls, and compliance with regulations, such as GDPR and HIPAA. Data integration solutions must offer robust security features, including data masking and role-based access, to protect sensitive information. For example, a healthcare provider managing patient data across cloud providers must ensure that only authorized personnel can access sensitive records, regardless of where the data is stored.

Strategies for effective multi-cloud and hybrid integration

In order to address the challenges of data integration in multi-cloud and hybrid environments, organizations can adopt several best practices and strategies that enable seamless data flows and improve data management.

The strategies are as follows:

- **Use a centralized data integration platform**: Implementing a centralized integration platform, such as MuleSoft, Talend, or Apache NiFi, provides a unified solution for managing data flows across different cloud providers. These platforms offer pre-built connectors, transformation tools, and monitoring capabilities that simplify the integration process. For example, MuleSoft's Anypoint Platform allows organizations to integrate AWS, Azure, and on-premises systems through a single interface, ensuring consistent data management and reducing complexity.

- **Implement data virtualization**: It allows organizations to create a unified, virtual view of data from different sources without physically moving it. This approach is especially useful in multi-cloud and hybrid environments, as it reduces the need for redundant data storage and enables real-time data access. By implementing data virtualization, a financial institution with data stored on both AWS and Google Cloud can provide analysts with a single view of customer data without duplicating it across systems. Data virtualization enables faster access to distributed data, improving efficiency and streamlining analysis.

- **Adopt real-time data streaming**: Real-time data streaming platforms, such as Apache Kafka, facilitate continuous data synchronization between cloud providers, minimizing latency and ensuring data accuracy across systems. Streaming is particularly valuable for applications that rely on real-time insights, such as fraud detection or supply chain monitoring. For example, a logistics company might use Kafka to synchronize shipment data across multiple cloud platforms, allowing it to track orders and optimize delivery routes in real-time. By using real-time streaming, organizations can maintain data consistency and reduce delays in data availability.

- **Establish data governance policies**: Data governance is critical for managing data quality, security, and compliance across cloud environments. Establishing governance policies ensures that data integration practices align with regulatory standards and organizational objectives. These policies should define data access controls, encryption standards, and audit requirements to protect data across platforms. For example, a healthcare organization might implement role-based access controls, ensuring that only authorized personnel can access patient data, regardless of the cloud provider. By enforcing governance policies, organizations can reduce security risks and ensure compliance with industry regulations.

The benefits of integrating data across multi-cloud and hybrid environments are evident in various industries. For example, a retail company might use AWS for data storage, Google Cloud for analytics, and an on-premises system for handling sensitive customer data. By integrating data from these sources, the retailer gains a comprehensive view of customer interactions, enabling personalized marketing and inventory optimization.

In the healthcare sector, multi-cloud integration allows providers to manage patient data across cloud and on-premises systems, supporting seamless access to medical records while maintaining compliance with data privacy regulations. For instance, a healthcare provider may store imaging data on AWS while keeping patient records in an on-premises database. Data integration enables doctors to access both types of information in real-time, improving care coordination and patient outcomes.

Similarly, financial institutions benefit from multi-cloud integration by achieving greater operational resilience and regulatory compliance. By distributing data across AWS, Azure, and on-premises platforms, banks can ensure data availability even if one platform experiences downtime. This setup allows banks to deliver uninterrupted service to customers while maintaining compliance with data privacy regulations.

Conclusion

Data integration has become a cornerstone of modern data engineering, enabling organizations to consolidate data from disparate sources into a unified, accessible, and actionable form. Throughout this chapter, we explored the critical role of integration across multi-cloud and hybrid environments, highlighting the strategies that support seamless data flows, ensure resilience, and enhance operational efficiency. By effectively managing integration across diverse cloud platforms, organizations can maximize their data's value, reduce operational complexity, and maintain a competitive edge.

This chapter builds on the foundations laid in earlier sections on data collection and ingestion, demonstrating how these integrated environments serve as conduits for diverse data streams. As data flows through multi-cloud ecosystems, ensuring its accessibility is only one part of the solution. Equally important is the quality of the data itself. Poor data quality can undermine integration efforts, compromise analytics, and create compliance risks, which is why maintaining high data quality is essential.

In the next chapter, we will focus on ensuring data quality and examining the frameworks, techniques, and tools that organizations need to maintain accuracy, consistency, and reliability. Data quality management will enhance the effectiveness of data integration, creating a stable foundation for subsequent processes, from analytics to AI-driven decision-making. By combining robust integration strategies with strong data quality practices, organizations can build scalable, trustworthy data ecosystems that support ongoing growth and innovation.

Join our book's Discord space

Join the book's Discord Workspace for Latest updates, Offers, Tech happenings around the world, New Release and Sessions with the Authors:

https://discord.bpbonline.com

CHAPTER 7
Ensuring Data Quality

Introduction

In the digital age, data is the foundation of decision-making, innovation, and efficiency. However, its value depends on quality. Poor data quality can lead to financial loss, reputational damage, and operational risks. Incorrect customer data can cause failed marketing campaigns, while erroneous transaction data may result in regulatory non-compliance. Ensuring accuracy, completeness, consistency, timeliness, and relevance is crucial.

Today's data ecosystems span multi-cloud platforms, hybrid environments, and diverse sources, making data integration complex. Data errors can arise at any stage,that is,collection, ingestion, transformation, or storage, causing failures in analytics, AI models, and business operations. High-velocity systems require immediate validation, while batch systems must ensure historical data integrity for compliance and analytics.

Beyond technical concerns, data quality impacts business success. Reliable data enables accurate predictions, trend identification, and informed decisions. Poor data quality leads to inefficiencies, lost opportunities, and increased costs. This chapter explores batch vs. streaming data quality, best practices, tools, and real-world examples. By implementing effective quality measures, organizations can build resilient data systems that ensure trust, efficiency, and long-term value.

Structure

The chapter contains the following topics:

- Data quality in batch vs. streaming
- Best practices and tools
- Impact on downstream users
- Real-world use cases of various sectors
- Tool comparison based on use cases

Objectives

By the end of this chapter, readers will have an understanding of how ensuring data quality is fundamental to maintaining reliable, accurate, and actionable data across an organization. This chapter aims to provide a comprehensive understanding of how data quality impacts business operations, analytics, and AI-driven decision-making. Readers will explore the key differences between batch and streaming data quality management, understanding how validation techniques vary based on processing methods. The chapter will introduce best practices for maintaining high-quality data, including automation, continuous monitoring, and governance policies. Additionally, a comparative analysis of leading data quality tools, such as Great Expectations, Deequ, and Apache Griffin, will highlight their strengths and real-world applications. By the end of this chapter, readers will gain practical insights into implementing effective data quality strategies, ensuring their data remains accurate, consistent, and trustworthy. These principles will serve as a foundation for the subsequent exploration of data analytics and visualization, where high-quality data translates into valuable business insights.

Data quality in batch vs. streaming

Data quality plays a pivotal role in ensuring the accuracy and reliability of insights generated from data. However, the approach to maintaining data quality varies significantly depending on whether the data is processed in batch or streaming pipelines. These two paradigms cater to different use cases, operational needs, and performance requirements, making it essential to understand their unique challenges and opportunities. This section explores the nuances of data quality in batch and streaming systems, offering a comprehensive view of how organizations can effectively manage quality across these distinct environments.

Effective data quality management involves multiple stages to ensure accuracy and reliability across data pipelines. The following flowchart illustrates the key phases of data quality management: data collection, validation, monitoring, and error correction, each playing a critical role in maintaining high-quality data in both batch and streaming environments:

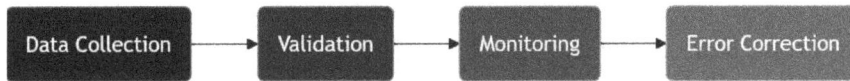

Figure 7.1: *Flowchart depicting the lifecycle of data quality management*

Batch data quality

Batch processing is a traditional approach where data is collected, processed, and validated in large chunks at scheduled intervals. This method is typically used for historical data analysis, periodic reporting, and long-term trend evaluation. Since batch pipelines work with datasets that are already available and complete, they afford engineers the opportunity to perform deep, comprehensive quality checks without the constraints of real-time processing.

One of the defining features of batch data quality is its ability to handle extensive validation. For example, batch pipelines allow for advanced checks such as:

- **Schema validation**: Ensuring that all data adheres to the predefined schema, including data types, column names, and constraints.

- **Deduplication**: Identifying and removing duplicate entries to maintain data uniqueness.

- **Aggregation**: Calculating metrics, such as sums, averages, and counts, which can be cross-validated against expected results.

- **Error correction**: Applying transformation rules to standardize formats, fill missing values, and handle outliers.

Imagine a retail company analyzing its monthly sales data to prepare financial reports. By using a batch processing system, the company can validate and aggregate sales records from multiple stores, ensuring that the final dataset is free from errors before analysis. This approach is ideal for non-urgent applications, where accuracy is prioritized over speed.

Despite its advantages, batch data quality comes with limitations. For instance, the reliance on periodic processing means that errors can persist in the system until the next batch cycle. If a critical error is introduced into a batch dataset, it may not be identified and corrected until the next processing window, potentially delaying decision-making. In order to mitigate this, organizations often implement interim monitoring systems that flag anomalies as they arise, even in batch workflows.

Streaming data quality

In contrast to batch systems, streaming pipelines are designed to handle data in motion. These pipelines process data in real-time or near real-time, enabling organizations to respond to events as they occur. Streaming is often employed in scenarios where time sensitivity is critical, such as fraud detection, live analytics, and IoT monitoring. However, the need for speed imposes unique challenges in maintaining data quality.

The real-time nature of streaming data necessitates lightweight and high-speed validation techniques. Unlike batch systems, which have the luxury of processing complete datasets, streaming pipelines must validate data as it arrives, often in small, incremental chunks. Common quality checks in streaming environments include:

- **Schema validation**: Ensuring that incoming data adheres to expected formats and structures.

- **Anomaly detection**: Identifying unusual patterns, such as abnormally high transaction values or sudden spikes in activity.

- **Filtering**: Removing corrupted, irrelevant, or incomplete records before they enter the pipeline.

- **Windowed aggregations**: Using sliding or tumbling windows to calculate metrics over defined time intervals, ensuring that data remains accurate even in continuous streams.

Consider a financial institution using a streaming pipeline for fraud detection. As transaction data flows into the system, lightweight validation rules are applied to flag anomalies, such as unusually large withdrawals or multiple transactions from different locations within a short period. These alerts are then routed to a risk management team for further investigation. In such cases, ensuring data quality in real-time is crucial to preventing financial loss and maintaining customer trust.

While streaming pipelines excel at providing immediate insights, they also pose significant challenges. For example, the lack of complete datasets in real-time makes it difficult to perform certain quality checks, such as deduplication and cross-validation. Additionally, the continuous nature of streaming systems demands robust monitoring and recovery mechanisms to handle errors without disrupting the flow of data.

Key differences between batch and streaming data quality

The distinctions between batch and streaming systems extend beyond their processing speeds, influencing how data quality is managed in each paradigm. These differences can be summarized, as follows:

- **Scope of validation**: Batch pipelines validate complete datasets, allowing for thorough checks and corrections. Streaming pipelines, by contrast, focus on incremental validation to ensure minimal latency.

- **Error handling**: Batch systems often include error correction as part of the pipeline, whereas streaming systems flag and redirect faulty records for separate processing.

- **Latency tolerance**: Batch systems can tolerate higher latencies since they are designed for scheduled processing. Streaming systems, on the other hand, prioritize low latency to maintain real-time responsiveness.

- **Use cases**: Batch pipelines are ideal for historical reporting, data warehousing, and compliance checks. Streaming pipelines are better suited for time-sensitive applications, such as real-time analytics and operational monitoring.

Table 7.1 is a structured comparison that provides a quick reference for selecting the appropriate data quality approach based on specific requirements:

Feature	Batch data quality	Streaming data quality
Scope of validation	Entire dataset at once	Incremental, real-time validation
Error handling	Corrects errors in bulk	Flags and redirects faulty records
Latency tolerance	High latency acceptable	Requires low-latency validation
Use cases	Historical reporting, compliance	Fraud detection, real-time analytics

Table 7.1: Comparison of batch vs. streaming data quality approaches

These differences highlight the importance of selecting the right approach based on the specific requirements of a use case. While batch systems offer the advantage of thorough validation, streaming systems enable organizations to act on data as it arrives, ensuring agility and responsiveness.

Balancing batch and streaming approaches

For many organizations, the choice between batch and streaming pipelines is not an either-or decision. Instead, they adopt a hybrid approach that leverages the strengths of both paradigms. For instance, raw data may be ingested and validated in real-time through a streaming pipeline to support immediate operational needs, while the same data is later aggregated and revalidated in a batch process for long-term analysis and storage.

Take the example of an e-commerce company managing customer orders. A streaming pipeline might validate incoming order data for real-time inventory updates and fraud detection, while a batch pipeline processes the same data at the end of the day to generate sales reports and calculate performance metrics. By combining batch and streaming approaches, the company ensures that data quality is maintained across both operational and analytical workflows.

Comparative analysis

Batch pipelines address the entire dataset, while streaming focuses on incremental changes. Batch systems correct errors in bulk, while streaming systems flag and redirect faulty records dynamically. Streaming pipelines require minimal latency, making them suitable for time-sensitive applications, whereas batch systems are designed for scheduled tasks. Balancing these approaches ensures organizations can handle both historical data accuracy and real-time operational reliability.

Best practices and tools

Maintaining high-quality data requires a combination of robust frameworks, systematic processes, and specialized tools. Organizations must establish a clear understanding of what constitutes quality data and implement measures to uphold these standards at every stage of the data lifecycle. From defining key quality metrics to automating validation and monitoring, best practices form the backbone of any successful data quality initiative.

Data engineers and decision-makers must prioritize building scalable, flexible systems that adapt to the evolving complexity of modern data ecosystems. This includes addressing issues, like inconsistent formats, duplicate records, and incomplete datasets, all of which can undermine analytics, machine learning, and operational efficiency. Leveraging advanced tools ensures that data pipelines are equipped to handle these challenges effectively, whether in batch or streaming environments.

Best practices for ensuring data quality

Data quality standards vary across industries and applications. Establishing clear metrics helps organizations evaluate and improve their data consistently. Common data quality dimensions include:

- **Accuracy**: Ensuring data reflects the real-world entities or events it represents.
- **Completeness**: Ensuring all required data is present, with no critical fields missing.
- **Consistency**: Ensuring data aligns across different systems and sources without conflicts.
- **Timeliness**: Ensuring data is up-to-date and available when needed.
- **Uniqueness**: Ensuring no duplicate records exist within datasets.

By aligning these metrics with organizational goals, data teams can prioritize their quality efforts and address critical issues effectively.

Automate validation and correction

Manual quality checks are time-consuming, error-prone, and unscalable, especially in environments with high data volumes. Automation ensures consistency and scalability in data quality management. Key automated processes include:

- **Schema validation**: Verifying that data conforms to pre-defined structures.
- **Range checks**: Ensuring numeric fields fall within acceptable limits.
- **Missing value handling**: Automatically inputting or flagging incomplete data.
- **Anomaly detection**: Using machine learning algorithms to identify irregular patterns.

Automation tools also integrate with data pipelines, providing real-time validation during ingestion and transformation, minimizing the risk of propagating errors downstream.

Implement continuous monitoring

Data quality issues often arise unexpectedly, especially in dynamic environments where data originates from multiple sources. Continuous monitoring helps organizations detect and address quality problems proactively. Key elements of effective monitoring include:

- **Alerts**: Automatic notifications for anomalies or validation failures.

- **Dashboards**: Visual displays of quality metrics for real-time insights.

- **Audit logs**: Comprehensive records of data changes, helping teams trace and resolve issues.

Real-time monitoring is particularly critical for streaming data systems, where delays in detecting issues can impact immediate decision-making.

Develop data governance policies

Data governance frameworks provide a structured approach to managing data quality. These policies define roles, responsibilities, and processes for ensuring data integrity. Governance encompasses the following policies, processes, and standards that ensure data integrity, security, compliance, and consistency across an organization's data ecosystem:

- **Access controls**: Restricting data access to authorized personnel.

- **Standardization**: Enforcing consistent formats and naming conventions across datasets.

- **Metadata management**: Documenting the origins, transformations, and usage of data.

- **Regulatory compliance**: Ensuring data handling aligns with laws, like the GDPR, HIPAA, or CCPA.

Governance policies establish accountability and help organizations maintain trust in their data systems.

Effective data governance is essential for maintaining consistency, security, and compliance across an organization's data landscape. By adopting well-established frameworks, businesses can ensure structured policies that align with industry best practices.

The following are data governance frameworks:

- **Data Management Body of Knowledge (DMBOK)**: Defines best practices for enterprise data governance.

- **ISO 8000**: Establishes international standards for data quality.

- **NIST Data Governance Framework**: Provides structured guidelines for secure and reliable data handling.

Address root causes

Data quality issues often originate from upstream processes, such as data collection or third-party integrations. Addressing these root causes prevents recurring errors and reduces the need for reactive fixes. For example, implementing stricter validation at data entry points can significantly reduce errors introduced during data collection.

Tools for data quality management

Tools are the cornerstone of effective data quality management, enabling organizations to implement best practices at scale. They simplify complex processes, such as validation, monitoring, and anomaly detection, ensuring data remains accurate and reliable across pipelines.

Great Expectations

Great Expectations is an open-source data quality framework that enables teams to define, validate, and document expectations for their data. It supports batch and streaming pipelines, offering flexible integration with tools, like *Pandas, Spark,* and *SQL-based systems*. The key features include:

- **Custom expectations**: Defining rules specific to organizational needs.
- **Validation as code**: Embed validation checks directly into data pipelines.
- **Data docs**: Automatically generate documentation summarizing validation results.
- **Use case**: An e-commerce company uses Great Expectations to validate transaction data for completeness and schema consistency before loading it into its analytics platform.

Deequ

Deequ, developed by *Amazon,* is a library built on *Apache Spark* for large-scale data quality management. It is designed for batch workflows and provides declarative checks for data validation and profiling. The key features include:

- **Metrics calculation**: Generating insights on data distributions and patterns.
- **Constraint validation**: Enforce rules such as uniqueness, ranges, and null checks.
- **Profiling**: Automatically identify quality issues across datasets.
- **Use case**: A financial institution integrates Deequ into its Spark pipeline to validate transaction logs and ensure regulatory compliance.

Apache Griffin

Apache Griffin is a data quality solution tailored for big data ecosystems, offering real-time monitoring, validation, and anomaly detection capabilities. Its strengths include:

- **Integration with big data frameworks**: It supports *Hadoop*, *Spark*, and *Kafka*.

- **Customizable quality rules**: Define rules for batch and streaming pipelines.

- **Real-time anomaly detection**: Identify issues as data flows through the system.

- **Use case**: An IoT company uses *Apache Griffin* to monitor sensor data streams, ensuring accurate and timely alerts for equipment maintenance.

Impact on downstream users

The quality of data has a cascading effect throughout an organization's operations and decision-making processes. High-quality data empowers downstream users, such as data analysts, data scientists, business leaders, and AI systems to generate accurate insights, drive strategic initiatives, and enhance customer experiences. Conversely, poor data quality can undermine trust, efficiency, and profitability. This section explores how downstream users are affected by data quality, highlights specific challenges they face, and emphasizes the importance of maintaining robust quality standards.

Role of downstream users

Downstream users are individuals or systems that consume processed data for analysis, decision-making, or operational purposes. Their reliance on data means that even minor quality issues can lead to significant disruptions.

The following are a few examples:

- **Data analysts**: Poor data quality results in skewed reports and inaccurate visualizations, which in turn lead to flawed business strategies.

- **Data scientists**: Inconsistent or incomplete datasets compromise the training and performance of machine learning models.

- **Business leaders**: Inaccurate forecasts based on erroneous data can lead to misinformed decisions and missed opportunities.

- **AI and automated systems**: Low-quality data can produce incorrect outputs, creating inefficiencies or harm, such as in fraud detection or medical diagnostics.

The role of downstream users highlights the ripple effect of data quality, where upstream issues magnify as they travel through the pipeline.

Consequences of poor data quality

Maintaining high data quality is essential for reliable decision-making, analytics, and operational efficiency. When data is inaccurate, incomplete, or inconsistent, it can have far-reaching consequences across an organization. Poor data quality not only skews insights and hampers AI model performance but also delays critical decisions, increases regulatory risks, and impacts customer satisfaction. The following sections explore these challenges in detail, highlighting the potential risks and implications of failing to ensure high-quality data.

Skewed insights and analytics

Analytics teams depend on clean and reliable data to derive actionable insights. Poor data quality can distort key metrics, such as sales performance, customer behavior trends, or financial forecasts. For example, duplicate customer records in a CRM system may result in overestimated sales projections, leading to overstocking or budget misallocations. Analysts often spend more time cleaning and verifying data than generating insights, reducing productivity and delaying critical decision-making.

Compromised AI model performance

Machine learning models rely heavily on high-quality training data to produce accurate predictions. When datasets contain inconsistencies, missing values, or incorrect labels, the model's performance suffers. For instance, an AI model designed to detect fraudulent transactions may underperform if its training data includes mislabeled examples or missing fields, resulting in missed fraud cases or false positives. Poor data quality not only undermines model accuracy but also increases the risk of biased or unethical outcomes.

Delayed decision-making

Low-quality data can slow down the decision-making processes by requiring additional time for validation and error correction. In fast-paced industries like e-commerce or financial services, delays caused by poor data quality can result in lost revenue and missed opportunities. For example, inaccurate inventory data may lead to delays in replenishment decisions, causing stockouts during peak demand periods. Business leaders depend on timely, accurate data to act quickly and stay competitive.

Regulatory and compliance risks

In industries with strict regulatory requirements, poor data quality poses significant compliance risks. Missing or inconsistent data can lead to inaccurate reporting, resulting in fines, legal actions, or reputational damage. For example, financial institutions that fail to provide accurate transaction records to regulators may face severe penalties. Maintaining high-quality data is critical to ensuring compliance with frameworks, like GDPR, HIPAA, and CCPA.

Customer dissatisfaction

Customer-facing systems, such as CRMs or recommendation engines, are particularly sensitive to data quality issues. Errors in customer records can result in duplicate communications, incorrect personalization, or unresolved service requests, negatively impacting the customer experience. For instance, a customer who receives irrelevant recommendations due to incorrect browsing history may disengage, reducing brand loyalty and lifetime value.

Best practices to minimize impact on downstream users

Ensuring high-quality data is crucial for minimizing disruptions and maintaining the reliability of downstream processes. Poor data quality can lead to inaccurate analytics, flawed AI models, compliance risks, and operational inefficiencies. To mitigate these challenges, organizations must implement proactive strategies that enhance data integrity, consistency, and accessibility.

The following best practices help safeguard data quality, ensuring that downstream users can trust and effectively utilize the data for decision-making and innovation:

- **Implement real-time validation**: By integrating real-time validation into data pipelines, organizations can catch and correct errors before they affect downstream users. For example, schema validation and anomaly detection during data ingestion ensure that faulty records are flagged and addressed immediately.

- **Maintain a single source of truth**: Centralizing data into a unified, consistent repository minimizes discrepancies and ensures that all downstream users work with the same dataset. Data warehouses or lakes serve as reliable sources, reducing the risk of conflicting reports or insights.

- **Automate data quality checks**: Automated tools like Great Expectations, Deequ, and Apache Griffin streamline the validation process, ensuring that data meets quality standards without requiring manual intervention. Automation also reduces the time spent on data cleaning, freeing analysts and data scientists to focus on generating value.

- **Enhance collaboration between teams**: Downstream users often rely on data engineering teams to provide high-quality data. Promoting collaboration and communication between these teams ensures that data quality requirements are clearly defined and consistently met. Regular feedback loops between data producers and consumers help identify and address recurring quality issues.

Real-world examples

By leveraging data quality tools and best practices, organizations have successfully addressed these issues, improving overall performance and customer satisfaction. The following examples illustrate how various industries, from e-commerce and finance to healthcare and telecommunications, have tackled data quality challenges and achieved measurable improvements.

Let us refer to some real-world examples:

- **E-commerce analytics and customer insights**: A leading e-commerce platform experienced customer dissatisfaction due to incorrect order status updates. The issue stemmed from poor data synchronization between its CRM and order management systems. By implementing Apache Griffin for real-time data validation, the company ensured accurate order tracking, reducing customer complaints by 25% and improving satisfaction metrics.

- **Financial compliance and risk management**: A multinational bank faced challenges in meeting regulatory reporting deadlines due to inconsistent transaction data. Using Deequ, the bank automated its data validation process, reducing errors in regulatory submissions by 20% and avoiding potential fines.

- **AI-powered fraud detection**: A fintech company's fraud detection model underperformed due to incomplete transaction datasets. By leveraging Great Expectations to validate training data for completeness and consistency, the company improved its model's accuracy, reducing false positives by 15%.

Long-term benefits of high-quality data

High-quality data benefits organizations beyond immediate operational improvements. It builds trust among stakeholders, enhances the accuracy of predictive systems, and strengthens regulatory compliance.

The following are some examples:

- **Improved decision-making**: Business leaders gain confidence in their insights, enabling faster and more accurate decisions.

- **Enhanced productivity**: Analysts and data scientists spend less time cleaning data, focusing instead on deriving value.

- **Customer trust and loyalty**: Accurate, personalized interactions enhance customer experiences, fostering long-term engagement.

Organizations that invest in data quality create a competitive advantage, as they can act faster, innovate more effectively, and build stronger relationships with their customers and stakeholders.

Real-world use cases of various sectors:

Real-world applications of data quality management highlight its importance in driving organizational success. Across industries, companies rely on clean, reliable data to make informed decisions, maintain regulatory compliance, and enhance operational efficiency. These examples showcase how organizations have implemented data quality practices and tools to overcome challenges, improve outcomes, and achieve strategic objectives.

High-quality data enables businesses to maintain a competitive edge in fast-evolving markets. Whether through improved customer insights, better compliance reporting, or optimized AI models, these use cases demonstrate the tangible benefits of prioritizing data quality.

E-commerce

An e-commerce company struggled with customer dissatisfaction due to inconsistent product inventory updates across its website and mobile app. This mismatch often led to situations where customers purchased items that were no longer available in stock. The root cause was traced to poor data synchronization between the inventory management system and the front-end applications.

In order to address the issue, the company implemented Apache Griffin to monitor and validate real-time data streams from its inventory system. By defining quality rules for consistency and accuracy, the tool ensured that product availability data matched across all channels. Real-time anomaly detection flagged discrepancies before they impacted customers, allowing teams to correct errors proactively.

The results were transformative. The company saw a 30% reduction in order cancellations due to out-of-stock items and a 20% improvement in customer satisfaction ratings. This example underscores the role of data quality in delivering seamless customer experiences and protecting brand reputation.

Finance

A multinational bank faced challenges in meeting stringent regulatory requirements due to inconsistent transaction data. The bank's manual processes for validating compliance reports were time-consuming and error-prone, often leading to late submissions and penalties. To streamline its data quality efforts, the bank adopted Deequ, a library built on Apache Spark, to automate data validation in its batch processing pipelines.

Deequ allowed the bank to define declarative checks for key quality metrics, including completeness, accuracy, and timeliness. These checks were integrated into the ETL workflow, ensuring that transaction data met regulatory standards before being submitted for reporting. The library's profiling capabilities also provided insights into data patterns, helping the bank identify recurring quality issues.

The impact was significant. The bank reduced errors in compliance reports by 25%, eliminated penalties for late submissions, and freed up resources for higher-value activities. This case highlights how automated tools can enhance data quality in heavily regulated industries, minimizing risks and boosting operational efficiency.

Healthcare

A regional healthcare provider struggled to deliver consistent patient care due to fragmented and inconsistent data across its EHR systems. Patient information, including medical histories, test results, and prescriptions, was often incomplete or duplicated, leading to delays in diagnosis and treatment.

The provider implemented Great Expectations to validate and document data quality rules across its EHR systems. Customizable expectations ensured that critical fields, such as patient identifiers and diagnosis codes, were accurate and complete. Automated validation checks flagged incomplete records, enabling healthcare staff to correct issues promptly.

By standardizing data quality practices, the provider improved care coordination and reduced diagnostic errors by 15%. Patients experienced faster treatment times, and physicians gained confidence in the accuracy of their decision-making. This case underscores the life-saving potential of high-quality data in healthcare.

Retail

A global retail chain faced challenges in managing its supply chain due to inconsistent supplier data. Delayed or inaccurate shipment updates often led to overstocking in some locations and stockouts in others, impacting revenue and customer satisfaction.

In order to address this, the retailer deployed Apache Griffin to monitor supplier data streams in real-time. Quality rules ensured that shipment statuses, delivery dates, and product quantities were accurate and consistent across the supply chain management system. The tool's anomaly detection capabilities flagged delays and mismatches, allowing the supply chain team to act quickly.

The results included a 20% reduction in inventory holding costs and a 25% improvement in on-time deliveries. By ensuring data quality, the retailer optimized its supply chain operations, enhanced customer satisfaction, and increased profitability.

Telecommunications

A telecommunications provider struggled with high customer churn rates, partly due to inaccurate and outdated customer profiles. Duplicate records and missing contact information made it difficult for the company to deliver personalized offers or respond to customer complaints effectively.

The company used Deequ to profile and validate its customer data. Quality checks focused on removing duplicates, filling in missing fields, and standardizing contact information formats. By enriching the dataset with accurate and complete profiles, the provider improved its ability to target at-risk customers with retention offers.

This initiative reduced churn by 18% and increased customer retention revenue by 12%. Clean data allowed the company to strengthen customer relationships and create more impactful marketing campaigns.

Energy

An energy company operating wind farms relies on IoT sensors to monitor equipment performance and predict maintenance needs. However, sensor data was often inconsistent due to hardware malfunctions or communication errors, leading to false alarms or missed maintenance schedules.

The company adopted Apache Griffin to validate IoT data streams in real-time. Quality rules ensured that sensor readings fell within expected ranges, and missing data points were flagged for follow-up. Anomaly detection identified faulty sensors, allowing maintenance teams to address issues promptly.

By improving data quality, the company reduced false alarms by 30% and extended the lifespan of its equipment. Predictive maintenance schedules became more accurate, minimizing downtime and operational costs.

Media and entertainment

A media streaming platform struggled to provide accurate content recommendations due to inconsistent metadata across its catalog. Missing or incorrect tags for genres, actors, and ratings negatively impacted the recommendation engine, leading to poor user engagement.

The platform used Great Expectations to validate metadata quality during ingestion. Custom expectations ensured that all fields were complete, consistent, and formatted correctly. Automated checks flagged errors in real-time, allowing content teams to correct issues before they affected users.

As a result, recommendation accuracy improved by 25%, and user engagement metrics, such as watch time and subscription renewals, increased significantly. This example highlights how data quality directly influences customer satisfaction in content-driven industries.

Tool comparison based on use cases

Choosing the right data quality tool depends on the specific needs of the organization and the nature of its data pipelines. Great Expectations excels in environments where flexibility and integration with diverse platforms, such as Pandas, Spark, or **structure query language** (**SQL**), are critical. It is particularly well-suited for validating schema consistency and documenting quality checks in hybrid pipelines. Deequ, built on Apache Spark, is ideal for batch processing in big data ecosystems, offering robust profiling and declarative quality checks for regulatory compliance and large-scale data validation. On the other hand, Apache Griffin shines in real-time streaming contexts, where anomaly detection and continuous monitoring are essential, such as the **Internet of Things** (**IoT**) or operational analytics. While Great Expectations focuses on ease of use and customization, Deequ emphasizes scalability for batch workflows, and Apache Griffin provides real-time assurance for high-velocity environments. Together, these tools cater to a broad spectrum of use cases, ensuring data quality in both static and dynamic systems.

Selecting the right tool requires understanding cost, complexity, and support availability. *Table 7.2* outlines the comparison:

Tool	Cost	Implementation complexity	Community support
Great Expectations	Free (open-source)	Medium, requires coding	Strong, active forums
Deequ	Free (open-source)	High, Spark-based setup	Moderate, AWS-focused
Apache Griffin	Free (open-source)	High, requires big data expertise	Moderate, growing adoption

Table 7.2: Comparison of data quality tools based on cost, complexity, and community support

Selecting the right data quality tool depends on specific use cases, whether for batch validation, real-time monitoring, or regulatory compliance. The following figure highlights the key strengths and applications of Great Expectations, Deequ, and Apache Griffin:

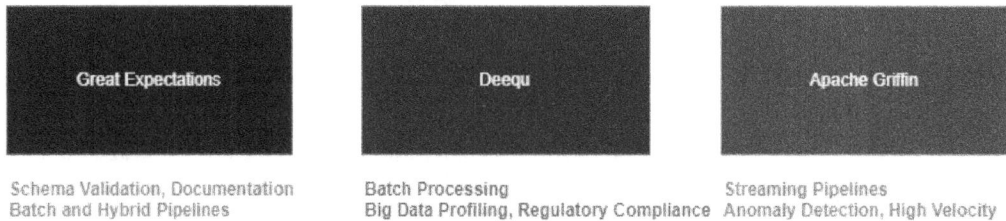

Great Expectations
Schema Validation, Documentation
Batch and Hybrid Pipelines

Deequ
Batch Processing
Big Data Profiling, Regulatory Compliance

Apache Griffin
Streaming Pipelines
Anomaly Detection, High Velocity

Figure 7.2: The strengths and use cases of popular tools

Conclusion

Ensuring data quality is a foundational element of modern data engineering, shaping every stage of the data lifecycle. This chapter has explored how maintaining high standards for accuracy, completeness, and consistency empowers organizations to drive impactful analytics, build trustworthy AI models, and enhance customer experiences. Through best practices, advanced tools, like Great Expectations, Deequ, and Apache Griffin, and real-world applications, we have seen how robust data quality practices directly impact operational efficiency, regulatory compliance, and strategic decision-making.

As we reflect on the techniques and tools for ensuring data quality, it is important to recognize its role as a bridge between data ingestion and analytics. The meticulous processes of validating, profiling, and transforming data prepare it for meaningful analysis and visualization. Poor data quality can derail these downstream processes, but a solid foundation ensures that every subsequent layer of the data pipeline operates seamlessly.

In the next chapter, we will focus on understanding data analytics, where clean, reliable data transforms into actionable insights and compelling narratives. This is where the hard work of ensuring data quality meets its purpose: informing strategies, uncovering opportunities, and driving innovation. As we transition to understanding how to make sense of data, we will explore how high-quality datasets amplify the value of analytics and visualization tools, bringing clarity and direction to complex problems. Prepare to see how data becomes a story that inspires decisions and shapes the future.

CHAPTER 8

Understanding Data Analytics

Introduction

Data analytics is the process of examining raw data to extract insights, patterns, and trends that drive informed decision-making. From early statistical analysis to modern AI-powered analytics, this field has continuously evolved to support business intelligence and automation. It is the bridge between raw data and meaningful insights, helping organizations make informed decisions, improve efficiency, and drive innovation. In today's data-driven world, the ability to analyze and apply data effectively provides a competitive advantage. Whether businesses are studying customer behavior, predicting market trends, or optimizing supply chains, data analytics transforms complex information into clear, strategic direction.

The power of analytics lies in its ability to uncover hidden patterns and trends. Retailers analyze purchasing data to manage inventory, healthcare providers use analytics to improve patient care, and financial institutions detect fraud by identifying anomalies. These examples highlight how analytics plays a crucial role across industries.

The process starts with data collection from sources like databases, IoT devices, and APIs. Raw data is cleaned and structured before analysis. Techniques range from descriptive analytics, which summarize historical trends, to predictive and prescriptive analytics, which forecast outcomes and suggest actions.

Advances in cloud computing, machine learning, and visualization tools like Tableau and Power BI have made analytics more accessible. However, challenges like data governance, security, and cost management remain. As we explore analytics in this chapter, we'll examine its key aspects, applications, and real-world impact across industries.

Structure

The chapter covers the following topics:

- Scale in data analytics
- Performance in data analytics
- Data governance in analytics
- Cost management in data analytics
- Impact on AI and business intelligence
- Real-life case studies

Objectives

By the end of this chapter, readers will have a comprehensive understanding of data analytics, its role in modern organizations, and the key principles that drive effective data-driven decision-making. Readers will learn how data analytics transforms raw data into actionable insights, enabling businesses to optimize operations, enhance customer experiences, and foster innovation. This chapter will explore essential topics such as scalability, performance optimization, governance, and cost management, critical aspects that ensure analytics systems remain efficient and reliable as data complexity grows.

Additionally, this chapter will highlight the relationship between data analytics, AI, and BI, demonstrating how analytics serves as the foundation for predictive modeling, automation, and strategic planning. Real-world case studies will illustrate practical applications across industries, from improving inventory management in retail to enhancing patient outcomes in healthcare and detecting fraud in financial services. A structured analytics maturity model helps organizations assess their capabilities across stages, descriptive (what happened), diagnostic (why it happened), predictive (what will happen), and prescriptive (what should be done).

Readers will understand how to design scalable and high-performance analytics systems while balancing governance and cost considerations. They will also appreciate the impact of analytics on AI and BI and how organizations leverage data to drive competitive advantage. This chapter sets the stage for exploring data privacy and ensuring ethical and secure analytics practices in the digital era.

Scale in data analytics

Scaling in data analytics is not just about handling larger datasets, it is about ensuring that data pipelines, platforms, and processes can deliver insights consistently and efficiently as data volumes, velocities, and varieties grow. Unlike general scalability concerns, analytics requires precise strategies that address the complexities of transforming raw data into actionable insights across diverse workloads. From high-velocity streaming data to massive batch jobs, the ability to scale analytics systems determines their reliability and relevance in modern organizations. Scaling patterns such as sharding for databases, auto-scaling for cloud workloads, and parallelization in Spark optimize performance while handling large datasets efficiently.

The growth of analytics workloads often comes with diverse challenges, such as handling real-time decision-making, expanding data source integrations, or supporting more users querying data simultaneously. Scaling data analytics is about adapting infrastructure, workflows, and tools to meet these evolving demands without compromising performance or accuracy. This section explores how scalability is applied specifically to data analytics workloads, covering both its types and techniques.

Importance of scalability in data analytics

In data analytics, scalability ensures that insights remain actionable regardless of the size or complexity of the data. Consider a streaming analytics pipeline monitoring financial transactions, as transaction volumes surge during market volatility, the pipeline must scale seamlessly to maintain real-time responsiveness. Similarly, a batch analytics system processing terabytes of historical data must adapt to accommodate growth without significantly extending job runtimes.

Scalability also enables broader accessibility. As analytics systems scale, they can support more users, from analysts and data scientists to decision-makers accessing and querying data simultaneously. This democratization of analytics ensures that every team within an organization can leverage data effectively, fostering a culture of informed decision-making.

Types of scalability

Scaling analytics systems typically involves two approaches: horizontal and vertical scalability. Each method offers distinct benefits in addressing the specific demands of data analytics.

Horizontal scaling in analytics workloads

Horizontal scaling distributes analytics workloads across multiple machines or nodes. This approach is fundamental to modern data analytics, where distributed systems handle immense data volumes and execute parallel computations, for example, consider a retail analytics system running on Apache Spark to analyze customer purchasing behavior. By distributing data across a cluster of machines, Spark executes complex transformations, such as aggregating sales by region or customer segment, much faster than a single-machine setup. This distributed model not only accelerates query performance but also ensures that the system can scale seamlessly as more data flows into the pipeline.

In the context of streaming analytics, horizontal scaling is critical. Platforms like Apache Kafka or Flink use partitioning to distribute data streams across nodes, enabling real-time processing even under high data velocities. For instance, a streaming pipeline monitoring IoT sensor data can horizontally scale to ingest and analyze millions of events per second, providing immediate insights for predictive maintenance.

Vertical scaling in analytics systems

Vertical scaling, while less common in large-scale analytics environments, involves enhancing the resources of an existing machine, such as adding more memory or processing power. This approach is suitable for smaller analytics systems or when workloads are concentrated on a single node.

An example of vertical scaling in analytics is enhancing a relational database server supporting ad-hoc queries. For a small team analyzing structured data, upgrading the server's hardware, such as adding CPUs or faster storage, can provide a cost-effective way to improve query performance without redesigning the system.

However, vertical scaling in analytics has limitations, particularly for dynamic or high-volume workloads. As datasets grow or query complexity increases, reliance on a single node can lead to performance bottlenecks, making horizontal scaling a more sustainable solution.

Challenges in scaling data analytics

Scaling data analytics systems presents unique challenges that go beyond general scalability issues. These challenges stem from the specific demands of analytics workloads, such as maintaining data quality, ensuring performance under heavy query loads, and balancing cost with computational efficiency, as follows:

- **Data partitioning and consistency**: Analytics workloads often involve partitioning large datasets across nodes to optimize performance. However, ensuring that partitioning strategies align with query patterns is critical. Poorly designed partitions can lead to uneven workload distribution, causing some nodes to become bottlenecks while others remain underutilized. Additionally, maintaining data consistency across partitions is vital, particularly in systems where frequent updates occur.

- **Query optimization at scale**: As datasets grow, the complexity of queries increases, resulting in longer execution times and higher resource consumption. Analytics systems must optimize queries by leveraging techniques, such as predicate pushdown, materialized views, and cost-based optimizers. Without these strategies, large-scale analytics pipelines risk becoming inefficient, delaying insights.

- **Real-time scalability challenges**: Real-time analytics pipelines require not only scalable ingestion and processing but also near-instantaneous response times. Handling spikes in data velocity, such as during financial market events or retail sales promotions, requires systems to scale elastically, provisioning resources dynamically while maintaining low latency.

- **Cost considerations**: Scaling analytics systems often incurs significant costs, especially in cloud environments, where infrastructure expenses scale with usage. Balancing scalability with cost efficiency requires careful planning, such as using serverless architectures for bursty workloads or selecting appropriate storage tiers for different data types.

  Techniques for achieving scalability achieving scalability in analytics systems involve implementing targeted techniques designed to address the unique demands of data processing, transformation, and querying.

Distributed computing for analytics

Distributed computing is a cornerstone of scalable analytics. Frameworks like Apache Spark and Hadoop enable parallel processing of large datasets, breaking down complex analytics workloads into smaller tasks that run simultaneously across nodes. This approach not only speeds up data processing but also ensures fault tolerance, as tasks can be reallocated to other nodes if failures occur.

For example, a telecom provider analyzing **call detail records** (**CDRs**) can distribute computations across multiple nodes using *Spark*, delivering aggregated metrics, such as call durations, peak usage times, and customer churn predictions in a fraction of the time required by single-node systems.

Partitioning for query optimization

Partitioning datasets based on usage patterns is essential for improving query performance in large-scale analytics systems. Techniques such as range partitioning (by date or region) and hash partitioning (by customer ID or product category) allow analytics engines to scan only relevant partitions, reducing query execution times.

For instance, a retail data warehouse partitioned by store locations enables regional managers to query sales data for their specific area without scanning the entire dataset.

Elastic resource scaling

Elastic scaling allows analytics platforms to dynamically allocate resources based on workload demands. Cloud-based services, like AWS Redshift and Google BigQuery, provide elastic scaling capabilities, enabling systems to handle peak workloads without over-provisioning infrastructure. For example, during *Black Friday* sales, an e-commerce company can temporarily scale its analytics cluster to process the surge in customer transaction data, scaling back once the peak subsides.

Scaling data analytics is a critical capability for organizations aiming to harness the full potential of their data. Whether through horizontal or vertical scaling, distributed computing, or caching, achieving scalability ensures that analytics systems remain robust, responsive, and ready to meet growing demands. While challenges, such as cost management and data consistency must be addressed, the benefits of scalable analytics, faster insights, enhanced decision-making, and greater adaptability make it an essential pillar of modern data engineering. As we explore the principles of data analytics, the next section will explore the importance of performance optimization, offering insights into how organizations maximize the efficiency of their analytics systems in diverse environments.

Performance in data analytics

Performance in data analytics refers to the efficiency and speed with which data systems process, transform, and deliver insights. In the context of analytics, performance optimization is critical to ensuring timely decision-making, maintaining system reliability, and meeting the growing demands of users. Whether it is enabling sub-second response times for real-time analytics or reducing query execution times for large datasets, performance in data analytics is the key to unlocking actionable insights.

As data grows in volume, velocity, and complexity, maintaining high performance becomes a significant challenge. This section discusses the factors influencing performance in data analytics, common bottlenecks, and strategies to optimize performance at various stages of the analytics pipeline. Optimizing performance involves indexing, query pruning, and distributed caching to reduce latency and improve data retrieval efficiency, ensuring real-time analytics scalability.

Importance of performance in data analytics

Performance in data analytics impacts every aspect of the data lifecycle, from ingestion to reporting. In modern analytics workflows, speed is often as critical as accuracy, for instance, a retail platform running recommendation systems relies on real-time analytics to present relevant products to customers. Any delay in delivering these insights could lead to lost sales opportunities. Similarly, financial trading platforms require low-latency analytics to make split-second decisions that affect profitability.

Performance optimization in analytics also ensures scalability. As organizations integrate new data sources, accommodate more users, or analyze larger datasets, systems must remain responsive. Poor performance can lead to delayed insights, dissatisfied users, and increased operational costs. By prioritizing performance, organizations can ensure that analytics systems not only meet current demands but also remain future-proof.

Key performance metrics in data analytics

Understanding and monitoring key performance metrics is essential for identifying bottlenecks and measuring the efficiency of analytics systems. These metrics include:

- **Query latency** refers to the time it takes for a system to process a query and return results. Low latency is especially critical in real-time analytics scenarios, where even slight delays can affect decision-making. For example, a logistics company using analytics to track shipments in real time requires instant query responses to re-route deliveries efficiently.

- **Throughput** measures the amount of data processed by a system within a given time frame. High throughput is essential for batch analytics workloads that involve processing large datasets. For instance, a social media platform analyzing millions of user interactions daily needs high throughput to generate insights quickly.

- **Data freshness** reflects how up-to-date the data is when it is analyzed. For real-time analytics, maintaining data freshness is critical. A streaming analytics pipeline monitoring IoT devices, for example, must process events as they occur to provide accurate insights for predictive maintenance.

- **System utilization** measures how effectively computing resources, such as CPU, memory, and storage, are used during analytics operations. Optimizing utilization ensures that resources are not wasted and that systems can handle peak workloads without degradation.

Common performance bottlenecks in data analytics

As data volumes grow and analytics systems become more complex, performance bottlenecks can significantly impact the speed and efficiency of data processing. These bottlenecks arise from various factors, including inefficient query execution, resource limitations, and data architecture constraints. Even with advancements in cloud computing and distributed processing, organizations often struggle with slow query performance, delayed insights, and high computational costs. Addressing these challenges requires a deep understanding of where inefficiencies occur and how they can be mitigated.

The following are some common performance bottlenecks in data analytics and strategies to overcome them:

- **Input/output (I/O) constraints**: I/O operations, such as reading and writing data to disk, are common sources of delays in analytics pipelines. Systems that rely on traditional storage solutions may struggle to handle large datasets, resulting in high query latency.

- **Inefficient query execution**: Poorly optimized queries can lead to excessive resource consumption and long execution times. For example, analytics workloads that scan entire datasets instead of filtering relevant partitions waste computational resources.

- **Resource contention**: In multi-user environments, resource contention occurs when multiple users or processes compete for the same resources, such as CPU or memory. This contention can degrade performance, especially during peak usage periods.

- **Network latency**: For distributed analytics systems, network latency can become a bottleneck. Transferring data between nodes in a cluster or between systems in different geographic locations adds overhead that affects performance.

Strategies for optimizing performance

Performance optimization in data analytics involves a combination of architectural improvements, query optimization techniques, and resource management strategies.

Some proven approaches to enhance analytics performance are as follows:

- **Indexing**: It improves query performance by organizing data in a way that facilitates faster retrieval. For example, creating indexes on frequently queried columns in a relational database can significantly reduce query execution times. In the context of analytics, indexing is particularly useful for ad-hoc queries and dashboards that rely on rapid data access.

- **Data partitioning**: It divides datasets into smaller, manageable segments based on specific criteria, such as date ranges or geographic regions. Analytics engines can then process only the relevant partitions, reducing the amount of data scanned. For instance, a data warehouse partitioned by time allows analysts to query recent data without accessing the entire dataset.

- **Caching**: It stores frequently accessed data in memory, reducing the need to fetch it repeatedly from slower storage layers. This is especially beneficial for real-time analytics workloads that involve repetitive queries. A financial institution analyzing live stock market data, for example, can use caching to accelerate the retrieval of recent price movements.

- **Query optimization**: Optimizing queries involves rewriting or restructuring them to improve execution efficiency. Techniques, such as predicate pushdown, materialized views, and query pruning help reduce the amount of data processed and enhance performance. For instance, an e-commerce platform analyzing customer behavior might optimize queries by pushing filters to the storage layer, minimizing the data retrieved.

- **Resource auto-scaling**: In cloud-based analytics platforms, resource auto-scaling adjusts computational capacity dynamically based on workload demands. This ensures that systems have sufficient resources during peak periods while minimizing costs during off-peak times. For example, a streaming analytics pipeline processing retail transactions can scale up during sales events and scale down afterward.

- **Monitoring and profiling**: Performance monitoring tools help identify bottlenecks and track key metrics in real-time. Profiling analytics pipelines provides insights into resource usage, query performance, and system behavior, enabling proactive optimization. Tools, like Apache Spark UI or AWS CloudWatch are commonly used for this purpose.

Performance in data analytics is not just about speed; it is about delivering insights at the right time to enable effective decision-making. By addressing common bottlenecks and implementing strategies, such as indexing, caching, and resource autoscaling, organizations can optimize their analytics systems to handle diverse workloads efficiently. As analytics environments grow more complex, maintaining high performance will remain a key priority, ensuring that data-driven strategies continue to drive value and innovation. In the next section, we will explore the role of data governance in analytics, highlighting its importance in maintaining data quality, security, and compliance across analytics pipelines.

Data governance in analytics

Data governance in analytics is the framework that ensures data is used effectively, securely, and ethically to support organizational goals. While governance encompasses a wide range of practices, in the context of data analytics, it focuses on maintaining the integrity, consistency, and usability of data as it flows through analytics pipelines. Without robust governance, even the most advanced analytics systems can falter, producing unreliable insights or exposing organizations to compliance risks.

Unlike general governance practices, data governance in analytics addresses challenges unique to the analytics lifecycle. These include managing data transformations, ensuring auditability of analytics processes, and aligning analytics outputs with business objectives. This section explores how governance frameworks are tailored to analytics environments, their critical components, and best practices for maintaining governance across complex data ecosystems.

Importance of data governance in analytics

In data analytics, governance is not just about compliance, it is a foundational requirement for delivering trustworthy and actionable insights. When governance is neglected, analytics systems risk operating on incomplete, inconsistent, or incorrect data, leading to flawed conclusions and poor decision-making. For example, if a financial institution's analytics system fails to detect duplicate transaction records due to poor governance, it could misrepresent revenue figures, impacting strategic decisions.

Governance also ensures that data analytics aligns with organizational priorities and regulatory requirements. With increasing scrutiny on data usage through regulations, such as the GDPR, CCPA, and HIPAA organizations must establish governance frameworks that not only safeguard data but also maintain transparency in how it is analyzed. This is especially critical in industries, like healthcare and finance, where analytics often involves sensitive or regulated data.

Moreover, governance frameworks enhance team collaboration, such as data engineers, analysts, and business stakeholders. By defining clear roles, policies, and processes, governance eliminates ambiguities and ensures that analytics systems deliver consistent and accurate outputs that align with business objectives.

Key components of data governance in analytics

Effective data governance frameworks in analytics revolve around several key components, each addressing specific challenges in the analytics lifecycle. Some of them are discussed in this section.

Metadata management

Metadata serves as the backbone of governance in analytics, providing information about the origins, structure, and transformations of data as it moves through pipelines. In analytics environments, metadata enables the following:

- **Lineage tracking**: Identifying how data is sourced, transformed, and consumed in analytics workflows.

- **Transparency**: Allowing analysts and stakeholders to understand the context of analytics outputs.

- **Quality assurance**: Detecting discrepancies or issues in data transformations.

An example is an e-commerce platform analyzing customer behavior uses metadata to track how raw clickstream data is transformed into actionable metrics, such as cart abandonment rates. This transparency ensures that stakeholders trust the analytics outputs.

The following figure illustrates the flow of metadata through the analytics lifecycle, highlighting its collection, enrichment, storage, and utilization by various stakeholders to ensure governance and transparency in data analytics processes:

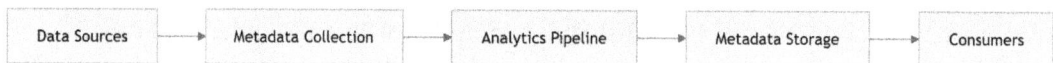

| Data Sources | → | Metadata Collection | → | Analytics Pipeline | → | Metadata Storage | → | Consumers |

Figure 8.1: Metadata management workflow in data analytics

Access controls

Access controls regulate who can view, modify, or analyze data, ensuring that sensitive information is protected while maintaining usability for authorized users. In analytics, granular access controls are essential for balancing data security with collaboration, for instance, in a healthcare analytics system, doctors may need access to patient health metrics but should be restricted from viewing financial or administrative data. RBAC ensures that each user only has access to the data they need for their role.

Data stewardship

Data stewardship assigns responsibility for maintaining the quality, security, and usability of data within analytics systems. Stewards play a critical role in ensuring that governance policies are implemented effectively and that analytics workflows adhere to organizational standards, for example, in a financial institution, a data steward may oversee the governance of transaction datasets used for fraud detection analytics. Their responsibilities include verifying the completeness of incoming data and resolving any discrepancies before analysis begins.

Audit trails

Audit trails provide a record of all actions performed on data, enabling organizations to monitor analytics activities and ensure accountability. In analytics systems, audit trails are crucial for:

- Tracking changes to data or analytics configurations.

- Investigating anomalies or discrepancies in analytics outputs.

- Demonstrating compliance with regulatory requirements.

For example, an audit trail in a logistics analytics system might show who modified delivery data and when ensuring transparency and accountability in decision-making.

Challenges in data governance for analytics

Despite its importance, implementing data governance in analytics systems presents unique challenges that stem from the dynamic and complex nature of analytics environments.

Some challenges are as follows:

- **Dynamic data pipelines**: Analytics pipelines often involve real-time data ingestion, frequent updates, and rapid transformations. Ensuring that governance policies keep pace with these dynamic processes can be difficult. For example, in streaming analytics systems, governance frameworks must address the continuous flow of data without introducing latency or bottlenecks.

- **Data silos**: In many organizations, data resides in disparate systems, leading to inconsistent governance practices across analytics workflows. Breaking down these silos to establish unified governance is critical for ensuring consistency in analytics outputs.

- **Balancing usability and security**: While governance emphasizes security, overly restrictive policies can hinder analytics teams from accessing the data they need. Striking the right balance between security and usability requires careful planning and collaboration.

Best practices for governance in analytics

Implementing governance in analytics systems requires a strategic approach that addresses the specific challenges of the analytics lifecycle.

Some best practices for maintaining effective governance are as follows:

- **Establish governance frameworks early**: Governance should be integrated into analytics systems from the outset, rather than being treated as an afterthought. By embedding governance policies into data pipelines, organizations can ensure consistent practices across all analytics workflows.

- **Automate governance processes**: Automation reduces the overhead of manual governance tasks, such as metadata management or access control enforcement. Tools, like Apache Atlas and AWS Lake Formation enable organizations to automate governance in analytics pipelines, improving efficiency and consistency.

- **Foster cross-team collaboration**: Governance frameworks should involve collaboration between data engineers, analysts, and business stakeholders. This ensures that governance policies align with both technical requirements and business objectives, fostering trust in analytics outputs.

- **Implement continuous monitoring**: Monitoring tools help organizations track compliance with governance policies and detect anomalies in analytics workflows. For example, a real-time monitoring system might flag unauthorized access to sensitive data or discrepancies in analytics results.

    Data governance in analytics is the cornerstone of delivering accurate, reliable, and secure insights. By focusing on components such as metadata management, access controls, and auditability, governance frameworks ensure that analytics systems align with organizational priorities and regulatory requirements. Despite challenges, such as dynamic pipelines and data silos, best practices like automation and cross-team collaboration can help organizations establish effective governance. As analytics continues to drive innovation, governance will remain essential in maintaining the trustworthiness and impact of data-driven decision-making. In the next section, we will explore *Cost management in analytics*, delving into strategies for optimizing analytics workflows without compromising performance or scalability. Frameworks like DAMA-DMBOK and NIST Data Governance provide structured approaches for managing data integrity, quality, and accountability in analytics workflows.

Cost management in data analytics

Cost management in data analytics involves optimizing resources, infrastructure, and workflows to ensure analytics systems remain both efficient and economically sustainable. With data analytics becoming an integral part of business operations, organizations are investing heavily in tools, cloud services, and personnel to derive insights. However, the rapid growth of analytics workloads can lead to escalating costs, especially in environments where data volumes and complexity are continuously increasing. Effectively managing these costs without compromising performance, scalability, or accuracy is a critical challenge.

Unlike general IT cost management, cost optimization in data analytics focuses specifically on expenses tied to data pipelines, storage, computational resources, and analytics tools. This section explores the major cost drivers in analytics, strategies to manage them, and the role of cost-efficient architectures in supporting analytics initiatives.

Importance of cost management in data analytics

In the context of data analytics, managing costs is not merely about reducing expenses,it is about achieving the maximum **return on investment** (ROI) from analytics systems. Analytics workloads often require significant computational power, large-scale data storage, and specialized tools, all of which can drive up costs rapidly. Without effective cost management, even well-designed analytics systems can become financially unsustainable.

Cost management is also critical for aligning analytics operations with organizational budgets. For example, a company deploying AI-driven analytics for customer segmentation may need to balance the cost of real-time predictions against the business value they generate. Proper cost management ensures that investments in analytics align with expected outcomes, fostering trust in the financial viability of data-driven initiatives.

Moreover, managing costs in analytics enables organizations to scale their systems responsibly. As analytics workloads grow, scalable and cost-efficient architectures allow businesses to expand their capabilities without overextending resources. This is particularly relevant in cloud-based environments, where costs are tied to usage and can fluctuate significantly.

Major cost drivers in data analytics

Understanding the primary sources of costs in data analytics is essential for identifying opportunities to optimize expenses.

The following cost drivers vary based on the organization's infrastructure, tools, and workload requirements:

- **Storage costs**: Analytics systems often require significant storage resources to handle large datasets. Costs increase as data volumes grow, particularly in environments with long-term data retention requirements. Cloud storage services, like AWS S3, Google Cloud Storage, or Azure Blob Storage, charge based on the volume of data stored, making storage a key cost driver.

- **Compute costs**: Computational resources used for data processing and analysis, such as CPUs and GPUs, represent another major cost. For instance, running machine learning models or processing large-scale ETL workflows can consume substantial computational power, driving up costs.

- **Data transfer costs**: In distributed analytics systems, data must often be transferred between nodes or regions. Cloud providers typically charge for data egress, meaning the transfer of data out of their platforms. For example, moving data between AWS regions or transferring analytics results to on-premises systems can incur significant costs.

- **Licensing and subscription fees**: Many analytics tools and platforms operate on a subscription or licensing model. Tools, like Tableau, Power BI, and Snowflake charge fees based on usage or user counts, which can add up in large organizations.

- **Personnel costs**: Skilled personnel, such as data engineers, analysts, and scientists, are essential for building and maintaining analytics systems. While not a direct infrastructure cost, personnel expenses contribute significantly to the overall cost of analytics.

Strategies for cost management in data analytics

Cost management in data analytics requires a multi-faceted approach that encompasses infrastructure optimization, resource planning, and workload management. Strategies that organizations can use to manage analytics costs effectively are as follows:

Optimize data storage

Efficient storage strategies can significantly reduce costs without compromising data availability or quality. Techniques include:

- **Storage tiering**: Using different storage tiers based on data access patterns. Frequently accessed data can be stored in high-performance tiers, while infrequently used data can be moved to lower-cost tiers.

- **Data compression**: Reducing the size of stored data to minimize storage requirements and costs.

- **Data lifecycle policies**: Automating data archiving and deletion based on pre-defined retention periods to avoid unnecessary storage costs.

Use serverless architectures

Serverless analytics platforms, such as AWS Athena or Google BigQuery, charge only for the resources consumed during query execution. This eliminates the need for provisioning and maintaining dedicated infrastructure, making it a cost-effective solution for intermittent analytics workloads.

Leverage spot and reserved instances

For cloud-based analytics systems, spot instances (unused compute capacity offered at discounted rates) and reserved instances (pre-purchased compute capacity at reduced rates) provide cost savings, for example, an organization running nightly batch analytics jobs can use spot instances to lower compute expenses.

Optimize query execution

Efficient query execution reduces compute costs by minimizing resource usage. Strategies include:

- **Predicate pushdown**: Filtering data at the storage layer to reduce the amount of data processed by queries.

- **Materialized views**: Pre-computing and storing frequently accessed query results to avoid redundant calculations.

- **Query scheduling**: Timing non-urgent queries during off-peak hours to leverage lower-cost compute resources.

Adopt cost monitoring tools

Monitoring tools provide visibility into cost drivers and help identify optimization opportunities. Tools, like AWS Cost Explorer, Google Cloud Billing, and third-party platforms, such as CloudHealth enable organizations to track spending, set budgets, and receive alerts for cost anomalies.

Balancing cost management with performance and scalability

Cost management in analytics must balance efficiency with other priorities, such as performance and scalability. Overly aggressive cost-cutting measures can compromise analytics performance or hinder the ability to scale. For example, reducing compute resources for real-time analytics could lead to slower query responses, impacting operational decision-making.

In order to achieve this balance, organizations should adopt a cost-aware architecture that integrates performance and scalability considerations. Techniques, such as autoscaling, dynamic resource allocation, and workload prioritization, ensure that analytics systems deliver value without exceeding budget constraints.

Cost management in data analytics is a critical enabler of sustainable data-driven operations. By understanding key cost drivers, implementing efficient storage and compute strategies, and leveraging cost monitoring tools, organizations can optimize their analytics workflows without compromising on quality or scalability. As analytics systems grow more complex, cost management will remain an essential discipline, ensuring that investments in analytics continue to deliver high ROI. In the next section, we will explore the impact of data analytics on artificial intelligence and business intelligence, highlighting how optimized analytics systems enhance AI and BI initiatives across industries.

Impact on AI and business intelligence

Data analytics is the backbone of both AI and BI, serving as the critical intermediary that transforms raw data into actionable insights and intelligent models. While BI focuses on descriptive and diagnostic analytics to guide decision-making, AI leverages predictive and prescriptive analytics to enable automation and intelligent decision-making. In both domains, the quality, scale, and efficiency of analytics pipelines directly influence the outcomes of AI and BI initiatives.

This section explores the multifaceted role of data analytics in shaping AI and BI, highlighting how optimized analytics pipelines enhance AI model performance and business intelligence strategies. By examining the interplay between these disciplines, we can better understand how data analytics enables innovation and drives success in data-driven organizations. AI-driven analytics enhances decision-making with anomaly detection, automated insights, and prescriptive recommendations, reducing manual intervention in data workflows.

Role of data analytics in AI

AI systems rely heavily on data analytics to provide the foundation for model training, evaluation, and real-time inference. High-quality analytics ensures that AI systems receive data that is clean, consistent, and representative of real-world scenarios. The power of data analytics is instrumental in shaping and fueling AI applications, as demonstrated in processes, as follows:

- **Feature engineering**: It is one of the most critical stages in AI development, where raw data is transformed into meaningful inputs for machine learning models. Data analytics plays a vital role in identifying patterns, correlations, and trends that inform the selection of features. For example, in predictive maintenance, analytics systems can process sensor data to identify variables, such as temperature, vibration levels, or operating hours, that serve as indicators of equipment failure.

- **Training data preparation**: The success of AI models depends on the quality of training data, and this is where data analytics pipelines shine. Tasks, such as deduplication, outlier detection, and data normalization, are essential for ensuring that the dataset is balanced and unbiased. For instance, an AI model designed for fraud detection requires analytics systems to pre-process historical transaction data, flagging fraudulent patterns without skewing the dataset toward one class.

- **Real-time AI**: In real-time AI systems, such as autonomous vehicles or fraud prevention platforms, data analytics pipelines enable rapid data ingestion, transformation, and feature generation. Streaming analytics platforms, like Apache Flink or Spark Streaming, ensure that AI models receive up-to-date inputs, enhancing their responsiveness and accuracy.

Role of data analytics in BI

BI focuses on turning historical and current data into actionable insights that inform strategic and operational decisions. Analytics systems form the backbone of BI by providing the tools and methodologies required to process and visualize data effectively.

Descriptive and diagnostic insights

Analytics systems are crucial for providing descriptive insights that summarize past performance and diagnostic insights that uncover the root causes of observed patterns. For instance, a BI dashboard powered by analytics pipelines might display **key performance indicators** (**KPIs**), such as revenue, churn rates, or customer satisfaction, allowing business leaders to diagnose issues and opportunities.

Predictive and prescriptive analytics in BI

While traditionally focused on past and present data, BI increasingly incorporates predictive and prescriptive analytics, bridging the gap with AI. Data analytics systems process historical trends to forecast future outcomes, such as projected sales or customer behavior. These forecasts are then used to recommend actions, such as inventory adjustments or marketing strategies.

Enhanced reporting and visualization

Data analytics tools, such as Tableau or Power BI, transform raw datasets into intuitive visualizations that make complex insights accessible to non-technical stakeholders. Analytics systems automate data preparation, ensuring that BI platforms always work with clean, accurate, and up-to-date data.

Synergy between AI, BI, and data analytics

In today's data-driven landscape, AI and BI are increasingly interconnected, with data analytics serving as the crucial link between them. While BI focuses on analyzing historical and real-time data to support business decision-making, AI extends these capabilities by enabling predictive and prescriptive insights. The integration of AI and BI is transforming how organizations derive value from their data, automating insights, improving efficiency, and enhancing decision-making processes.

This section explores how AI enhances BI, how BI informs AI development, and real-world case studies demonstrating the impact of data analytics across industries.

AI-enhanced BI

Modern BI platforms increasingly integrate AI capabilities, such as **natural language processing** (**NLP**) for query generation or machine learning models for automated forecasting. Analytics pipelines are critical to these integrations, providing the data flows required to train AI models and validate their outputs. For example, a retail company might use an AI-enhanced BI platform to analyze customer feedback through sentiment analysis, identifying trends that inform product development.

BI-driven AI

Conversely, BI insights often serve as the starting point for AI initiatives. By identifying patterns and gaps in historical data, BI platforms inform the design of AI models. For instance, a bank using BI to track loan default trends may leverage these insights to build a machine-learning model that predicts default risks, enabling proactive risk management.

Real-life case studies

Data analytics has revolutionized how organizations approach decision-making, optimize processes, and innovate across industries. Each case study illustrates how advanced analytics systems have been implemented to solve complex challenges, yielding transformative outcomes. The following detailed case studies provide insights into the application of data analytics in retail, healthcare, and financial services. Additional applications include AI-driven anomaly detection in manufacturing, real-time fraud prevention in banking, and predictive maintenance in logistics.

Enhancing inventory management in retail

A global retail chain with hundreds of outlets across multiple regions faced significant challenges in managing its inventory. The lack of accurate demand forecasting led to frequent stockouts and overstock situations, impacting both revenue and customer satisfaction. Additionally, disparate systems across regional warehouses made it difficult to consolidate and analyze inventory data effectively.

Analytics solution

The retailer implemented a data analytics platform powered by Apache Spark to process historical sales data, seasonal trends, and regional demand patterns. The platform is integrated with POS systems, supplier databases, and external market data sources, such as local weather and holiday calendars. A machine learning model was trained using processed data to predict demand trends for each product category.

The platform also enabled real-time analytics to monitor inventory levels across all outlets. By leveraging predictive analytics, the system provided actionable insights to managers, such as restocking schedules and inventory transfers between stores.

The results are as follows:

- **Reduction in stockouts**: By forecasting demand more accurately, the chain reduced stockouts by 35%, ensuring that high-demand items were consistently available.

- **Cost savings**: Overstock situations were minimized, leading to a 20% reduction in inventory carrying costs.

- **Improved customer satisfaction**: Availability of desired products increased, resulting in higher customer loyalty and repeat purchases.

Takeaways

This case highlights how data analytics can optimize inventory management by leveraging predictive models and integrating real-time monitoring, ensuring that supply chains align with customer demand effectively. By implementing a data-driven approach, the retailer not only reduced inefficiencies but also enhanced decision-making at every level of inventory management.

Furthermore, the integration of machine learning models allowed for proactive inventory adjustments, minimizing revenue losses from stockouts and excess inventory. The ability to forecast demand with precision enabled better coordination between suppliers and store managers, leading to a more agile and responsive supply chain.

Beyond operational benefits, this transformation also improved customer experience, as consumers found their preferred products readily available, strengthening brand trust and loyalty. This case exemplifies how businesses can harness data analytics to create a more resilient, cost-efficient, and customer-centric retail ecosystem.

Transforming patient outcomes in healthcare

A regional healthcare provider managing multiple hospitals struggled with inconsistent patient data and delays in treatment due to inefficient analytics workflows. Critical information, such as patient histories and diagnostic results, was siloed across departments, making it difficult for physicians to access the data needed for timely decisions.

Analytics solution

The provider deployed a centralized analytics platform built on Azure Synapse Analytics. The system aggregated data from EHR, diagnostic labs, and IoT devices, such as wearable health monitors. Advanced data cleaning and normalization processes ensured that all records were consistent and complete.

Using the analytics platform, the healthcare provider implemented real-time patient monitoring dashboards. Predictive analytics models analyzed vital signs and historical data to detect early warning signs of critical conditions, such as sepsis or heart failure.

The results are as follows:

- **Faster diagnosis**: Physicians gained access to comprehensive patient profiles, reducing the time required to diagnose complex cases by 30%.

- **Improved outcomes**: Predictive analytics enabled proactive interventions, resulting in a 25% reduction in readmission rates.

- **Operational efficiency**: Centralizing analytics workflows reduced the administrative burden on staff, freeing up more time for patient care.

Takeaways

This case demonstrates how data analytics can bridge silos in healthcare, delivering actionable insights that improve patient outcomes and streamline clinical operations. By integrating data from multiple sources into a centralized analytics platform, the healthcare provider eliminated inefficiencies that previously hindered timely decision-making.

The ability to consolidate and standardize patient records across departments empowered physicians with a comprehensive view of patient histories, enabling faster and more accurate diagnoses. Predictive analytics played a crucial role in identifying early warning signs of life-threatening conditions, allowing for timely interventions that improved survival rates and reduced hospital readmissions.

Beyond enhancing patient care, the implementation of real-time monitoring dashboards and automated workflows significantly increased operational efficiency. Physicians and healthcare staff spend less time manually gathering and verifying data, allowing them to focus more on patient care and treatment planning.

Furthermore, the improved accessibility of high-quality data fostered better collaboration among healthcare professionals, ensuring coordinated efforts in patient management. This case highlights how leveraging data analytics in healthcare not only improves clinical outcomes but also optimizes hospital resource utilization, reduces treatment delays, and enhances the overall patient experience. It underscores the potential of data-driven strategies to transform modern healthcare systems and drive continuous improvements in medical care.

Real-time fraud detection in financial services

A multinational financial institution faced rising cases of fraudulent transactions, costing millions in losses annually. Traditional batch processing analytics systems could not keep up with the need for real-time fraud detection, allowing fraudulent activities to go unnoticed until after they occurred.

The following figure showcases the real-time fraud detection pipeline, detailing how transaction data flows through various stages, including ingestion, processing, anomaly detection, and feedback loops for continuous model improvement:

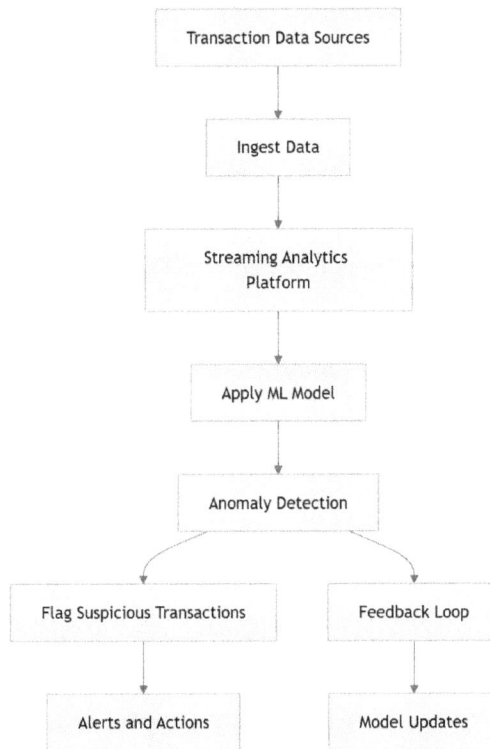

Figure 8.2: Real-time fraud detection pipeline

Analytics solution

The institution implemented a streaming analytics pipeline using Apache Flink to process and analyze transaction data in real time. The pipeline ingested data from multiple sources, including credit card networks, customer profiles, and merchant databases.

A machine learning model trained on historical fraud patterns was integrated into the pipeline. Real-time anomaly detection flagged suspicious transactions, triggering alerts for further investigation. The system also provided a feedback loop, continuously improving the model by incorporating new fraud patterns.

The results are as follows:

- **Faster fraud detection**: Fraudulent transactions were identified and flagged within milliseconds, allowing the institution to block them before completion.

- **Reduced losses**: The financial institution saved approximately $20 million in potential fraud losses within the first year of implementation.

- **Enhanced customer trust**: The system's accuracy reduced false positives, ensuring legitimate transactions were not disrupted, which improved customer satisfaction.

Takeaways

This case underscores the importance of real-time analytics in high-stakes industries like finance, where rapid responses to anomalies can prevent significant losses and enhance trust. By implementing a streaming analytics pipeline powered by Apache Flink, the financial institution was able to shift from a reactive fraud detection approach to a proactive, real-time monitoring system that identifies suspicious transactions within milliseconds.

The integration of machine learning models into the fraud detection pipeline enabled continuous learning and adaptation, allowing the system to evolve alongside emerging fraud techniques. This not only reduced financial losses but also strengthened the institution's ability to detect and mitigate fraudulent activities before they could cause substantial damage.

Beyond security, real-time fraud detection significantly improved customer experience. By reducing false positives, the system ensured that legitimate transactions were processed smoothly, minimizing disruptions for customers and enhancing their trust in the financial institution.

Additionally, the automated feedback loop streamlined the institution's fraud detection operations, reducing manual intervention and allowing fraud analysts to focus on high-risk cases requiring human oversight. This case highlights how real-time data analytics transform financial security, enabling institutions to protect assets, maintain compliance, and build a more resilient and trustworthy banking ecosystem.

Conclusion

These case studies illustrate the transformative potential of data analytics across different sectors. In retail, analytics optimized inventory management, ensuring that products matched customer demand. In healthcare, it bridged silos to improve patient outcomes and operational efficiency. In financial services, real-time analytics provided a robust defense against fraud, saving millions in losses. Together, these examples highlight the versatility and power of data analytics in solving complex challenges and driving success across industries.

In the next chapter, we will explore ensuring data privacy in analytics, exploring how organizations balance data-driven innovation with the need for security and compliance.

CHAPTER 9
Data Visualization and Reporting

Introduction

Data visualization is the art of converting raw data into meaningful insights. In today's data-driven world, simply collecting and processing data is not enough; its real value lies in how it is presented to inform, persuade, and empower decision-makers. Visualizations serve as a bridge between complex data and actionable insights, enabling organizations to navigate challenges effectively.

Previous chapters explored the data journey, from collection and ingestion to real-time storage and scalable processing, highlighting the need for efficiency to support AI, business intelligence, and operational decision-making. This chapter extends that journey, demonstrating how data is transformed into impactful visual stories that drive action and innovation. It also sets the stage for subsequent discussions on analysis and security.

Data visualization plays a crucial role in connecting technical teams with decision-makers. Engineers and analysts ensure seamless data flows, while executives rely on clear reports to guide strategies. Effective visualizations translate intricate data processes into digestible insights. By the end of this chapter, readers will understand visualization fundamentals and learn to use tools like Tableau, Power BI, and D3.js to create insightful dashboards.

As we move forward, the connection between scalable data architectures and real-world applications will become evident, showing how visualization enhances clarity, transparency, and strategic decision-making.

Structure

The chapter covers the following topics:

- Fundamentals of data visualization
- Tools and technologies
- Real-life examples and case studies

Objectives

By the end of this chapter, readers will have a comprehensive understanding of data visualization as a crucial element in the data analytics lifecycle. Readers will learn how to transform raw data into meaningful, visually compelling insights that drive informed decision-making. The chapter highlights the importance of visualization in bridging the gap between technical data processes and business strategy, ensuring that complex data is presented in a clear, actionable manner.

Building on previous discussions of data collection, ingestion, storage, and processing, this chapter explores how visualization brings data to life. It emphasizes the role of visualization in AI-driven analytics, business intelligence, and operational monitoring, demonstrating its impact across industries. Through practical insights, readers will learn to leverage tools such as Tableau, Power BI, and D3.js to create effective dashboards and reports.

Additionally, this chapter sets the stage for discussions on data analysis and security by showcasing how visualization aids in monitoring data governance, compliance, and privacy. By the end, readers will not only grasp the fundamentals of data visualization but also understand its strategic significance in enhancing clarity, transparency, and data-driven decision-making across organizations.

Fundamentals of data visualization

Data visualization is a powerful method of communicating insights from data by converting abstract numbers and complex datasets into visual representations. Humans are inherently visual creatures; we process visual information faster and retain it longer than textual or numerical data. Effective data visualization leverages this cognitive trait to make data accessible, comprehensible, and actionable.

At its core, data visualization serves to address three key objectives: identifying current trends, analyzing underlying causes, and predicting future outcomes. Achieving these objectives requires more than the creation of visually appealing representations; it necessitates a thorough comprehension of both the data and the intended audience. This section provides a solid foundation for both beginners and experienced professionals, ensuring that readers at all levels can effectively interpret and apply visualization principles.

Figure 9.1 illustrates the end-to-end workflow for creating effective data visualizations. It starts with raw data sources, moves through stages, like data preparation and processing, and concludes with creating interactive dashboards or reports. The flow highlights how each step transforms data into actionable insights, bridging the gap between technical data engineering processes and decision-making.

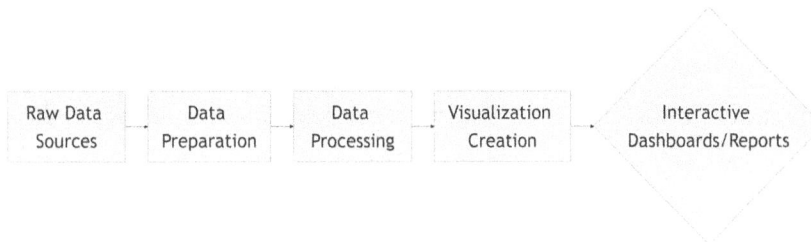

Figure 9.1: *Workflow for creating effective data visualizations*

Purpose of data visualization

The primary purpose of data visualization is to simplify complexity. In modern data engineering, where systems generate and store terabytes of data daily, identifying patterns, trends, and outliers is crucial. Visualization acts as a lens, focusing attention on critical insights while filtering out noise. By highlighting relationships between data points, it allows organizations to make decisions faster and more accurately.

Beyond simplification, data visualization enhances communication. Stakeholders often come from diverse backgrounds, with varying levels of technical expertise. While a data engineer might appreciate the raw details of a dataset, a business executive might only need a high-level summary. Visualization bridges this gap, presenting data in ways that resonate with different audiences.

Types of data visualizations

Effective data visualization requires selecting the right representation to convey insights accurately and efficiently. Different types of visualizations serve distinct purposes, ranging from simple comparisons to complex analytical interpretations. Choosing the appropriate visualization depends on factors such as the nature of the data, the relationships being analyzed, and the audience's needs.

Data visualizations can be categorized into three main types: **basic charts**, which provide straightforward comparisons and trends; **complex visualizations**, which reveal patterns and relationships in multidimensional data; and **specialized visualizations**, which cater to specific analytical needs such as geospatial analysis and network mapping.

The following are the categories in detail, highlighting their applications and advantages in data-driven decision-making:

- **Basic charts**:
  - ○ **Bar charts**: Ideal for comparing categorical data across different groups.
  - ○ **Line charts**: Useful for showing trends over time.
  - ○ **Pie charts**: Often used to represent proportions or percentages, but should be employed sparingly due to potential misinterpretations.
- **Complex visualizations**:
  - ○ **Scatter plots**: Highlight relationships or correlations between variables.
  - ○ **Heatmaps**: Represent data intensity using colors, often applied in analytics.
  - ○ **Tree maps**: Display hierarchical data through nested rectangles.
- **Specialized visualizations**:
  - ○ **Geospatial maps**: Combine location data with metrics, useful for industries like logistics and retail.
  - ○ **Network graphs**: Showcase relationships and connections, particularly in social media and graph databases.
  - ○ **AI, driven visualizations**: Automatically generated insights using machine learning models.

Principles of effective visualization

In order to create impactful visualizations, it is essential to follow key principles that ensure clarity, accuracy, and usability, as follows:

- **Understand your audience**: Every visualization must be tailored to its audience. For instance, a technical team might benefit from detailed scatter plots, while senior management might prefer concise dashboards summarizing key metrics.
- **Focus on the data's story**: A great visualization tells a story. Avoid overloading visuals with unnecessary details. Instead, focus on the narrative, whether it is identifying trends, comparing performance, or highlighting anomalies.
- **Choose the right visualization type**: Each type of chart or graph serves a specific purpose. Using the wrong type can lead to misinterpretation. For example, a pie chart is not ideal for showing trends over time.
- **Simplify without oversimplifying**: Strive for simplicity, but not at the cost of losing critical information. Strike a balance between minimalism and informativeness.
- **Ensure accessibility**: Visualizations should be accessible to all users, including those with color blindness or other impairments. Using high-contrast color palettes and providing textual descriptions ensure inclusivity.

- **Leverage visual hierarchies**: Use size, color, and position to emphasize important aspects of the data. For instance, larger fonts or brighter colors can draw attention to key values.

- **Validate and test**: Always validate the accuracy of your visualization against the original dataset. Testing visualizations with sample users can reveal misunderstandings or areas for improvement.

Common pitfalls in data visualization

While data visualization can be highly effective, there are common pitfalls that can undermine its purpose, as follows:

- **Cherry, picking data**: Selecting only favorable data points while ignoring the complete dataset leads to biased interpretations.

- **Misleading scales**: Manipulating axes to exaggerate trends or differences can mislead viewers.

- **Overcomplication**: Cluttering visuals with too many data points or design elements detracts from their readability.

- **Ignoring context**: Visuals should always provide context, such as timeframes, units, or baselines, to avoid ambiguity.

A dedicated focus on responsible visualization is essential, covering biases, misleading scales, and manipulation risks to ensure transparency and ethical data representation.

Tools and technologies for visualization

Advancements in technology have significantly enhanced the accessibility and capabilities of data visualization, enabling users to create dynamic, interactive, and insightful representations of complex datasets. The choice of tools depends on the complexity of the data, the level of customization required, and the technical expertise of the user. Visualization tools can be broadly categorized into the following three groups:

- **Traditional tools**:
  - **Tableau and Power BI**: Widely used for creating interactive dashboards and reports.
  - **Excel**: Still a popular choice for basic visualizations.

- **Open, source libraries**:
  - **D3.js**: A JavaScript library for creating custom visualizations.
  - **Matplotlib and Seaborn**: Python libraries for generating static, publication, and quality graphics.

- **AI, driven tools**:

  o **AutoML visualization**: Tools, like Google AutoML generate insights directly from machine learning models.

  o **TensorBoard**: Visualizes deep learning metrics, such as loss and accuracy curves.

Role of AI in visualization

AI has introduced a paradigm shift in how we approach data visualization. By analyzing patterns, AI-driven tools can suggest optimal visualization types, highlight anomalies, and predict future trends, for example, ML models can transform a sales dataset into a dashboard that reports past performance and predicts future outcomes.

AI-powered visualization tools leverage **natural language processing (NLP)** and computer vision to automate complex tasks that once required human expertise. This automation reduces the time spent on data preparation and accelerates insight generation. Tools like Power BI's Key Influencer Analysis or Tableau's integration with Einstein Analytics demonstrate how AI can detect hidden drivers behind metrics, offering deeper, data-backed narratives that would otherwise go unnoticed.

Moreover, AI enables real-time visualization, continuously updating dashboards as new data flows in. This is particularly valuable in industries like healthcare and finance, where rapid decision-making is crucial. For instance, AI-driven monitoring systems in hospitals can visualize patient vitals and alert medical staff to critical anomalies, ensuring timely interventions.

AI also enhances predictive analytics by visualizing not just historical data but forecasted trends. Retailers can visualize demand patterns for the upcoming quarter, while manufacturers can track equipment wear and predict failures before they happen, preventing costly downtime. Such proactive insights allow businesses to stay ahead of challenges, optimize resource allocation, and improve operational efficiency.

As AI continues to evolve, it is likely to democratize data visualization, making sophisticated tools more accessible to non-technical users. Conversational AI interfaces are emerging, enabling users to ask questions and receive data-driven visual answers in return simply. This bridges the gap between data analysts and decision-makers, fostering a culture of self-service analytics across organizations.

Mastering the fundamentals of data visualization is critical for ensuring that insights are communicated effectively. As datasets grow in size and complexity, these fundamentals act as a guiding framework, helping professionals design visuals that are both impactful and actionable.

AI-driven real-time updates are transforming industries like healthcare and finance, enabling faster anomaly detection, predictive insights, and timely decision-making.

Tools and technologies

When it comes to data visualization and business intelligence, selecting the right tool is essential for transforming raw data into meaningful insights. Different tools excel in different areas, from user-friendly drag-and-drop interfaces to fully customizable coding environments. This section explores four of the most prominent tools in the field, Tableau, Power BI, Looker, and D3.js, highlighting their strengths, limitations, and best use cases.

Tableau

Tableau is a leading data visualization tool that focuses on creating interactive and shareable dashboards. Its drag-and-drop interface allows users to quickly create compelling visualizations from complex datasets. Tableau supports integrations with a wide range of databases and excels in handling large datasets with minimal latency. The platform offers advanced features like calculated fields, storytelling dashboards, and live data connections, making it a favorite for business intelligence professionals.

Let us look at some strengths and limitations:

- **Strengths**:
  - o Intuitive drag and drop functionality.
  - o Extensive support for database integration.
  - o Advanced visualization options like geospatial mapping.

- **Limitations**:
  - o High cost for enterprise licenses.
  - o Steeper learning curve for beginners.

Power BI

Power BI, developed by *Microsoft*, provides a robust ecosystem for creating interactive dashboards and reports. It integrates seamlessly with other Microsoft tools, like Excel, Azure, and Teams, making it highly versatile for businesses already using the Microsoft ecosystem. Power BI's AI-powered analytics, such as Q&A visualizations and key influencer analysis, are major highlights.

Let us look at some strengths and limitations:

- **Strengths**:
  - o Affordable pricing with a free version for individuals.
  - o Seamless integration with *Microsoft* tools.
  - o Built-in AI features for advanced analytics.

- **Limitations**:
  - o Limited customization compared to tools like D3.js.
  - o Performance issues with very large datasets.

Looker

Looker is a cloud-based business intelligence tool designed for modern data workflows. It excels in real-time analytics and integrates directly with SQL databases, enabling data analysts to query data in its raw form. Looker's modeling layer, *LookML*, allows for advanced customizations and dynamic reports.

Some of the strengths and limitations are as follows:

- **Strengths**:
  - o Direct integration with databases for real-time analytics.
  - o Customizable metrics and reports via LookML.
  - o User-friendly interface for team collaboration.

- **Limitations**:
  - o Requires technical expertise for advanced customizations.
  - o Limited offline support due to its cloud-based nature.

D3.js

Data Driven Documents (D3.js) is an open, source JavaScript library that provides unparalleled flexibility for creating custom visualizations. Unlike Tableau or Power BI, D3.js requires coding knowledge but offers complete control over the visualization's appearance and interactivity. It is often used for creating unique, web-based visualizations that cannot be replicated **prebuilt** tools.

Some of the strengths and limitations are as follows:

- **Strengths**:
  - o Full customization of visualizations.
  - o Ideal for web-based, interactive graphics.
  - o Extensive community support and examples.

- **Limitations**:
  - o Requires significant coding expertise.
  - o Time-consuming compared to drag-and-drop tools.

Each tool serves a unique purpose. For example, Tableau and Power BI are ideal for organizations seeking ease of use and rapid deployment, while Looker and D3.js cater to those needing highly customizable, technical solutions.

Integration with AI, driven tools for predictive insights

The next frontier in data visualization involves integrating AI to derive predictive insights. Tools like Tableau and Power BI have built AI features, such as NLP and anomaly detection. For example, Power BI's Key Influencer Analysis automatically identifies the factors driving a particular metric, while Tableau's integration with Einstein Analytics offers predictive modeling capabilities.

The key integrations are as follows:

- **AI in Tableau**: Integrates with Salesforce Einstein for predictive analytics and uses AI to recommend the best visualization types.

- **AI in Power BI**: Offers Q&A visualization, where users can ask natural language questions, and predictive models for forecasting trends.

- **AI with D3.js**: Although D3.js does not have built-in AI, it allows seamless integration with external AI models and APIs to create visualizations driven by ML outcomes.

AI-enhanced visualizations go beyond traditional dashboards. They enable businesses to predict future trends, detect anomalies, and make data-driven decisions in real-time. As organizations increasingly adopt AI, these integrations will become vital for maintaining a competitive edge.

By combining the strengths of visualization tools with AI-driven insights, businesses can unlock deeper understanding and foresight, transforming raw data into a powerful strategic asset.

The visualization of AI-driven insights plays a crucial role in transforming raw predictions and anomaly detections into actionable dashboards. By focusing on outputs like heatmaps, scatter plots, and trend forecasts, visualization tools ensure that complex data is presented in an intuitive and digestible format for decision-makers.

The following figure highlights how AI-driven analytics flow directly into various visualization forms, ultimately converging into interactive dashboards:

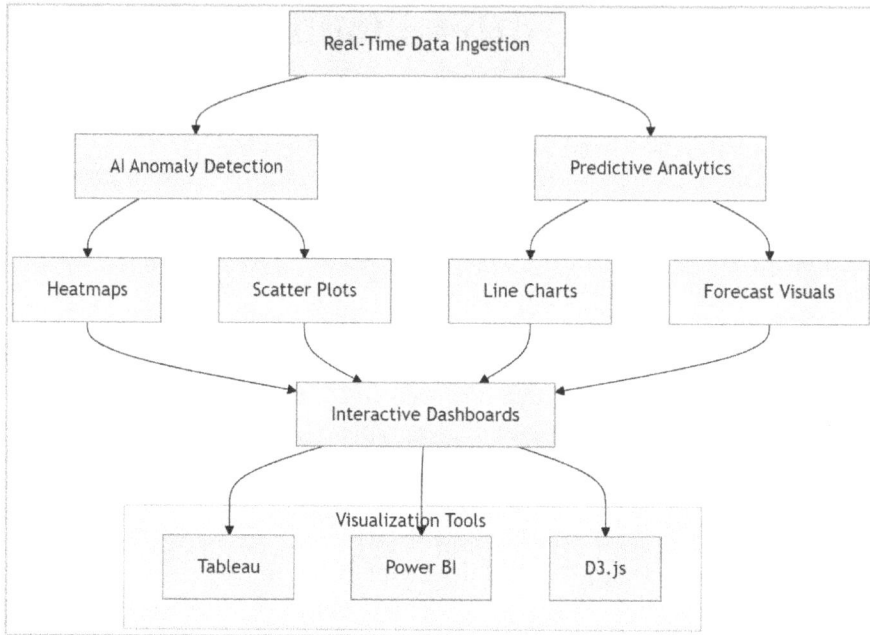

Figure 9.2: *Visualization workflow for AI-driven anomaly detection and predictive analytics*

AI-driven visualization techniques

AI has revolutionized the field of data visualization, enabling users to uncover patterns, detect anomalies, and forecast trends with greater precision and speed than ever before. Unlike traditional static visualizations, AI-driven techniques dynamically adapt to the data, providing richer, actionable insights tailored to specific needs. This section explores how AI enhances anomaly detection and predictive analytics, along with real-world examples that demonstrate its transformative power.

Anomaly detection

Anomalies are deviations from expected patterns in data, often signaling critical issues such as fraud, system failures, or emerging opportunities. Traditional approaches to anomaly detection rely on predefined rules or thresholds. However, these methods are limited by their inability to adapt to complex and evolving datasets. AI-driven anomaly detection leverages machine learning models to identify outliers dynamically by analyzing patterns, behaviors, and relationships within the data.

The following figure showcases the workflow for AI-driven anomaly detection, starting with raw data from sensors or transactions. It illustrates the stages of pre-processing, feeding data into AI/ML models, and identifying anomalies, which are then visualized using advanced tools. A feedback loop ensures continuous model improvement based on new insights from the visualizations.

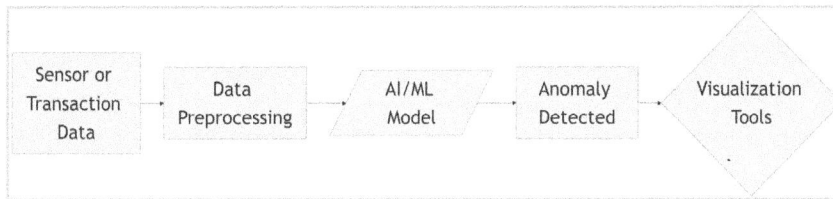

Figure 9.3: *Workflow of AI, driven anomaly detection*

Consider a financial institution monitoring transactions for potential fraud. A rule-based system might flag transactions above a specific dollar amount, but this approach can lead to both false positives and missed anomalies. AI, on the other hand, examines the entire dataset, identifying unusual behaviors, such as an unusual frequency of small transactions from a single account, that might otherwise go unnoticed. Visualizing these anomalies through heatmaps or scatter plots makes them immediately apparent˙ to analysts, facilitating quicker and more informed decision-making.

Predictive trends

Predictive analytics involves using historical data to forecast future outcomes. AI enhances this process by building models that continuously learn and improve over time, offering increasingly accurate predictions. Visualizing predictive trends is particularly useful in industries such as retail, where demand forecasting plays a pivotal role in inventory management and sales planning, for example, a retail company might use AI-powered visualizations to forecast product demand based on factors like seasonal trends, economic conditions, and consumer behavior. A line chart with predictive overlays could show not only past sales but also anticipated demand spikes during upcoming holiday seasons. These insights allow decision-makers to optimize stock levels, reducing waste and maximizing revenue.

Real-world examples of AI in visual analytics

AI-driven visual analytics is revolutionizing industries by enabling real-time insights, predictive capabilities, and automated data interpretation. Traditional visualization techniques often rely on historical data and manual analysis, whereas AI-powered solutions dynamically process vast datasets, uncover hidden patterns, and generate real-time visualizations. These advancements help organizations optimize decision-making, enhance operational efficiency, and mitigate risks.

The real-world examples of how AI transforms visual analytics are as follows:

- **Healthcare**: AI-driven visualizations are transforming the healthcare industry by enabling real-time monitoring of patient health. For instance, wearable devices generate continuous streams of data, such as heart rate and activity levels. AI algorithms analyze this data for anomalies, such as irregular heartbeats, and present the findings through dashboards with red flags indicating potential health issues. Physicians can quickly identify patients requiring immediate attention, improving outcomes.

- **Manufacturing**: In manufacturing, predictive maintenance is a critical application of AI-driven visualization. Machine sensors generate massive amounts of operational data. AI models analyze this data to predict equipment failures before they occur. Visualizing these predictions in dashboards with color-coded alerts helps maintenance teams prioritize repairs, minimizing downtime and costs.

- **E-commerce**: These platforms use AI to visualize customer behavior and predict future trends. For example, a heatmap generated by AI might show areas of a website where customers spend the most time, helping designers optimize page layouts. Predictive visualizations also forecast future purchase patterns, enabling targeted marketing campaigns.

- **Finance**: Financial institutions employ AI to create real-time dashboards that track stock market movements and predict potential market shifts. These visualizations enable traders to make informed decisions faster, capitalizing on emerging opportunities while mitigating risks.

Advantages of AI-driven visualization techniques

AI-driven visualization techniques enhance the efficiency, scalability, and accuracy of data representation by leveraging ML and automation. Unlike traditional visualization methods, which rely on static charts and manual updates, AI-powered tools can process vast datasets, detect complex patterns, and generate dynamic insights in real time. These advancements enable organizations to extract deeper value from their data, improve decision-making, and automate reporting processes.

The following are the key advantages of AI-driven visualization, demonstrating its impact on scalability, adaptability, and automation:

- **Scalability**: AI-driven tools can handle vast datasets, making them ideal for organizations dealing with big data. The ability to process millions of data points in real-time ensures that visualizations remain accurate and relevant.

- **Dynamic adaptation**: Unlike static charts, AI-driven visualizations update dynamically as new data flows in. This is particularly useful for monitoring live systems, such as website performance or manufacturing processes.

- **Enhanced insights**: AI uncovers patterns and correlations that might be overlooked by traditional methods. For instance, clustering algorithms can group customers based on purchasing behavior, visualizing these clusters in intuitive diagrams.

- **Automation**: Many AI tools automate the visualization process, reducing the need for manual intervention. Automated dashboards powered by AI provide real-time insights without requiring constant updates from analysts.

Challenges and considerations

While AI-driven visualization offers significant benefits, it is not without challenges. One major consideration is ensuring data quality. AI models are only as good as the data they are trained on; poor-quality data can lead to misleading insights. Additionally, there is a learning curve associated with implementing AI tools, particularly for organizations without prior expertise in machine learning.

Another critical factor is interpretability. AI-driven visualizations often rely on complex algorithms, making it difficult for non-technical users to understand how conclusions are drawn. To address this, many tools now include explainability features, breaking down the logic behind predictions and anomalies in simple terms.

Future trends in AI

The future of AI-driven visualization lies in its integration with other emerging technologies. For example, **augmented reality** (**AR**) and **virtual reality** (**VR**) are being explored as platforms for immersive visualizations, enabling users to interact with data in three-dimensional spaces. Voice, activated interfaces powered by AI are also gaining traction, allowing users to query datasets and receive visual outputs in real-time.

Another exciting trend is the use of generative AI in visualization design. Tools, like ChatGPT and similar models are being adapted to assist in creating visualizations based on user prompts, further democratizing access to advanced analytics.

AI-driven visualization techniques represent a paradigm shift in how we interact with data. By combining the strengths of AI with intuitive visual interfaces, these tools empower organizations to make smarter, faster decisions. Whether it is detecting anomalies, forecasting trends, or uncovering hidden insights, AI is transforming data visualization into a cornerstone of modern analytics.

Best practices for effective visualization

Creating effective visualizations is as much an art as it is a science. While tools and technologies provide the foundation, it is the careful application of best practices that ensures visualizations convey the right insights to the right audience. This section explores how to tailor visualizations to audience needs, ensure accessibility and readability, and leverage automation to improve reporting workflows. These guidelines ensure that visualizations are not only clear and accessible but also actionable, improving interpretation across different platforms and audiences.

Tailoring visualizations to audience needs

The first step in creating impactful visualizations is understanding your audience. Different stakeholders have different levels of technical expertise, varying needs, and distinct ways of interpreting data. A detailed scatter plot may be perfect for a data scientist analyzing correlations, but a high-level dashboard might better serve a business executive. Identifying these requirements helps ensure your visualizations resonate.

For instance, consider a sales report, sales managers may need detailed trends broken down by product and region, while executives may prefer a summary of total revenue and growth rates. Designing visuals that address these specific needs increases engagement and ensures your message is effectively communicated.

Tailoring visualizations involves not only selecting the right type of chart or graph but also choosing the appropriate level of granularity. Striking this balance ensures that the insights are neither overwhelming nor overly simplified.

When you align your visualizations with the audience's expectations, you foster better understanding and informed decision-making. This approach builds trust and maximizes the impact of your data storytelling.

Ensuring accessibility and readability

Accessibility is a critical aspect of visualization design that ensures your insights are available to everyone, regardless of ability. Approximately 8% of men and 0.5% of women worldwide are colorblind, highlighting the importance of using color palettes that are both inclusive and distinguishable. Tools like Tableau and Power BI include colorblind, friendly templates, making it easier to create visuals that accommodate diverse users.

Readability is equally important. Overly complex visualizations can confuse users and detract from the message. Use clear labels, appropriate font sizes, and sufficient spacing between elements. For example, a bar chart comparing quarterly revenues should include axis labels and values directly on the bars for easier interpretation.

When designing a visualization, it is essential to consider the intended medium of consumption, whether it is a printed report, a presentation, or an interactive dashboard. Each format has distinct requirements that influence design choices. Printed materials necessitate clear layouts with minimal clutter and appropriately sized fonts for readability. Presentations require visually engaging graphics that effectively communicate key insights at a glance. Interactive dashboards enable user exploration but must incorporate intuitive navigation to ensure accessibility and usability.

Accessible and readable visualizations not only broaden your audience but also enhance their ability to quickly extract insights. These practices should be central to your design process.

Automation in reporting and updates

Manual updates to reports and dashboards can be time-consuming and prone to errors. Automation streamlines this process, ensuring your visualizations are always up to date with the latest data. Tools like Power BI and Tableau offer features for connecting directly to live data sources, and automatically refreshing dashboards as new information becomes available.

For example, a real-time dashboard monitoring website traffic can pull data directly from Google Analytics. This ensures that metrics like page views and bounce rates are updated in near real-time, providing decision-makers with the most current insights.

Automation also supports scalability. As data grows in volume and complexity, manually updating reports becomes impractical. Automated workflows, such as scheduling daily or weekly updates, free up time for analysts to focus on interpreting insights rather than maintaining visuals.

By leveraging automation, you not only increase efficiency but also ensure consistency and accuracy in your reporting. This reduces the risk of outdated or incorrect information impacting decisions.

Real-life examples and case studies

Real-life examples and case studies bring theory to life by showcasing how organizations across industries leverage data visualization to solve problems, make informed decisions, and achieve strategic goals. These examples highlight not only the power of visualization tools but also the impact of combining them with best practices and AI-driven techniques.

Case study 1: Visualizing sales data for performance

A prominent e-commerce company faced challenges in understanding why certain product categories were underperforming in specific regions. Their existing reports provided sales figures but lacked actionable insights to identify root causes. To address this issue, the company implemented Tableau to create a dynamic, interactive dashboard.

The dashboard aggregated sales data from multiple sources, including regional sales reports, seasonal trends, and customer demographics. The use of heatmaps highlighted areas with declining sales, while bar and line charts displayed sales trends over time. Filters allowed decision-makers to drill down into specific regions and product categories.

Results

The company discovered that underperforming regions often experienced supply chain delays due to logistical bottlenecks. By reallocating resources and improving logistics in these regions, they achieved a 15% increase in sales within six months. The insights derived from the dashboard not only addressed immediate problems but also informed future strategies for supply chain optimization.

This case study discusses the importance of visualizing data at a granular level to uncover actionable insights. With the right tools and visualizations, even complex issues can be broken down and addressed effectively.

Case study 2: Using dashboards for predictive maintenance

A manufacturing firm with multiple plants worldwide struggled with unplanned machine failures, which resulted in costly downtime and disrupted production schedules. The company turned to Power BI to build a real-time dashboard that integrated data from IoT sensors attached to their machinery.

The dashboard visualized critical metrics such as vibration levels, temperature, pressure, and usage rates. By applying machine learning models to the sensor data, the company predicted equipment failures before they occurred. The dashboard featured color-coded alerts that highlighted machines requiring immediate attention.

Results

Over a six-month period, the firm reduced unplanned downtime by 25% and saved hundreds of thousands of dollars in repair and operational costs. Additionally, proactive maintenance improved worker safety and increased production efficiency.

This example underscores the value of combining real-time visualizations with predictive analytics. By transforming raw sensor data into actionable dashboards, organizations can transition from reactive to proactive operations.

Case study 3: Real-time analytics for financial trading

A global financial services firm needed a way to monitor stock market trends in real-time and provide insights to their trading teams. Static reports were insufficient in the fast-paced trading environment where decisions must be made within seconds. The firm implemented Looker to create a real-time analytics dashboard.

The dashboard integrated data from multiple sources, including stock exchanges, financial news APIs, and historical trading records. It visualized market movements through candlestick charts, scatter plots for correlations, and heat maps for sector performance.

Results

Traders used the dashboard to identify emerging trends and make timely decisions, resulting in a 12% increase in trading efficiency. The firm also reduced the time spent on manual data gathering and analysis, allowing traders to focus on strategy rather than data preparation.

This case highlights the importance of speed and precision in data visualization. For industries like finance, where milliseconds can make a difference, real-time analytics dashboards are indispensable.

Case study 4: Monitoring customer engagement in retail

A major retail chain aimed to improve customer engagement across its brick-and-mortar and online stores. Using Tableau, the company developed a dashboard that visualized data from customer surveys, loyalty programs, and web analytics.

The dashboard included a geospatial map showing customer engagement by region, line charts tracking loyalty program participation over time, and bar graphs displaying product categories with the highest customer satisfaction. AI-driven sentiment analysis provided insights from customer feedback, which were visualized as word clouds and bar charts.

Results

The dashboard revealed that customers in urban areas were less satisfied with delivery times compared to suburban customers. The company addressed this by partnering with local courier services, leading to a 20% improvement in delivery satisfaction ratings. Additionally, insights from sentiment analysis informed marketing campaigns, resulting in increased loyalty program participation.

This case demonstrates how combining traditional visualization methods with AI-driven insights can help organizations address customer needs effectively.

Case study 5: Optimizing patient care in healthcare

A hospital system sought to improve patient care by visualizing data from EHRs, wearable devices, and patient feedback. Using Power BI, the hospital created dashboards that integrated real-time data streams from wearable health monitors and historical patient data.

The dashboards displayed key metrics such as patient vitals, treatment progress, and bed occupancy rates. Predictive models flagged patients at high risk for readmission, and the results were visualized through interactive dashboards, allowing healthcare providers to intervene proactively.

Results

The hospital reduced readmission rates by 18% and improved overall patient satisfaction scores. Nurses and doctors reported that the dashboards saved time by providing a single source of truth for patient data, enabling more efficient care delivery.

This example highlights how data visualization can improve outcomes in critical fields like healthcare. By presenting data in a user-friendly format, organizations can make better decisions and improve their services.

Case study 6: Energy efficiency in smart grids

A utility company managing a smart grid network is needed to optimize energy distribution and reduce outages. The company implemented D3.js to create a custom visualization system that displayed energy usage patterns, grid performance, and outage predictions.

The visualization system included interactive geospatial maps showing grid coverage, line charts for energy consumption trends, and network graphs highlighting potential bottlenecks in energy distribution. AI models were integrated to predict high-demand periods and identify vulnerable nodes in the grid.

Results

The utility company reduced outages by 22% and improved energy efficiency by 15%. Interactive visualizations also helped engineers prioritize maintenance tasks, ensuring that critical infrastructure was addressed first.

This case underscores the importance of customization in visualization. D3.js allowed the company to build a tailored solution that met the unique needs of its smart grid operations.

Some key lessons from the case studies are as follows:

- **Actionable insights**: Effective visualizations focus on delivering actionable insights rather than overwhelming users with data. Each of these case studies demonstrated how organizations used visualizations to solve specific problems.

- **Real-time applications**: Dashboards that update in real-time provide organizations with the agility to respond to changes quickly. This is especially critical in industries like finance and manufacturing, where delays can lead to significant losses.

- **AI integration**: Combining traditional visualization techniques with AI enhances the ability to uncover hidden patterns and predict future outcomes. This approach ensures that visualizations are not just descriptive but also prescriptive.

- **Tailored solutions**: Customization plays a crucial role in meeting unique business needs. Whether it is a real-time trading dashboard or an energy efficiency map, tailored visualizations deliver maximum value.

By understanding and applying these lessons, organizations can leverage data visualization to drive success in their respective fields. Each of these case studies highlights the transformative power of well-designed, actionable, and intelligent visualizations.

Conclusion

Data visualization is more than just a technical capability; it is a critical tool that transforms raw data into actionable insights. This chapter has explored how effective visualization enhances understanding, empowers decision-makers, and drives organizational success. Whether through basic charts or AI-driven analytics, every visualization serves a purpose bringing clarity, precision, and impact to data. We began by examining how visualization translates complex data into a universally understandable format. A well-crafted visualization is not just about presenting numbers but telling a story that inspires action. Whether a simple bar chart summarizes sales performance or an advanced heatmap detects anomalies, these visual representations help organizations make informed decisions.

AI-driven visualization techniques have further expanded traditional methods, offering real-time anomaly detection and predictive insights. Organizations in industries such as healthcare, retail, and finance are leveraging these capabilities to optimize operations and improve strategic decision-making. A key takeaway from this chapter is the importance of designing visualizations tailored to the audience. Effective reporting requires balancing detail and simplicity, ensuring that stakeholders receive meaningful insights without being overwhelmed by excessive data. Additionally, automation and real-time updates are now essential, as static reports often fail to capture the fast-paced nature of business operations.

Real-world case studies demonstrated the transformative potential of visualization, from improving patient outcomes in healthcare to preventing fraud in financial services. These examples reinforce that data visualization is not just a reporting tool, it is a strategic asset that enhances efficiency, innovation, and problem-solving across industries. As we conclude this chapter, it is important to recognize that visualizations are only as valuable as the data they represent. With increasing reliance on data for critical decision-making, ensuring its security is paramount.

In the next chapter, we will explore how organizations protect data integrity, privacy, and compliance in an ever-evolving digital landscape.

Join our book's Discord space

Join the book's Discord Workspace for Latest updates, Offers, Tech happenings around the world, New Release and Sessions with the Authors:

https://discord.bpbonline.com

CHAPTER 10

Operational Data Security

Introduction

In the previous chapter, we explored how data visualization transforms raw information into actionable insights, enabling organizations to make informed decisions. However, the effectiveness of visualization depends on the integrity and security of the underlying data. Without robust security measures, data remains vulnerable to breaches, unauthorized access, and manipulation, compromising its reliability. This chapter focuses on operational data security, a critical aspect of safeguarding data across its lifecycle.

Operational data security ensures that data remains protected at rest, in transit, and during processing. Whether stored in on-premise databases, transferred between systems, or processed in the cloud, security measures must be in place to mitigate risks. Additionally, organizations must adopt incident response strategies and adhere to evolving regulations to maintain compliance and trust.

This chapter explores practical techniques for securing data, covering encryption, access controls, cloud security best practices, and compliance frameworks. It also introduces incident response planning to address potential security breaches effectively.

As we navigate through this chapter, we set the foundation for the next discussion on data privacy, which focuses on ethical and legal responsibilities in handling sensitive data. Together, these topics provide a comprehensive approach to responsible data management, ensuring security, privacy, and trust in an increasingly complex digital landscape.

By the end of this chapter, you will have a robust understanding of operational data security, empowering you to create secure, resilient, and trustworthy systems that serve as the backbone of modern data-driven decision-making.

Structure

The chapter covers the following topics:

- Securing data at rest
- Securing data in transit
- Incident response and data breach management
- Compliance and regulatory considerations
- Case studies and real-world examples

Objectives

By the end of this chapter, readers will have a comprehensive understanding of operational data security and its role in protecting data across its lifecycle. As organizations increasingly rely on data for decision-making, analytics, and visualization, ensuring the confidentiality, integrity, and availability of data becomes critical. This chapter explores how security measures safeguard data at rest, in transit, and during processing, preventing unauthorized access, breaches, and data manipulation.

Readers will gain insights into core security principles, including encryption, access control mechanisms, authentication protocols, and best practices for securing cloud environments. Additionally, the chapter will cover compliance frameworks helping organizations align security strategies with regulatory requirements.

Beyond preventive measures, the chapter introduces incident response planning, emphasizing the importance of detecting, mitigating, and recovering from security breaches. It highlights strategies to establish proactive security monitoring and response workflows, ensuring resilience against cyber threats.

Finally, this chapter lays the groundwork for the next discussion on data privacy, which focuses on ethical and legal considerations in managing personal and sensitive data. By the end of this chapter, readers will understand how operational security serves as the first line of defense in protecting organizational data, and ensuring trust and compliance in an evolving digital landscape.

Securing data at rest

Data at rest refers to information that is stored in a static location, such as databases, data lakes, file systems, or backup servers. It contrasts with data in transit, which is actively being transferred between locations or systems. While at rest, data is particularly vulnerable to unauthorized access, theft, or compromise because it is often stored in centralized locations where attackers can target it. Ensuring the security of data at rest is a fundamental responsibility for data engineers, scientists, and IT professionals, as it protects the foundation of any data-driven operation.

The following figure outlines the core stages of the security lifecycle, showcasing how data transitions through various states and the critical role of incident response and compliance in maintaining continuous protection:

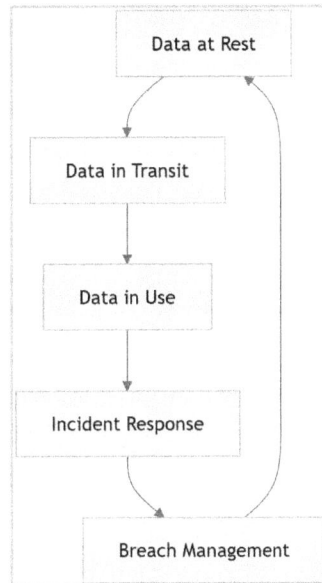

Figure 10.1: Security lifecycle, a continuous process that safeguards data across different phases

In this section, we will explore various strategies and best practices to secure data at rest, ranging from encryption and access controls to advanced techniques like tokenization and masking. These measures not only protect sensitive information but also ensure compliance with regulatory requirements and industry standards.

Securing data at rest matters

Data at rest often contains sensitive or valuable information, such as customer records, financial data, intellectual property, or confidential business strategies. If this data is compromised, the consequences can be severe, such as:

- **Financial loss**: Data breaches can result in hefty fines, legal costs, and lost revenue.
- **Reputation damage**: A single breach can erode trust with customers and stakeholders.
- **Operational disruption**: Compromised data can lead to downtime, impacting business continuity.

- **Regulatory penalties**: Non-compliance with data security regulations, such as GDPR or CCPA, can result in significant fines.

Techniques for securing data at rest

Effective security measures for data at rest involve a combination of encryption, access controls, data masking, tokenization, secure backups, and continuous monitoring. These techniques prevent unauthorized access while maintaining data integrity and compliance with industry regulations.

The following are the key strategies organizations can implement to secure stored data, reduce risks, and ensure that only authorized personnel can access critical information:

- **Encryption**: It is one of the most effective methods for securing data at rest. By converting plaintext data into an unreadable format, encryption ensures that even if attackers gain access to the data, they cannot interpret it without the decryption key.

  o **Encryption standards**: **Advanced Encryption Standard** (**AES256**) is a widely used and highly secure protocol for encrypting sensitive data.

  o **Database encryption**: Most modern database systems, such as MySQL, PostgreSQL, and Oracle, offer built-in encryption features to secure stored data.

  o **File system encryption**: Encrypting entire file systems using tools like BitLocker (Windows) or LUKS (Linux) provides an additional layer of security.

  o **Example**: A financial institution encrypts its customer records stored in a database. Even if an unauthorized user accesses the database, they cannot read the encrypted information without the proper key.

- **Access control**: It involves implementing policies and mechanisms that limit who can access data at rest. It ensures that only authorized personnel can view, modify, or delete sensitive information.

  o **Role-based access control (RBAC)**: It assigns permissions based on user roles, ensuring that employees can only access the data necessary for their job functions.

  o **Multi-factor authentication (MFA)**: It adds an extra layer of security by requiring users to verify their identity through multiple factors, such as passwords and biometrics.

  o **Least privilege principle**: It grants users the minimum level of access needed to perform their tasks.

  o **Example**: A healthcare provider implements RBAC to ensure that only authorized doctors and nurses can access patient medical records, while administrative staff can only view billing information.

- **Data masking**: It replaces sensitive information with fictional data that resembles the original but is not real. It is commonly used in non-production environments like testing or development.

  o **Static masking**: It alters the data in a database or file permanently for use in non, production settings.

  o **Dynamic masking**: It temporarily masks data during retrieval, keeping the original data intact.

  o **Example**: A retail company uses data masking to anonymize customer information in its development environment, ensuring that developers do not have access to real customer data.

- **Tokenization**: It replaces sensitive data with unique identifiers or tokens. Unlike encryption, tokens do not have a mathematical relationship with the original data, making them useless to attackers.

  o **Use case**: It is commonly used for securing payment information, such as credit card numbers, in compliance with PCI DSS standards.

  o **Token vault**: A secure database stores the relationship between tokens and original data.

  o **Example**: An e-commerce platform tokenizes customer credit card details, storing the tokens in its operational database while keeping the original data in a secure vault.

- **Backup security**: Backups are essential for data recovery, but they can also be a vulnerability if not secured properly. A compromised backup can provide attackers with access to sensitive information.

  o **Encryption**: All backups should be encrypted to prevent unauthorized access.

  o **Geographically distributed storage**: Storing backups in multiple locations ensures resilience against physical threats like natural disasters.

  o **Access restrictions**: Limit access to backup systems to a small group of trusted personnel.

  o **Example**: A SaaS company encrypts its daily backups and stores them in multiple cloud regions. This ensures that even in the event of a ransomware attack, the company can restore operations quickly and securely.

- **Monitoring and auditing**: Continuous monitoring and regular audits help detect unauthorized access or unusual activity in data storage systems. These practices provide early warnings and ensure compliance with security policies.

  o **Monitoring tools**: Use tools like Splunk or AWS CloudWatch to monitor database and file access.

o **Audit logs**: Maintain detailed logs of access events, including who accessed the data, when, and for what purpose.

o **Example**: An energy company uses audit logs to track access to its operational data, ensuring that only authorized personnel can modify critical systems.

Real-world examples of securing data at rest

Implementing strong data security measures is essential across industries to protect sensitive information from unauthorized access and cyber threats. Organizations leverage encryption, tokenization, and access controls to ensure data remains secure, even in the event of a breach. The following examples illustrate how different sectors apply these techniques to safeguard stored data and maintain compliance with security standards:

- **Healthcare industry**: A hospital encrypts its patient records and implements RBAC to limit access to sensitive data. When an attempted breach targets the hospital's database, the encryption and access controls prevent the attackers from retrieving any meaningful information.

- **Financial services**: A bank tokenizes customer account numbers to secure transactions. Even if a cyberattack compromises the transaction database, the tokens are meaningless without access to the secure vault.

- **E-commerce**: An online retailer uses dynamic masking to anonymize customer data displayed on operational dashboards. This ensures that employees can view trends and insights without exposing sensitive customer information.

Challenges in securing data at rest

Encryption, tokenization, and access controls offer strong protection for stored data, but implementing these security measures presents several challenges. Organizations must balance security with cost, performance, and operational complexity to ensure data remains both protected and accessible. In highly regulated industries, compliance with security standards adds another layer of difficulty, requiring continuous monitoring and updates to security protocols.

The following challenges highlight key obstacles organizations face when securing data at rest and the considerations needed to maintain both security and efficiency:

- **Cost**: Encryption and secure storage solutions can be expensive to implement and maintain.

- **Complexity**: Managing encryption keys, access controls, and secure backups requires specialized expertise.

- **Performance impact**: Encryption and masking can slow down database queries and data retrieval, especially for large datasets.

The following figure illustrates the primary techniques used to secure data at rest. These approaches, including encryption, access control, and tokenization, form independent layers that collectively minimize vulnerabilities in stored data.

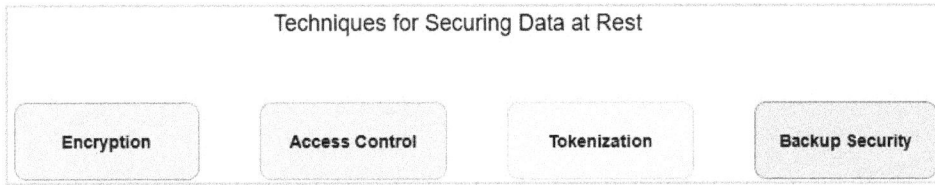

Figure 10.2: *Techniques for securing data at rest, a visual breakdown of the core strategies*

Despite these challenges, securing data at rest is non-negotiable for organizations that prioritize trust, compliance, and operational efficiency.

Securing data at rest is not an isolated task; it is foundational to the entire data lifecycle. Once data is securely stored, it becomes easier to protect it during transit and in cloud environments. Moreover, robust security measures at this stage lay the groundwork for compliance with privacy regulations and ensure that data remains trustworthy for downstream processes like visualization and AI-driven analytics.

As we transition to the next topic *Securing data in transit*, we shift our focus to protecting data as it moves across systems and networks. Together, these strategies create a comprehensive framework for securing data, no matter its state.

Securing data in transit

Data in transit refers to information being transferred between locations, whether across internal systems, external networks, or between devices and users. Unlike data at rest, data in transit is exposed to unique risks such as interception, eavesdropping, and tampering. Securing data in transit is critical for ensuring the confidentiality, integrity, and authenticity of the information being transmitted. As organizations increasingly rely on interconnected systems, APIs, and real-time data exchanges, the need for robust transit security has become more vital than ever.

Building upon the previous section on securing data at rest, this topic emphasizes protecting data as it flows through various channels. Whether it is transferring sensitive files between servers, transmitting analytics results to dashboards, or syncing data with cloud storage, securing data in transit ensures that it remains protected against unauthorized access and manipulation.

Risks associated with data in transit

Data in transit is particularly vulnerable to interception and manipulation as it moves between systems, applications, or networks. Unlike data at rest, which can be secured through encryption and access controls, transmitted data is exposed to a variety of cyber threats that can compromise confidentiality, integrity, and authenticity. Attackers exploit unsecured communication channels to eavesdrop, alter, or replay transmitted data, leading to financial loss, identity theft, or operational disruptions.

Understanding these risks is essential before implementing security measures. The following are common threats that organizations face when transmitting data across networks, along with examples illustrating their impact:

- **Interception (Eavesdropping)**: Attackers can intercept data packets over unsecured networks, gaining access to sensitive information, such as login credentials or financial details. For example, using an unsecured public Wi-Fi network to transfer files exposes the data to interception by nearby attackers.

- **Man in the middle (MITM) attacks**: In this attack, a malicious actor positions themselves between two communicating parties to intercept, alter, or steal data without either party's knowledge. For example, an attacker intercepts an HTTPS session to steal sensitive user credentials.

- **Data tempering**: Unauthorized modifications to data during transmission compromise its integrity, potentially leading to incorrect or malicious results. For example, tampering with financial transaction data during transmission between banking systems.

- **Replay attacks**: Attackers capture valid data transmissions and replay them later to deceive systems into processing them as legitimate. For example, reusing an intercepted payment transaction request to fraudulently extract funds.

Best practices for securing data in transit

Ensuring the security of data during transmission is critical to preventing unauthorized access, interception, and tampering. Without proper safeguards, sensitive information traveling between systems, applications, or networks is vulnerable to cyber threats, such as eavesdropping, data tampering, and replay attacks.

To mitigate these risks, organizations must implement strong encryption protocols, secure communication channels, and robust authentication mechanisms. The following best practices outline essential strategies for protecting data in transit, ensuring confidentiality, integrity, and authenticity throughout its journey:

- **End-to-end encryption**: It ensures that data remains encrypted from the source to the destination, with only authorized endpoints having the decryption keys.

- **Transport layer security (TLS)/ secured socket layer (SSL)** : A widely used encryption protocol for securing web traffic and APIs.

- **Virtual private network (VPN)**: It encrypts data before it leaves the device, ensuring secure communication over public or private networks.

Example: SaaS company encrypts all API communications between its web application and cloud database using TLS to prevent interception.

- **Secure communication protocols**: Adopting secure protocols ensures that data is transmitted safely.

- **Hypertext Transfer Protocol Secure (HTTPS)**: It encrypts web traffic, protecting user interactions with websites.

- **Secure File Transfer Protocol (SFTP)**: It secures file transfers between systems.

- **Secure Shell (SSH)**: It protects remote administrative access.

  Example: An e-commerce platform uses HTTPS to encrypt customer payment data during checkout.

- **Authentication and authorization**: Implementing strong authentication and authorization mechanisms ensures that only verified users or systems can initiate or receive data transmissions.

- **OAuth 2.0 and OpenID Connect**: It secures a framework for authenticating users in web and mobile applications.

- **Mutual TLS**: It requires both client and server to present certificates, verifying each other's identity.

  Example: A fintech app uses OAuth 2.0 to authenticate users before initiating secure API calls for financial transactions.

- **Data integrity verification** It ensures the integrity of transmitted data and prevents tampering or corruption during transit.

- **Checksums**: Verify data consistency by comparing the checksum value before and after transmission.

- **Digital signatures**: Cryptographically sign data packets, allowing recipients to validate their authenticity.

  Example: A logistics company uses checksums to verify the integrity of shipment tracking data transmitted between systems.

- **Network security measures** Securing the networks through which data travels adds additional protection.

- **Firewalls**: Monitor and control incoming and outgoing traffic based on predefined security rules.

- **Intrusion detection systems (IDS)**: Identify and alert suspicious activities within the network.

- **VPNs**: Create secure tunnels for transmitting sensitive data over public networks.

  Example: A multinational organization uses VPNs to secure communications between its regional offices.

- **Limiting data exposure**: Minimize the exposure of sensitive data during transmission.

- **Masking**: Mask sensitive fields like credit card numbers before transmitting them.

- **Tokenization**: Replace sensitive information with tokens that are meaningless without access to a secure vault.

  Example: A payment processor tokenizes customer credit card data before transmitting it to ensure security.

Real-world examples of securing data in transit

As data moves between devices, applications, and cloud environments, ensuring its security during transmission is critical to preventing interception, tampering, or unauthorized access. Industries handling sensitive information, such as healthcare, financial services, and retail, implement strong encryption protocols, authentication mechanisms, and secure transmission channels to safeguard data integrity and confidentiality.

The following examples demonstrate how organizations across different sectors apply end-to-end encryption, HTTPS, tokenization, and digital signatures to protect data in transit and ensure compliance with security standards:

- **Healthcare industry**: A hospital system transfers patient data between wearable health devices and its central database for real-time monitoring. By implementing end-to-end encryption with TLS and mutual TLS for authentication, the hospital ensures that patient vitals remain confidential and untampered.

- **Financial services**: A global bank uses HTTPS and digital signatures to secure transactions between its mobile banking app and backend systems. This ensures that customer account details remain confidential while validating the integrity of each transaction.

- **Retail sector**: An e-commerce company encrypts all payment data transmitted between its web servers and payment gateway using TLS. Additionally, they tokenize customer card details, reducing the risk of exposing sensitive information even if the transmission is intercepted.

Emerging technologies for securing data in transit

As cyber threats become more sophisticated, traditional security measures must evolve to keep pace with emerging risks. Advancements in encryption, authentication, and network security are reshaping how data is protected during transmission. Modern approaches focus on eliminating trust assumptions, enhancing cryptographic strength, and leveraging innovative technologies to safeguard sensitive information. As technology evolves, new methods for enhancing transit security are emerging.

Some are as follows:

- **Quantum encryption**: Uses the principles of quantum mechanics to provide ultra-secure communication channels, for example, research institutions are exploring quantum key distribution to secure transmissions of highly sensitive data.

- **Zero-trust architecture**: Assumes that no network, device, or user is inherently trustworthy, implementing strict verification at every access point.

These innovations promise to further strengthen data security, especially in high-risk environments like financial trading or defense.

Challenges in securing data in transit

Despite the effectiveness of encryption, authentication, and secure communication protocols, ensuring data security during transmission presents several challenges. Organizations must address these obstacles to maintain confidentiality, integrity, and availability while balancing performance and compliance requirements.

Some of these challenges are as follows:

- **Cost and complexity**: Deploying advanced encryption and secure protocols may require significant investment in hardware, software, and expertise.

- **Performance impact**: Encrypting data can introduce latency, especially in real-time systems where speed is critical.

- **Scalability**: Ensuring secure data transmission in large-scale, distributed systems requires careful planning and optimization.

Despite these challenges, the benefits of securing data in transit far outweigh the costs. The risks of interception or tampering are simply too great to ignore.

Securing data in transit is critical because it acts as the bridge between systems, users, and devices. Without robust transit security, even the most secure stored data becomes vulnerable once it begins to move. By protecting data during transmission, organizations ensure that their insights remain trustworthy, their operations are uninterrupted, and their customers' privacy is respected.

Data security in the cloud

The cloud has revolutionized how organizations store, process, and access data. It offers unmatched scalability, flexibility, cost, and effectiveness, enabling businesses to innovate and grow faster. However, with these advantages come unique security challenges. Cloud environments are inherently shared, with multiple users and organizations leveraging the same infrastructure. This creates risks that require specific strategies to ensure data security.

Building upon the foundational concepts of securing data at rest and in transit, this chapter explores how to safeguard data within cloud environments. As organizations migrate their workloads to the cloud, understanding and implementing cloud security practices is essential for protecting sensitive information and maintaining compliance with regulatory requirements.

Cloud security matters

As organizations increasingly migrate to cloud environments, securing data presents unique challenges compared to traditional on-premises systems. Cloud infrastructure is dynamic, distributed, and often involves multiple stakeholders, requiring a proactive security approach. Unlike on-premises setups, cloud security operates under a shared responsibility model, where both cloud providers and customers play distinct roles in protecting data. Additionally, the global distribution of cloud resources expands the potential attack surface, making security misconfigurations a critical risk. Ensuring compliance with regulations such as the GDPR, HIPAA, and CCPA further adds to the complexity, requiring strict security controls and continuous monitoring.

The following key considerations highlight the unique security challenges and responsibilities in cloud environments:

- **Shared responsibility model**: Cloud providers secure the infrastructure, but customers are responsible for securing their data, applications, and access controls. For example, while AWS encrypts data on its storage disks, the customer must configure proper permissions for their files.

- **Distributed nature**: Cloud data often spans multiple regions and systems, increasing the attack surface.

- **External dependencies**: Relying on third parties introduces potential vulnerabilities, such as insider threats or misconfigurations.

- **Compliance requirements**: Cloud systems must adhere to data protection regulations like GDPR, HIPAA, and CCPA, which impose stringent security standards.

Key principles of cloud data security

Securing data in the cloud requires a multi-layered approach that protects information throughout its lifecycle. Unlike traditional on-premises security models, cloud environments introduce unique challenges, such as shared infrastructure, remote accessibility, and compliance with global regulations. Organizations must implement encryption, identity management, real-time monitoring, data loss prevention, and backup strategies to mitigate risks and maintain data integrity.

The following key principles outline essential security measures that organizations can adopt to safeguard their cloud-stored data, prevent unauthorized access, and ensure resilience against evolving threats:

- **Encryption across the lifecycle**:
  - **At rest**: Encrypt data stored in cloud databases, file storage, and backups using provider, native tools like AWS **Key Management Service** (**KMS**) or Azure Disk Encryption.
  - **In transit**: Use TLS/SSL for secure connections between cloud services and external systems.
  - **In use**: Emerging technologies, like confidential computing, encrypt data while it is being processed, preventing exposure even in memory.
  - **Example**: A financial services company uses AWS KMS to encrypt sensitive customer data stored in S3 buckets, ensuring compliance with PCI DSS.
- **Identity and access management (IAM)**: Effective IAM ensures that only authorized users can access cloud resources.
  - **Role-based access control (RBAC)**: It assigns permissions based on roles, such as admin, developer, or auditor.
  - **Multi-factor authentication (MFA)**: It requires users to authenticate with multiple factors, such as passwords and biometrics.
  - **Least privilege principle**: It minimizes access rights to what is strictly necessary.
  - **Example**: A healthcare provider uses Azure Active Directory to enforce RBAC and MFA for its staff accessing patient data in the cloud.
- **Monitoring and threat detection**: Continuous monitoring helps detect and respond to potential security threats in real time.
- **Cloud-native tools**: Services like AWS CloudTrail, Azure Security Center, and Google Cloud Operations Suite provide visibility into user activity, system performance, and anomalies.
- **Anomaly detection**: Leverage AI to identify unusual patterns, such as excessive access attempts or data exfiltration.
- **Example**: A retail company uses Google Cloud Operations Suite to monitor API activity and detect unauthorized attempts to access customer order data.
- **Data loss prevention (DLP)**: These tools prevent sensitive data from leaving the organization or being exposed inadvertently.

o **Tagging and classification**: Label sensitive data to apply appropriate security policies.

o **Automated rules**: Block or alert on unauthorized sharing or downloading of classified data.

o **Example**: A tech company implements DLP on Microsoft 365 to prevent employees from emailing customer data to personal addresses.

- **Backup and disaster recovery** Ensuring data redundancy and regular backups safeguards against accidental loss, ransomware, or system failures.

o **Geo-redundant backups**: Store data copies in multiple regions to protect against regional outages.

o **Automated backup policies**: Schedule regular backups using tools like AWS Backup or Azure Recovery Services.

o **Example**: A media streaming service uses geo-redundant backups to ensure uninterrupted content delivery during regional outages.

Common challenges in cloud security

Cloud platforms provide advanced security tools and frameworks, but organizations still face several challenges in securing cloud environments. The dynamic nature of cloud computing, shared infrastructure, and complex configurations introduces risks that require continuous monitoring and proactive security measures.

Misconfigurations, insider threats, and multi-cloud complexity can expose sensitive data to cyberattacks or unauthorized access. Additionally, organizations operating in multi-tenant environments must safeguard against risks associated with shared resources.

The following challenges highlight key security concerns that organizations must address to ensure robust cloud security:

- **Misconfigurations**: These permissions, exposed storage buckets, or open ports can leave cloud resources vulnerable to attack.

  For example, a storage bucket with public access enabled can expose sensitive files to anyone on the internet.

- **Shared infrastructure risks**: Multi-tenant environments introduce the possibility of side-channel attacks or unauthorized cross-tenant data access.

- **Complexity of multi-cloud environments**: Organizations using multiple cloud providers (e.g., AWS, Azure, Google Cloud) may struggle to maintain consistent security policies across platforms.

- **Insider threats**: Malicious or negligent actions by employees or contractors can compromise data security.

Best practices for cloud data security

Ensuring robust cloud security requires a proactive approach that aligns with evolving threats and compliance requirements. Organizations must implement strategies that minimize risks, enforce strict access controls, and ensure data integrity across cloud environments.

Adopting the shared responsibility model, automating security enforcement, conducting regular audits, and following a zero-trust architecture can significantly enhance cloud security. Additionally, securing third-party integrations and external services is crucial to prevent supply chain vulnerabilities.

The following best practices outline key measures organizations should implement to strengthen cloud data security and protect sensitive information:

- **Leverage the shared responsibility model**: Understand what your cloud provider secures versus what you are responsible for. Use provider documentation and security tools to fill gaps.

- **Automate security practices**: Use IaC tools, like Terraform to enforce consistent security configurations, reducing the likelihood of human error.

- **Perform regular audits**: Conduct audits to identify vulnerabilities, misconfigurations, and compliance gaps. Use tools, like AWS Trusted Advisor or Azure Security Center.

- **Zero-trust architecture**: Adopt a zero-trust approach, where no entity (user, device, or application) is inherently trusted. Verify every access request and enforce strict policies.

- **Secure third-party integrations**: Evaluate third-party services for security and compliance. Use API gateways to manage and secure data exchanges with external providers.

Real-world examples of cloud security

Cloud security is essential for protecting sensitive data across industries, ensuring compliance, and mitigating cyber threats. Organizations implement encryption, identity management, monitoring tools, and backup strategies to safeguard their cloud environments. Various sectors, including healthcare, finance, and retail, have successfully deployed cloud security measures to prevent data breaches, detect anomalies, and ensure business continuity. The following examples highlight how different industries utilize cloud security to protect critical data and maintain regulatory compliance:

- **Healthcare industry**: A hospital uses AWS to store patient records and leverages encryption, IAM, and CloudTrail for compliance with HIPAA. When a breach attempt targeted the system, encryption ensured no data was exposed.

- **Financial sector**: A bank implements Azure Sentinel for threat detection and response. It identifies anomalous login attempts from unusual locations and prevents unauthorized access to sensitive financial records.

- **Retail industry**: An e-commerce platform secures customer order data on Google Cloud by encrypting it at rest, applying RBAC, and using geo-redundant backups. These measures protect against data loss during a regional outage.

The emerging trends in cloud security are as follows:

- **Confidential computing**: Technologies like Intel SGX and AMD SEV encrypt data in use, providing an additional layer of protection during processing.

- **AI-driven threat detection**: AI-powered tools continuously analyze cloud activity to detect sophisticated attacks and automate responses.

- **Serverless security**: As organizations adopt serverless architectures (e.g., AWS Lambda, Azure Functions), securing ephemeral compute environments becomes crucial.

Cloud security is the backbone of modern data-driven operations. As organizations increasingly rely on the cloud, ensuring the confidentiality, integrity, and availability of data is paramount. By implementing robust cloud security practices, organizations can confidently leverage the cloud's potential while safeguarding their most valuable asset: data.

Incident response and data breach management

Despite robust security measures, no organization is immune to the risk of a data breach. Attackers are constantly evolving their techniques, and even the most secure systems can be compromised by vulnerabilities, misconfigurations, or insider threats. This reality makes incident response and data breach management critical components of any operational data security strategy.

Incident response involves a systematic approach to detecting, containing, and mitigating security incidents, while breach management focuses on minimizing the damage and recovering from the fallout of a breach. Together, they ensure that organizations can respond swiftly and effectively, preserving trust and continuity.

In this section, we will explore the key stages of incident response, best practices for managing breaches, and real, world examples that highlight the importance of preparation and resilience.

Understanding incident response

Incident response is a structured approach to handling security events, aiming to minimize damage and restore normal operations as quickly as possible. The process typically follows a lifecycle consisting of six stages:

1. **Preparation**

    - **Goal**: Equip the organization with the tools, processes, and policies needed to handle security incidents.

    - **Activities**: Develop an incident response plan, form an incident response team, and conduct regular training and simulations.

    - **Example**: A financial institution creates a detailed incident response playbook, outlining steps for responding to phishing attacks and ransomware incidents.

2. **Detection and analysis**

    - **Goal**: Identify potential incidents and assess their scope and impact.

    - **Activities**: Use monitoring tools, **intrusion detection systems** (**IDS**), and threat intelligence to detect anomalies. Analyze logs, alerts, and forensic evidence to confirm incidents.

    - **Example**: A retail company's IDS detects unusual login attempts from multiple geographies. The security team analyzes logs to confirm a brute, force attack on user accounts.

3. **Containment**

    - **Goal**: Limit the spread and impact of the incident.

    - **Activities**: Isolate affected systems, disable compromised accounts, and block malicious IP addresses. Choose between short, term containment (immediate response) and long, term containment (mitigating root causes).

    - **Example**: A healthcare provider isolates a compromised server to prevent ransomware from spreading to other systems.

4. **Eradication**

    - **Goal**: Eliminate the root cause of the incident.

    - **Activities**: Remove malware, patch vulnerabilities, and revoke compromised credentials.

    - **Example**: After identifying the use of an unpatched software vulnerability, a logistics company patches its systems and removes the malicious payload.

5. **Recovery**

  - **Goal**: Restore systems and operations to normal while ensuring no residual threats remain.

  - **Activities**: Validate system integrity, recover from backups, and monitor for signs of recurrence.

  - **Example**: A media company restores its data from encrypted backups after a ransomware attack, ensuring systems are clean before resuming operations.

6. **Post-incident review**

  - **Goal**: Learn from the incident to improve future response efforts.

  - **Activities**: Conduct a post-mortem analysis to identify weaknesses and update security policies and response plans.

  - **Example**: An e-commerce platform conducts a review after a credential stuffing attack, identifying the need for stronger password policies and MFA.

Key elements of a successful incident response plan

In today's rapidly evolving threat landscape, organizations must be prepared to detect, contain, and mitigate security incidents with precision. A well-structured **incident response plan** (IRP) is essential for minimizing damage, ensuring business continuity, and maintaining stakeholder trust.

The following are the critical components that form the foundation of a successful incident response strategy:

- **Incident response team (IRT)**
  - Composed of security professionals, IT staff, legal advisors, and communications personnel.
  - Responsibilities include detecting incidents, coordinating responses, and communicating with stakeholders.

- **Clear roles and responsibilities**
  - Define roles for team members, such as incident commander, forensic analyst, and public relations officer.
  - Ensure accountability and streamline decision, making during crises.

- **Incident classification and prioritization**
  - Categorize incidents based on severity, such as minor disruptions, data breaches, or full, scale attacks.

- o Prioritize responses based on potential impact on operations, customers, and compliance.
- **Communication plans**
  - o Establish protocols for internal and external communication during incidents.
  - o Ensure clear messaging to customers, regulators, and the media to maintain trust and transparency.

Managing data breaches

A data breach occurs when sensitive information is accessed or disclosed without authorization. Effective breach management focuses on limiting the damage, addressing stakeholder concerns, and ensuring compliance with legal requirements, as follows:

- **Immediate actions**
  - o Identify and contain the breach.
  - o Secure affected systems and prevent further data loss.
  - o Notify the incident response team and relevant stakeholders.
- **Impact assessment**
  - o Determine the scope of the breach, including affected systems, data types, and stakeholders.
  - o Assess potential legal, financial, and reputational damage.
- **Legal and regulatory compliance**
  - o Notify affected parties and regulatory bodies as required by laws such as GDPR, HIPAA, or CCPA.
  - o Ensure timely and transparent disclosure to avoid penalties.
  - o **Example**: A financial services firm notifies customers within 72 hours of a breach to comply with GDPR requirements.
- **Customer communication**
  - o Provide clear and honest information to customers about the breach and its impact.
  - o Offer support, such as credit monitoring services, to mitigate the consequences.
- **Long, term mitigation**
  - o Implement additional security measures to prevent recurrence, such as enhanced monitoring, regular audits, and updated policies.

Real-world examples

Cybersecurity breaches can have devastating consequences, impacting businesses, customers, and public trust. Effective incident response and breach management are essential to mitigate damage, restore operations, and strengthen defenses against future threats.

The following real-world cases highlight key lessons from major security incidents, demonstrating the importance of early detection, rapid response, and transparent communication in crisis management:

- **Target Data Breach (2013)**
  - **What happened**: Hackers exploited a vulnerability in Target's payment system, stealing credit card information of 40 million customers.
  - **Response**: Target implemented enhanced monitoring and offered free credit monitoring to affected customers. However, delays in detection and response led to reputational damage.
  - **Lesson**: Early detection and rapid response are critical to minimizing the impact of breaches.

- **Maersk Ransomware Attack (2017)**
  - **What happened**: The NotPetya ransomware attack disrupted Maersk's operations, forcing the company to rebuild its IT systems.
  - **Response**: Maersk isolated affected systems, restored operations using backups, and strengthened its cybersecurity defenses.
  - **Lesson**: A robust backup strategy is essential for recovering from ransomware attacks.

- **Equifax Data Breach (2017)**
  - **What happened**: Hackers exploited a vulnerability to access personal information of 147 million individuals.
  - **Response**: Equifax faced criticism for delayed disclosure and poor customer support. The breach resulted in significant fines and a damaged reputation.
  - **Lesson**: Transparent communication and regulatory compliance are critical for maintaining trust.

Challenges

Despite having robust security measures, organizations face several challenges in effectively responding to cyber incidents. Attackers continuously evolve their tactics, while internal and external factors complicate response efforts.

The following are some key challenges that organizations must navigate to ensure a swift and effective incident response:

- **Sophisticated threats**
  - o Attackers use advanced techniques like AI, powered malware and zero, day exploits, making detection and response more difficult.

- **Coordination across teams**
  - o Large organizations may struggle to coordinate responses across security, IT, legal, and PR teams.

- **Regulatory complexity**
  - o Different jurisdictions have varying notification requirements, creating challenges for global organizations.

- **Customer expectations**
  - o Delayed or inadequate communication can erode trust, leading to long, term reputational damage.

Best practices

To effectively mitigate cyber threats, organizations must adopt proactive measures that enhance their incident response capabilities. From leveraging advanced detection tools to refining response strategies through simulations, the following best practices help strengthen resilience against evolving cyber risks:

- **Invest in detection and monitoring tools**
  - o Deploy SIEM systems to identify and analyze incidents in real time.

- **Conduct regular simulations**
  - o Test incident response plans through tabletop exercises and red team/blue team simulations.

- **Partner with cybersecurity experts**
  - o Engage third, party experts to assist with breach investigations and forensic analysis.

- **Focus on continuous improvement**
  - o Use lessons learned from incidents to update policies, tools, and training programs.

Importance of incident response and breach management

In an era of increasing cyber threats, incident response and breach management are no longer optional, they are essential. A well-prepared organization can mitigate the impact of incidents, recover quickly, and maintain stakeholder trust. These strategies ensure that even in the face of challenges, organizations remain resilient and focused on their goals.

Emerging security challenges in AI/ML pipelines

As AI and ML pipelines become integral to modern data systems, they introduce unique security challenges that traditional data security practices are not equipped to handle. These pipelines process sensitive data, generate critical insights, and power decision-making across industries. While they bring tremendous value, they also create new attack surfaces for malicious actors.

This section explores emerging threats to AI/ML systems, including adversarial attacks, data poisoning, and model extraction, and outlines strategies to mitigate these risks.

Key security challenges in AI/ML pipelines

As AI and ML become integral to various industries, they also introduce new security vulnerabilities that adversaries can exploit. From adversarial manipulation to data privacy breaches, these challenges pose significant risks to the integrity, fairness, and trustworthiness of AI models. Some of the most pressing security threats in AI/ML pipelines and their real-world implications are as follows:

- **Adversarial attacks**
  - Adversarial attacks involve feeding AI models deliberately crafted inputs that cause them to produce incorrect or unexpected outputs.
  - **Example**: An attacker subtly alters a road sign image, causing an autonomous vehicle to misclassify a stop sign as a speed limit sign.
  - **Impact**: These attacks can lead to misinformed decisions in critical applications like healthcare diagnostics, autonomous systems, and fraud detection.

- **Data poisoning**
  - Attackers inject malicious data into the training dataset, skewing the model's learning process.
  - **Example**: Poisoning an e-commerce recommendation system's training data to promote specific products unfairly.
  - **Impact**: Corrupted training data results in biased or ineffective models, potentially undermining trust and causing financial losses.

- **Model inversion**
  - Model inversion attacks use a trained model to infer sensitive information about its training data.

- o **Example**: Extracting private patient health records from a machine learning model trained on medical data.

- o **Impact**: Such attacks compromise user privacy and may violate data protection regulations like GDPR or HIPAA.

- **Model theft or extraction**

  - o Attackers replicate a deployed model by querying it and analyzing its responses.

  - o **Example**: Reverse, engineering a proprietary fraud detection algorithm to bypass it.

  - o **Impact**: Model theft undermines intellectual property protections and allows attackers to exploit system vulnerabilities.

- **Bias amplification**

  - o AI models can inadvertently amplify biases present in the training data, leading to discriminatory or unfair outcomes.

  - o **Example**: A hiring algorithm favoring candidates based on biased historical hiring practices.

  - o **Impact**: This can lead to reputational damage and legal challenges for organizations.

Strategies to mitigate security challenges in AI/ ML pipelines

Securing AI/ML pipelines requires a proactive approach that integrates robust data practices, model protections, and continuous monitoring. The following strategies help organizations strengthen their AI systems against adversarial attacks, data poisoning, model theft, and bias amplification while ensuring fairness, privacy, and integrity:

- **Robust model training**

  - o Use diverse, high, quality datasets to minimize the risk of bias and poisoning.

  - o Regularly update training data to reflect current patterns and trends.

  - o Incorporate adversarial training techniques to improve model resilience.

    Example: A healthcare AI company includes adversarial examples in its training data to strengthen its diagnostic model against malicious inputs.

- **Secure data preprocessing**

  - o Implement strict controls over data sources to ensure their authenticity.

  - o Use hashing and validation techniques to verify dataset integrity before training.

Example: A financial institution validates all incoming transaction data using cryptographic hashes before adding it to the training pipeline.

- **Differential privacy**

  o Add controlled noise to training data or model outputs to protect sensitive information.

  o Differential privacy ensures that individual data points cannot be extracted from the model.

    Example: A tech company deploying an AI, powered survey tool applies differential privacy to anonymize user responses.

- **Model watermarking**

  o Embed unique watermarks into AI models to detect and prove unauthorized use or theft.

  o Watermarking can also serve as a deterrent to attackers.

    Example: An AI startup adds watermarks to its proprietary recommendation algorithm to protect its intellectual property.

- **Monitoring and anomaly detection**

  o Monitor model performance and predictions for anomalies that could indicate an attack.

  o Use tools like AI, based IDS to flag unusual activity in real time.

    Example: An autonomous vehicle company implements anomaly detection to identify and mitigate adversarial inputs during operations.

- **Post-deployment testing**

  o Continuously test deployed models against adversarial inputs to identify vulnerabilities.

  o Update and retrain models as new threats emerge.

  o **Example**: A fraud detection system undergoes periodic testing with simulated attacks to ensure its defenses remain effective.

Future directions in AI/ML security

As AI and ML systems become more widespread, their security must evolve to address increasingly sophisticated threats. Emerging trends in AI/ML security include:

- **Federated learning**

  o Allows models to be trained across multiple decentralized devices without sharing raw data, reducing the risk of data leakage.

- o **Example**: A healthcare consortium uses federated learning to train models on patient data from multiple hospitals without transferring sensitive information.

- **Explainable AI (XAI)**
  - o Enhances model transparency by providing insights into how decisions are made.
  - o **Example**: Explainable fraud detection algorithms help financial institutions understand and defend against adversarial attacks.

- **AI-driven security for AI systems**
  - o AI models are being used to detect and prevent attacks on other AI systems, creating a layered defense mechanism.
  - o **Example**: An AI-powered monitoring tool flags potential data poisoning attempts during the training phase.

Compliance and regulatory considerations

In the digital age, the responsibility of safeguarding data goes beyond technical implementations, it extends into the legal and ethical domains. Organizations must align their data security practices with global regulations to ensure compliance, avoid penalties, and maintain customer trust. Regulations such as the GDPR, HIPAA, and CCPA mandate specific measures to protect sensitive information, including personal data, financial records, and health information.

Compliance is not merely a box-checking exercise; it requires a comprehensive understanding of the laws, adherence to prescribed protocols, and continuous monitoring to adapt to changing requirements.

Key regulations

To ensure compliance and protect sensitive data, organizations must adhere to various regulations that govern privacy, security, and ethical AI usage. These frameworks establish guidelines for handling personal and financial data, enforcing transparency, and mitigating cybersecurity risks.

The following are some of the most critical regulations impacting AI-driven businesses:

- **GDPR**:
  - o Applicable to organizations handling the personal data of EU citizens, GDPR emphasizes transparency, data minimization, and user consent.
  - o **Requirements**: Organizations must ensure user rights such as data access, rectification, and erasure, and report breaches within 72 hours.

- **Example**: A SaaS provider encrypts customer data and implements robust breach notification processes to comply with GDPR.

- **CCPA**:

  - Grants California residents' rights over their personal information, including the right to know, delete, and opt, out of the sale of their data.

  - **Requirements**: Organizations must provide clear privacy notices, honor consumer requests, and avoid penalizing users for exercising their rights.

- **HIPAA**:

  - Ensures the confidentiality and security of health information in the U.S.

  - **Requirements**: Implement safeguards for storing, transmitting, and sharing **protected health information (PHI)**.

    Example: A healthcare provider encrypts patient records and restricts access using role, based permissions.

- **Payment Card Industry Data Security Standard (PCI DSS)**:

  - Focused on securing payment card information, this standard applies to all organizations handling credit card transactions.

  - **Requirements**: Tokenization, encryption, and monitoring of cardholder data.

Achieving and maintaining compliance

Ensuring compliance with data protection and security regulations requires a proactive approach that integrates regular assessments, employee education, and technological safeguards. Organizations must continuously monitor and refine their practices to stay aligned with evolving legal requirements.

The following are the key strategies to achieve and sustain regulatory compliance:

- **Regular audits and assessments**:

  - Conduct internal and external audits to identify gaps and ensure adherence to compliance standards.

  - **Example**: An e-commerce company partners with third-party auditors to verify its GDPR compliance.

- **Privacy impact assessments (PIAs)**:

  - Evaluate the potential privacy risks associated with new data processing activities.

  - **Example**: A social media platform conducts PIAs before rolling out a new feature that collects user location data.

- **Employee training**:

  o Train employees on compliance requirements, ethical data handling, and breach response protocols.

  o **Example**: A multinational corporation conducts annual GDPR and CCPA workshops for its staff.

- **Data mapping**:

  o Maintain detailed records of data flow within the organization to ensure visibility and control over sensitive information.

- **Technology and automation**:

  o Leverage tools such as DLP systems, encryption, and automated compliance reporting.

Case studies and real-world examples

Organizations across industries face unique challenges in adhering to key regulations like the GDPR, CCPA, and HIPAA. The following examples showcase the importance of proactive security measures, transparent data handling, and alignment with regulatory standards:

Case study 1: GDPR compliance in e-commerce

- **Challenge**: An online retailer needed to comply with GDPR while managing large-scale customer data.

- **Solution**: The company implemented robust encryption, developed user, friendly interfaces for data access requests, and automated breach notifications.

- **Outcome**: The retailer avoided fines and improved customer trust through transparent data handling practices.

Case study 2: HIPAA compliance in healthcare

- **Challenge**: A hospital struggled with ensuring HIPAA compliance while adopting cloud, based health record systems.

- **Solution**: By encrypting data, implementing strict role, based access controls, and using AWS HealthLake for secure storage, the hospital ensured compliance.

- **Outcome**: Improved patient data security and seamless regulatory audits.

Case study 3: CCPA compliance in retail

- **Challenge**: A U.S., based retail chain needed to align its data practices with CCPA.

- **Solution**: The company created a centralized privacy dashboard allowing customers to manage their data preferences, including opting out of data sales.

- **Outcome**: Enhanced customer engagement and successful navigation of regulatory audits.

Case study 4: Breach management at Equifax

- **Challenge**: Following a major data breach, Equifax faced intense regulatory scrutiny and reputational damage.

- **Solution**: The company revamped its cybersecurity infrastructure, invested in employee training, and improved compliance monitoring.

- **Outcome**: Although recovery took time, the measures improved resilience and regulatory compliance.

Challenges in compliance and real-world application

While compliance frameworks provide guidelines, organizations face challenges such as:

- **Evolving regulations**: Laws like GDPR and CCPA are frequently updated, requiring continuous monitoring.

- **Resource constraints**: Smaller organizations may struggle to allocate resources for compliance activities.

- **Global variability**: Operating across jurisdictions complicates compliance due to differing regulatory requirements.

Conclusion

Operational data security serves as the bedrock for ensuring the integrity and reliability of data across its lifecycle, from storage to transit and into the cloud. By implementing robust security measures, organizations safeguard their data from breaches, ensure compliance, and build resilience against evolving threats. As data grows in scale and complexity, operational security provides the necessary framework to protect insights that drive decision-making. However, security alone is not enough; ensuring data privacy is equally critical.

In the next chapter, we will explore the ethical, legal, and regulatory dimensions of data privacy, highlighting how organizations can align data protection with user rights and transparency. Together, operational security and data privacy form a comprehensive strategy for responsible data management in the modern landscape.

CHAPTER 11
Protecting Data Privacy

Introduction

As the digital landscape evolves, data has become the cornerstone of business innovation, driving advanced analytics, personalization, and **artificial intelligence** (**AI**) development. However, with the growing reliance on data comes an increasing responsibility to ensure its protection and ethical use. Building upon *Chapter 10, Operational Data Security*, which highlighted techniques to safeguard data in transit, at rest, and during processing, this chapter explores a critical, yet often understated facet: protecting data privacy.

Operational data security serves as the foundation, shielding data from external threats and unauthorized access. However, data privacy introduces the ethical dimension, ensuring that the data collected, stored, and processed adheres to regulatory guidelines and respects the rights of individuals. Operational security concerns itself with firewalls and encryption, privacy involves policies, consent mechanisms, and the minimization of data collection itself.

This chapter acts as a bridge to the next, which focuses on case studies and real-world examples. By understanding privacy as not just a legal requirement but a core aspect of data engineering, businesses can foster trust, ensure compliance, and mitigate potential legal liabilities.

Topics, such as the fundamentals of data privacy, practical approaches to managing personal and sensitive data, and privacy challenges in the cloud, will be explored. In addition, emerging risks introduced by AI systems, including unintentional data leakage, will be discussed alongside potential solutions and strategies for deploying AI in private environments.

By the end of this chapter, readers will gain comprehensive insights into data privacy principles, practical techniques, and cutting-edge technologies that enable organizations to thrive in an era increasingly defined by stringent privacy expectations and regulations.

Structure

The chapter covers the following topics:

- Fundamentals of data privacy
- Data privacy in practice
- Managing personal and sensitive data
- Data privacy in the cloud
- AI and data privacy
- Case studies and industry insights

Objectives

By the end of this chapter, readers will have a comprehensive understanding of data privacy, its significance, and the frameworks necessary for its implementation. Data privacy is distinct from security, focusing on the ethical and legal management of personal and sensitive data. Core principles such as data minimization, purpose limitation, transparency, and user consent ensure responsible data handling. Organizations must recognize data privacy as a critical component of compliance, trust-building, and risk mitigation. Failure to implement privacy measures can lead to reputational damage, legal consequences, and financial losses. Key regulatory frameworks, including the GDPR, the CCPA, and the HIPAA, impose strict requirements on data collection, processing, and retention.

Understanding these regulations helps organizations align their practices with legal mandates. This chapter also explores practical strategies such as data anonymization, encryption, access controls, and **privacy-enhancing technologies** (**PETs**) to safeguard information. Additionally, the intersection of AI and data privacy presents new challenges, including data leakage and model inference attacks, necessitating privacy-preserving techniques like differential privacy and federated learning. By the end of this chapter, readers will be equipped with actionable insights to establish strong privacy frameworks, ensuring compliance, security, and ethical data stewardship in an evolving digital landscape.

Fundamentals of data privacy

In today's digital age, data serves as the backbone of innovation, driving advancements in artificial intelligence, customer engagement, and business analytics. Organizations continuously collect, analyze, and store vast amounts of personal and sensitive data to stay competitive and offer personalized services. However, as the volume of data grows, so do the risks associated with its misuse, loss, or unauthorized access. The concept of data privacy has emerged as a fundamental aspect of responsible data management, ensuring that personal data is handled ethically, securely, and in compliance with global regulations. This chapter explores the core principles of data privacy, exploring why it matters, key regulatory frameworks, and the foundational steps organizations can take to build robust privacy frameworks.

Understanding data privacy

Data privacy encompasses the policies, processes, and technologies that govern how personal data is collected, processed, stored, and shared. Unlike data security, which focuses on protecting data from external threats, data privacy emphasizes the ethical use of data and the rights of individuals to control their information.

At its core, data privacy ensures that individuals have transparency and autonomy over how their data is handled. This involves obtaining user consent, limiting data collection to what is necessary, and safeguarding personal information throughout its lifecycle. Organizations that prioritize data privacy not only comply with legal mandates but also build trust and foster long-term relationships with their customers.

Importance of data privacy

Data privacy is not merely a legal obligation but a cornerstone of sustainable business practices. Companies that fail to implement adequate data privacy measures face significant risks, ranging from reputational damage to severe financial penalties. Conversely, those who embed privacy into their operations can differentiate themselves and gain a competitive edge.

Ensuring data privacy is no longer an option but a necessity in the modern digital landscape. As organizations increasingly rely on vast amounts of personal and sensitive data, safeguarding this information becomes crucial to maintaining compliance, trust, and operational integrity. Effective data privacy frameworks not only protect organizations from regulatory penalties but also foster long-term customer relationships and enhance brand reputation. Beyond legal mandates, responsible data management is an ethical obligation that aligns with societal expectations and corporate governance principles.

The following key reasons highlight why data privacy should be a fundamental priority for any organization handling sensitive information:

- **Regulatory compliance:** Governments worldwide have introduced stringent regulations, such as the GDPR, the CCPA, and the HIPAA. These laws impose strict requirements on data collection, usage, and disclosure. Non-compliance can result in substantial fines and legal action.

- **Trust and reputation:** Transparent data practices build customer trust and enhance brand reputation. Consumers are more likely to engage with organizations that prioritize the privacy and protection of their personal information.

- **Risk mitigation:** Effective data privacy frameworks reduce the likelihood of data breaches, insider threats, and accidental leaks. By limiting data access and implementing encryption, organizations can minimize exposure to potential risks.

- **Ethical responsibility:** Upholding data privacy reflects an organization's commitment to ethical business practices and the protection of individual rights. This aligns with broader societal expectations and corporate social responsibility initiatives.

Core principles of data privacy

Establishing a strong foundation for data privacy requires adherence to key principles that guide responsible data handling. As organizations collect, store, and process vast amounts of personal and sensitive information, ensuring compliance with global privacy regulations and ethical standards is essential. These principles serve as a framework for organizations to protect data integrity, maintain user trust, and mitigate risks associated with improper data management. By incorporating transparency, accountability, and security measures, businesses can navigate the complexities of data privacy while aligning with industry best practices.

The following core principles outline the fundamental strategies organizations must adopt to safeguard data privacy and ensure responsible data stewardship:

- **Data minimization:** Organizations should collect only the data necessary to fulfill a specific purpose. Reducing the scope of data collection not only limits exposure but also aligns with regulatory requirements. For example, an e-commerce platform might collect customer shipping addresses but avoid gathering unnecessary demographic information.

- **Purpose limitation:** Data must be collected for explicit, legitimate purposes and should not be further processed in a manner that is incompatible with those purposes. A healthcare provider, for instance, may collect patient data for treatment but should refrain from using it for marketing campaigns.

- **Transparency:** Organizations must communicate how data is collected, stored, and shared. Users should be informed of their rights and the reasons for data collection through easily accessible privacy policies, for example, mobile applications often provide pop-up notifications explaining data collection practices.

- **Data accuracy:** Maintaining accurate and up-to-date data prevents errors and ensures that individuals can rectify inaccuracies. Financial institutions, for example, allow customers to update their contact details through secure online portals to ensure account accuracy.

- **Accountability:** Organizations are responsible for ensuring compliance with data privacy regulations and must demonstrate their efforts to protect personal data. This often involves appointing a **Data Protection Officer** (**DPO**) and conducting regular privacy audits.

- **Security:** Data privacy cannot exist without strong security measures. Encryption, access controls, and secure storage practices are essential to protect sensitive data from unauthorized access. A cloud services provider, for example, may encrypt all stored data to prevent breaches.

- **User control and consent:** Users should have control over their data, with the ability to grant or withdraw consent at any time. Streaming services, for instance, allow users to manage their data-sharing preferences through account settings.

Data privacy and regulatory frameworks

As the digital economy expands, data privacy has become a critical concern for governments and regulatory bodies worldwide. To safeguard personal information and ensure responsible data handling, various legal frameworks have been established to impose strict guidelines on how organizations collect, store, process, and share data. Compliance with these regulations is essential for businesses operating across multiple jurisdictions, as failure to adhere to legal requirements can lead to severe financial penalties and reputational damage. The following regulatory frameworks GDPR, CCPA, and HIPAA, illustrate the global efforts to enforce data privacy, protect individual rights, and enhance consumer trust in the digital landscape:

- **GDPR:**
  - **Jurisdiction: European Union (EU)**
  - **Key requirements:** User consent, data breach notification, right to erasure, and data portability.
  - **Impact:** Applies to any organization that processes the data of EU citizens, regardless of location.

- **CCPA:**
  - **Jurisdiction:** California, USA
  - **Key requirements:** Right to know, right to delete, and the right to opt out of data sales.
  - **Impact:** Provides California residents with greater control over their personal information.

- **HIPAA:**

  - **Jurisdiction:** USA (Healthcare sector)

  - **Key requirements**: Protects patient health data and enforces strict security measures for data storage and transmission.

  - **Impact:** Non-compliance can result in heavy fines and reputational damage.

Building data privacy framework

Implementing a comprehensive data privacy framework is essential for achieving regulatory compliance and safeguarding personal information.

The following steps outline how organizations can develop and maintain effective privacy programs:

1. **Data mapping and inventory:** Conducting data mapping exercises helps organizations identify all data assets, their locations, and how they flow across departments. This process uncovers potential vulnerabilities and ensures that all data is accounted for. For example, a financial institution may track sensitive data from customer onboarding through to service delivery.

2. **Privacy policies and procedures:** Establishing clear privacy policies defines how data is collected, processed, and retained. These policies should align with industry standards and be readily available to users. A software company, for instance, might outline data retention practices in its terms of service.

3. **Risk assessments and audits:** Regular risk assessments and privacy audits identify gaps in compliance and help organizations address potential threats. An e-commerce retailer might conduct annual audits to ensure data privacy measures remain effective.

4. **Employee training and awareness:** Educating employees about data privacy fosters a culture of responsibility and reduces the risk of human error. A cloud services provider could implement quarterly training sessions to ensure staff stay informed on evolving regulations.

5. **Incident response and breach management:** Developing an incident response plan enables organizations to act swiftly in the event of a data breach. A healthcare institution, for example, might establish protocols for notifying affected patients and regulatory authorities.

Data privacy in practice

While understanding the fundamentals of data privacy sets the stage, the real challenge lies in implementing these principles across organizational processes and systems. Data privacy in practice focuses on the tangible steps, tools, and strategies organizations can use to safeguard sensitive information, ensuring compliance with laws and maintaining user trust. This section explored practical applications, policies, and frameworks that translate privacy theory into actionable processes.

Establishing a privacy-first culture

Data privacy is both a legal mandate and an ethical obligation; organizations must go beyond compliance to cultivate a privacy-first culture. This approach integrates data protection into the fabric of daily operations, treating it as a fundamental business value rather than an afterthought. Establishing such a culture requires active commitment from leadership, comprehensive employee training, and transparent communication with stakeholders. By embedding privacy into every aspect of decision-making and operations, organizations can not only meet regulatory requirements but also build trust, foster accountability, and enhance their reputation.

The following key elements outline how businesses can establish a privacy-first culture that aligns with evolving societal expectations and strengthens their competitive edge:

- **Leadership buy-in:** Privacy must be championed by senior executives to gain traction across departments. Executives should publicly prioritize privacy initiatives and allocate resources to support privacy-related projects. By modeling privacy-conscious behavior, leadership can influence company-wide adoption.

- **Employee training:** Conduct regular workshops to educate employees on handling personal data responsibly. Provide real-world scenarios during training to help employees recognize potential privacy breaches and respond appropriately. Consider certifications to ensure knowledge retention.

- **Data ethics committees:** Form committees to evaluate data collection, retention, and usage, ensuring ethical considerations align with business goals. Regularly review data handling practices, ensuring they reflect evolving regulations and societal expectations.

- **Transparency in policies:** Communicate data privacy policies to both employees and customers, fostering trust and accountability. Publish easy-to-understand privacy notices and keep stakeholders informed of policy changes.

- **Example:** A financial services firm instituted a quarterly privacy audit, requiring managers to report how customer data is stored, processed, and shared. This proactive approach reduced inadvertent data exposure and increased client confidence.

Data mapping and inventory

In order to protect data effectively, organizations must first understand what data they hold, where it resides, and how it flows across systems. This process, known as **data mapping**, is essential for identifying vulnerabilities and ensuring compliance with regulations like the GDPR or CCPA.

The steps in data mapping are as follows:

1. **Catalog data sources:** Identify all databases, cloud storage, employee devices, and third-party services that collect or process data. Conduct a comprehensive audit to ensure that no data source is overlooked.

2. **Classify data:** Separate sensitive data, such as financial records or health information, from less critical datasets. Assign sensitivity labels and track the access permissions associated with each category.

3. **Track data flows:** Map how data moves internally and externally, highlighting points of entry, storage, and sharing. Visual tools can simplify this process, making it easier to communicate data flows to non-technical stakeholders.

4. **Assess risk:** Evaluate each stage for potential security gaps and implement access controls to minimize exposure. Create risk scores for each data set, prioritizing protection efforts based on data sensitivity.

5. **Example:** A healthcare provider mapped patient data flows from intake to insurance claims, identifying multiple unnecessary copies across systems. By streamlining storage locations, the provider minimized exposure and improved compliance.

The following figure outlines the data mapping process, starting from identifying data sources to classifying, tracking, and assessing risks. It highlights key steps such as mapping data flows, identifying storage locations, and managing access. The process culminates in risk assessment, with paths leading to either remediation or documentation and audit for compliance.

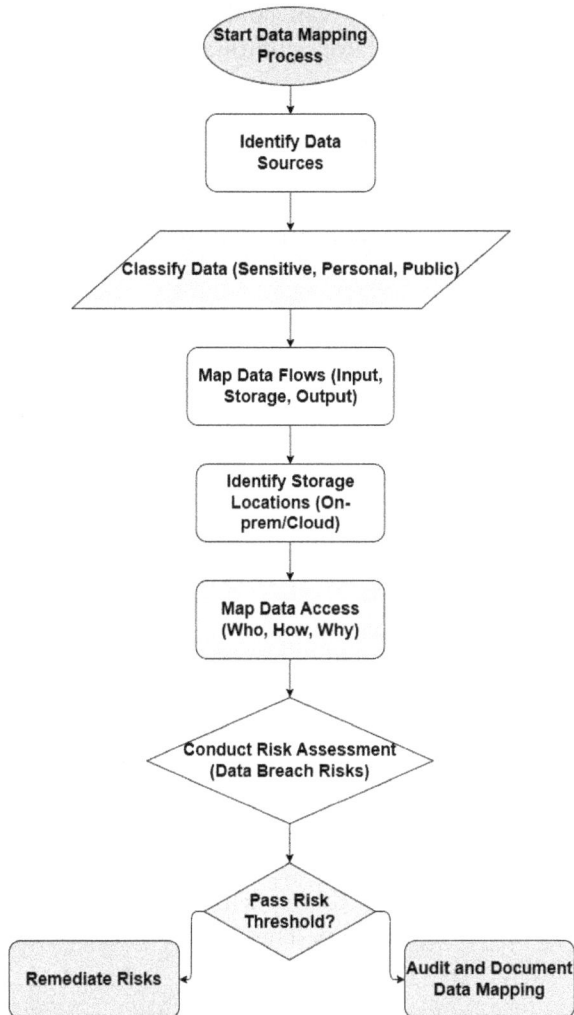

Figure 11.1: Data mapping and flow process for privacy and compliance

Implementing data minimization and anonymization

In an increasingly data-driven world, organizations must balance the need for valuable insights with the imperative to protect user privacy. Implementing data minimization and anonymization techniques reduces the risk of data breaches while ensuring compliance with privacy regulations. Data minimization focuses on collecting only the necessary information, limiting retention, and restricting access to sensitive details. Meanwhile, anonymization techniques, such as generalization, randomization, and tokenization, further safeguard data by removing or obscuring personally identifiable elements. By adopting these practices, organizations can continue to leverage data analytics while upholding ethical standards and regulatory compliance.

The following methods outline how businesses can effectively implement data minimization and anonymization in their operations:

- **Data minimization techniques:**

  o **Limit collection:** Gather only the data necessary to fulfill specific business functions. Regularly assess data collection practices to ensure adherence to this principle.

  o **Retention policies:** Delete data that is no longer required for operational or legal purposes. Automate deletion processes where feasible to ensure consistency.

  o **Pseudonymization:** Replace **personally identifiable information (PII)** with artificial identifiers to limit exposure. Ensure pseudonymized data is stored separately from the keys needed to re-identify it.

  o **Example:** A healthcare organization collects patient data for medical research but replaces patient names and Social Security numbers with unique identifiers. The original identifiers are stored in a separate, highly secured database accessible only to authorized personnel. This ensures that even if the research data is exposed, it cannot be linked back to individual patients without access to the separate key database, maintaining patient confidentiality while allowing valuable medical studies to continue.

- **Anonymization techniques:**

  o **Generalization:** Broaden the specificity of data points (e.g., replacing exact age with an age range). This makes data useful for analysis without compromising privacy.

  o **Randomization:** Add noise or random variations to datasets, preventing the re-identification of individuals. Use this technique for large-scale analytics without affecting trends.

  o **Tokenization:** Substitute sensitive data with non-sensitive equivalents, maintaining referential integrity without exposing real data. Tokens can be stored in secure vaults to ensure high-level protection.

  o **Example:** An e-commerce platform anonymized customer data for its analytics department, ensuring that purchasing trends could be analyzed without exposing individual identities.

Embedding privacy by design

Privacy by design is a foundational approach that embeds privacy considerations into the core of system architecture, ensuring that data protection is not an afterthought but a fundamental requirement. By integrating privacy measures from the initial stages of development, businesses can mitigate risks, comply with regulatory standards, and build trust with users. This methodology emphasizes minimizing data collection, enforcing strict security controls, and continuously monitoring for potential privacy breaches.

The principles of privacy by design are as follows:

- **Default privacy settings:** Systems should default to the highest privacy levels unless the user specifies otherwise. Include opt-in rather than opt-out settings for data-sharing features.

- **Minimal data use:** Design applications to function with the least amount of personal data possible. Evaluate product features regularly to identify and eliminate unnecessary data processing.

- **Continuous monitoring:** Implement automated tools to detect potential data privacy violations throughout the system lifecycle. Use real-time alerts to mitigate breaches before they escalate.

- **Example:** A mobile app developer integrated privacy by design by requiring explicit consent for location tracking and providing granular controls for users to manage permissions.

Privacy impact assessments

As organizations increasingly handle vast amounts of personal and sensitive data, assessing privacy risks before launching new systems, products, or initiatives has become essential. A **privacy impact assessment (PIA)** serves as a proactive measure to identify, evaluate, and mitigate potential privacy threats, ensuring compliance with regulations and safeguarding user trust. By systematically analyzing how data is collected, processed, and shared, PIAs help organizations implement necessary safeguards before risks materialize. This structured approach not only minimizes legal and reputational risks but also fosters a privacy-conscious culture that prioritizes responsible data handling.

The following key components outline the steps involved in conducting an effective PIA, ensuring privacy remains integral to business operations and technology development:

- **Scope definition:** Determine the type of data involved and the systems interacting with it. Clearly outline the objectives of the PIA to ensure alignment across teams.

- **Risk analysis:** Assess the likelihood and impact of potential privacy breaches. Establishment frameworks like the **National Institute of Standards and Technology (NIST)** or the **International Organization for Standardization (ISO)** can be used to guide the risk analysis process.

- **Mitigation strategies:** Develop technical and administrative controls to address identified risks. Document these strategies and assign responsibility for their implementation.

- **Stakeholder engagement:** Consult legal, compliance, and IT teams throughout the assessment. Engage external privacy consultants for high-risk projects.

- **Example:** Before launching a smart home device, a technology firm conducted a PIA to assess potential privacy risks associated with audio data. By encrypting data at rest and in transit, the company reduced the chance of unauthorized access.

Managing vendor and third-party relationships

Vendors and third-party services often process or store sensitive data on behalf of organizations. Managing these relationships is crucial to ensure privacy standards extend beyond internal systems.

The best practices for vendor management are as follows:

- **Due diligence:** Assess the data privacy policies of potential vendors before engagement. Require vendors to demonstrate compliance with relevant regulations.

- **Contractual safeguards:** Include data protection clauses in vendor contracts, specifying responsibilities and penalties for non-compliance. Ensure contracts address breach notification timelines.

- **Audits and reviews:** Conduct regular audits to verify that third parties adhere to the agreed-upon privacy practices. Use audit findings to drive continuous improvement.

- **Example:** A retail chain worked closely with its logistics provider to implement encrypted data sharing, reducing exposure to supply chain breaches.

Leveraging privacy-enhancing technologies

As organizations handle vast amounts of sensitive data, ensuring privacy while maintaining analytical capabilities has become a significant challenge. PETs offer advanced methods to protect data throughout its lifecycle, enabling secure processing, storage, and sharing. These technologies allow organizations to extract valuable insights without exposing or compromising individual data points. By integrating PETs, businesses can comply with stringent data privacy regulations while fostering trust and minimizing security risks.

The following PETs illustrate how innovative techniques can safeguard privacy without limiting the usability of data:

- **Homomorphic encryption:** It allows computations on encrypted data without decrypting it. This ensures privacy is maintained throughout data processing.

- **Secure multi-party computation:** It enables collaborative data analysis while preserving confidentiality. Ideal for cross-organization projects.

- **Differential privacy:** It introduces controlled noise to datasets, preventing individual data points from being re-identified. This is valuable for public data releases.

  For example, a government agency used homomorphic encryption to analyze census data without exposing personal details, preserving privacy while gaining insights.

Managing personal and sensitive data

Managing personal and sensitive data is at the heart of modern data privacy efforts. Organizations deal with vast amounts of personal data daily, from customer profiles to employee records. The effective management of this data is essential not only to meet legal and regulatory requirements but also to maintain trust and build a secure operational environment.

Understanding the distinction between personal and sensitive data is essential for developing effective security measures and ensuring regulatory compliance. Personal data refers to any information that can identify an individual, either directly or indirectly. This includes basic identifiers, such as names, email addresses, and phone numbers. Sensitive data, however, carries a higher risk if exposed and typically involves information, like medical records, financial details, or biometric identifiers. The classification of data dictates the level of protection required and influences data handling policies within organizations.

Personal data may relate to identifiable characteristics specific to an individual, such as physical or behavioral traits. In contrast, sensitive data often pertains to categories explicitly protected under privacy regulations, including information about racial or ethnic origin, religious beliefs, or criminal records. Proper classification is crucial for prioritizing security measures and aligning with both operational needs and regulatory frameworks.

The examples of personal data are as follows:

- Full name
- Email address
- Phone number
- Location data (IP address, GPS)

The examples of sensitive data are as follows:

- Genetic and biometric data
- Criminal records
- Health conditions or medical history
- Financial account numbers

By clearly defining and categorizing data, organizations can enhance their ability to protect sensitive information, mitigate risks, and comply with evolving data privacy laws.

This foundational step supports broader privacy initiatives and ensures responsible data stewardship.

Data collection and minimization

Data collection and minimization play a critical role in ensuring that organizations handle personal and sensitive data responsibly. This principle emphasizes limiting the scope and volume of data collected to only what is necessary for achieving specific, legitimate purposes. By reducing the amount of data collected, organizations can mitigate the risks associated with breaches, data leaks, and unauthorized access, fostering a more secure data environment.

Importance of data minimization

Minimizing data collection reduces an organization's overall data footprint, making it easier to manage and secure sensitive information. Excessive data collection not only increases the attack surface but can also lead to regulatory violations and loss of customer trust. Adopting data minimization helps organizations comply with privacy regulations, like the GDPR and CCPA, both of which stress the need for proportionality in data processing.

The key benefits of data minimization are as follows:

- **Reduced risk exposure:** Less data means fewer targets for hackers and lower consequences in the event of a breach.

- **Operational efficiency:** Streamlining data collection improves data processing times and reduces storage costs.

- **Regulatory compliance:** Data minimization aligns with legal mandates, protecting organizations from non-compliance penalties.

- **Enhanced user trust:** Collecting only necessary data reassures users that their privacy is respected and safeguarded.

Implementing data minimization

Implementing data minimization requires a structured approach to assess current data collection practices and identify areas for reduction. Organizations should evaluate each data point's relevance and necessity across the data lifecycle.

The steps to implement data minimization are as follows:

- **Conduct data audits:** Regularly review existing datasets to identify redundant or unnecessary information. Determine if each piece of data serves a clear and critical purpose.

- **Define clear collection policies:** Develop policies that outline the specific types of data that can be collected based on operational needs and legal obligations.

- **Limit data fields:** Reduce the number of required fields in forms and surveys to gather only essential information. For example, request age ranges instead of exact birth dates.

- **Regularly review and purge data:** Establish automated data retention schedules to delete obsolete or irrelevant data. Periodic data cleansing reduces clutter and mitigates privacy risks.

- **Example:** A financial services company previously collected extensive personal information during online account creation, including detailed employment histories and educational backgrounds. After a data audit, the firm reduced its form to only collect essential information like names, addresses, and income brackets, cutting data storage by 30% and minimizing breach exposure.

Anonymization and pseudonymization

Data minimization can be further strengthened through anonymization and pseudonymization, ensuring that personal data is transformed to prevent direct identification. By transforming identifiable data into de-identified formats, businesses can comply with privacy regulations and protect user information without sacrificing insights.

The following approaches illustrate how anonymization and pseudonymization contribute to secure data management:

- **Anonymization:** It irreversibly removes identifying information from datasets, making it impossible to trace data back to individuals.

- **Pseudonymization:** It replaces identifying fields with artificial identifiers or pseudonyms, allowing the data to remain useful while reducing privacy risks.

- **Example:** An e-commerce company analyzes purchasing trends by anonymizing customer profiles, ensuring that insights can be drawn without compromising personal privacy.

Challenges in data minimization

While the benefits of data minimization are significant, challenges may arise in balancing operational needs with privacy requirements. Businesses often feel compelled to gather large amounts of data for analytics and personalization purposes. However, through innovative technologies like differential privacy and privacy-enhancing computation, organizations can strike the right balance.

By embedding data minimization into the core of data governance frameworks, organizations not only protect sensitive information but also create more resilient, trustworthy systems that enhance long-term growth and security. In order to manage personal data responsibly, organizations should adhere to the principle of data minimization, collecting only the data necessary for specific, legitimate purposes. This limits exposure and reduces the risk of breaches.

The key steps to implement data minimization are as follows:

- Conduct data audits to identify unnecessary data collection.

- Establish clear policies regarding the data collection process.

- Regularly review and purge redundant data.

- **Example:** An online retailer, instead of collecting exact birth dates, asks customers to select an age range, minimizing sensitive information while still gaining useful demographic insights.

Data classification and tagging

Data classification and tagging are foundational practices for effective data governance and privacy management. By categorizing data according to its sensitivity and applying appropriate tags, organizations can enforce granular access controls, enhance security, and ensure compliance with regulatory frameworks. This process allows businesses to prioritize protection efforts, focusing on the most sensitive and high-risk information.

The classification levels are as follows:

- **Public data:** Information that can be freely shared without risk, such as press releases or marketing materials.

- **Internal data:** Proprietary information intended for internal use only, such as operational procedures or employee communications.

- **Confidential data:** Sensitive personal data or business-critical information that could cause significant harm if exposed, such as intellectual property or client records.

- **Restricted data:** The highest level of sensitivity, including financial records, health information, and trade secrets, which require the strictest access controls.

The key steps for effective data classification and tagging are as follows:

- **Identify data sources:** It catalogs all data repositories, including databases, cloud storage, and external platforms, to ensure comprehensive classification coverage.

- **Define classification criteria:** It establishes clear parameters for each classification level based on data type, regulatory requirements, and organizational risk appetite.

- **Automate tagging:** It leverages automated tools to consistently tag data as it is created or modified, reducing human error and ensuring scalability.

- **Monitor and update classifications:** It regularly reviews data classifications and adjusts as necessary to reflect changes in regulatory landscapes or business needs.

- **Example:** A multinational healthcare provider implemented automated classification tools that tagged patient medical records as restricted and internal reports as confidential. this ensured that sensitive health data was encrypted and accessible only to authorized personnel, reducing the likelihood of accidental disclosure or cyberattacks.

By embedding classification and tagging into their data lifecycle management strategies, organizations not only mitigate risk but also build a robust framework for managing data responsibly across diverse environments. Classifying data according to sensitivity levels ensures that higher-risk information receives the appropriate protection measures. Organizations can use automated tools to tag data, ensuring it is handled, stored, and transmitted according to its classification.

The classification levels are as follows:

- **Public data:** Information accessible to everyone.

- **Internal data:** Information restricted to employees.

- **Confidential data:** Business-critical or sensitive personal data.

- **Example:** A healthcare provider tags medical records as confidential and applies stringent access controls, allowing only authorized personnel to view them.

Data access and control policies

Limiting access to sensitive data is a cornerstone of data privacy, ensuring that only authorized individuals can interact with personal or confidential information. Effective data access and control policies reduce the risk of accidental exposure, data leaks, or malicious insider threats. Organizations must adopt comprehensive access frameworks that regulate permissions, enforce authentication, and maintain oversight through continuous monitoring.

The principles of access control are as follows:

- **Least privilege principle (LPP):** Users are granted the minimum access necessary to perform their job functions. This minimizes the potential impact of a compromised account.

- **Separation of duties:** Sensitive operations are divided among multiple users to prevent any single point of failure or abuse. For example, one employee may handle data entry while another reviews and approves transactions.

- **Role-based access control (RBAC):** Access is assigned based on predefined roles within the organization, streamlining permission management and ensuring consistency.

- **Attribute-based access control (ABAC):** Permissions are determined by evaluating multiple attributes, such as user location, device type, or time of access, providing a more granular level of control.

Implementing effective access policies

Effective access control is a fundamental aspect of data privacy, ensuring that only authorized individuals can interact with sensitive information. Without proper access policies, organizations risk data breaches, insider threats, and unauthorized exposure. Implementing robust identity verification, data segmentation, and monitoring mechanisms helps mitigate these risks while maintaining compliance with security regulations.

The following strategies outline key practices for enforcing secure and controlled access to critical data assets:

- **User identity verification:** Implement strong identity verification processes, such as MFA, to prevent unauthorized logins.

- **Data segmentation:** Segment data repositories based on sensitivity, restricting access to confidential data to higher-clearance personnel only.

- **Audit trails and monitoring:** Maintain detailed logs of all access attempts, successful or failed. Automated tools are used to analyze logs and detect unusual patterns or anomalies.

- **Time-limited access:** Provide temporary access for specific tasks, automatically revoking permissions once the task is completed.

Real-world example

A multinational bank implemented RBAC and enforced MFA for all employees accessing customer financial records. By doing so, unauthorized access attempts dropped by 30%, and the bank enhanced its compliance with financial data protection regulations.

Challenges and considerations

While access control policies significantly improve data security, challenges may arise in large organizations with complex hierarchical structures. Managing access across cloud environments, remote teams, and third-party vendors requires dynamic policy adjustments and regular reviews to ensure policies remain aligned with evolving risks.

Regular employee training and simulations further reinforce access control practices, ensuring that all personnel understand the importance of safeguarding sensitive data through proper access management. Limiting access to sensitive data is crucial for preventing unauthorized exposure. Organizations should implement robust access control mechanisms that operate on the principle of least privilege.

The best practices are as follows:

- Use RBAC to restrict data access based on job functions.
- Implement MFA for accessing sensitive data.
- Maintain logs to monitor data access and detect anomalies.

- **Example:** A financial services firm allows only senior financial analysts to access credit score data, while administrative staff have limited access to customer contact information.

Encryption and secure storage

Encrypting personal and sensitive data, both at rest and in transit, ensures that even if data is intercepted or accessed by unauthorized users, it remains unreadable.

The encryption techniques are as follows:

- **At Rest:** Encrypt databases and files where data is stored.

- **In Transit:** Use TLS/SSL encryption for data being transmitted.

- **Example:** A cloud-based application encrypts user passwords with AES-256 encryption and uses HTTPS for all communications.

Retention and disposal policies

Retention and disposal policies are critical components of data lifecycle management, ensuring that personal and sensitive data is not kept longer than necessary. Proper retention safeguards data from unauthorized access while ensuring compliance with regulatory requirements. Additionally, timely disposal reduces the risk of breaches by minimizing the volume of data stored. Organizations must establish clear guidelines that dictate how long data should be retained based on its purpose and legal obligations.

The steps to develop and implement retention policies are as follows:

- **Categorize data by sensitivity and usage:** Distinguish between different types of data and assign retention periods based on regulatory requirements and operational needs.

- **Define retention schedules:** Set specific timelines for retaining personal data, sensitive records, and operational information.

- **Automate deletion processes:** Leverage automated tools to delete data once retention periods expire. This minimizes human error and ensures consistency.

- **Secure disposal methods:** Use secure disposal techniques such as shredding physical records, digital wiping, or degaussing for electronic media to ensure data cannot be reconstructed.

- **Regular audits and updates:** Periodically review retention policies to ensure alignment with evolving laws and business processes.

- **Example:** A university implements a policy to retain student application data for two years post-graduation. After this period, records are securely purged, with anonymized data retained for analytical purposes. This approach not only mitigates potential privacy risks but also streamlines data storage practices.

By enforcing structured retention and disposal policies, organizations not only enhance data privacy but also foster trust with clients and stakeholders by demonstrating a commitment to responsible data management. Data should not be retained longer than necessary. Establishing retention schedules ensures that data is purged once its operational or legal necessity expires.

The steps to develop retention policies are as follows:

1. Categorize data based on retention needs.

2. Automate data deletion for expired records.

3. Ensure secure disposal methods, such as shredding or digital wiping.

    For example, a university deletes student application data two years after graduation, retaining only anonymized records for analysis.

Incident response and breach management

Incident response and breach management are critical pillars of an organization's overall data security strategy. Despite robust preventive measures, no system is entirely immune to breaches. An effective incident response plan not only mitigates damage but also ensures compliance with regulatory obligations, preserving the trust and confidence of stakeholders.

Key phases of incident response

A well-defined incident response plan is essential for mitigating the impact of security breaches and ensuring business continuity. Effective response strategies enable organizations to quickly detect, contain, and recover from security incidents while minimizing data loss and reputational damage. A structured approach to incident response ensures that security teams can act swiftly and efficiently, reducing downtime and exposure.

The key phases of incident response provide a systematic framework for handling security breaches. From preparation and detection to containment and recovery, each phase plays a crucial role in maintaining data integrity and regulatory compliance. Organizations that follow a structured incident response process can better anticipate cyber threats, improve response times, and refine security measures based on past incidents. Incident response is typically structured around the following key phases:

1. **Preparation:**

    - Develop and document comprehensive incident response policies.

    - Assemble an **incident response team** (**IRT**) with defined roles and responsibilities.

- Conduct regular training and simulate breach scenarios to refine the response process.

2. **Detection and analysis:**

   - Monitor networks, systems, and applications continuously for unusual activity.

   - Leverage automated threat detection tools and establish clear criteria for identifying potential incidents.

   - Analyze alerts and anomalies to determine the severity and scope of the breach.

3. **Containment:**

   - Implement immediate measures to prevent the breach from spreading, such as isolating affected systems.

   - Apply short-term containment to stabilize the situation while planning for long-term remediation.

4. **Eradication:**

   - Identify and remove the root cause of the breach, such as malicious software or compromised user accounts.

   - Patch vulnerabilities and update systems to prevent recurrence.

5. **Recovery:**

   - Restore affected systems and validate that they are functioning securely.

   - Monitor for any signs of residual threats to ensure complete remediation.

   - Resume normal operations in a phased approach to minimize further risks.

6. **Post-incident review:**

   - Conduct a thorough post-mortem analysis to evaluate the effectiveness of the response.

   - Document lessons learned and update incident response plans accordingly.

Share findings with relevant stakeholders and use insights to strengthen security protocols.

Communication and transparency

Effective communication is a cornerstone of breach management. Organizations must develop communication plans that outline. The following key elements outline the essential components of a robust breach communication strategy:

- How to notify affected individuals promptly and transparently.

- When to inform regulatory bodies in accordance with data protection laws (e.g., GDPR, HIPAA).

- The messaging strategy for media and public relations to maintain customer trust.

The following pie chart provides a visual representation of the primary causes of data breaches, highlighting the significant role of phishing attacks, weak passwords, insider threats, malware/ransomware, physical theft, and other factors:

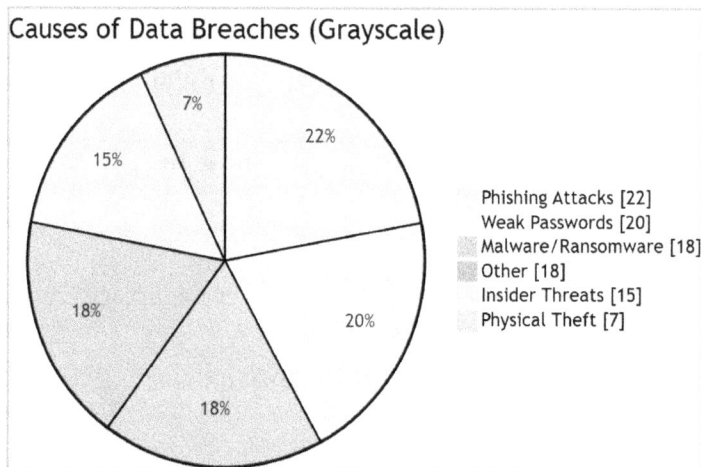

Causes of Data Breaches (Grayscale)

Phishing Attacks [22]
Weak Passwords [20]
Malware/Ransomware [18]
Other [18]
Insider Threats [15]
Physical Theft [7]

Figure 11.2: Distribution of causes of data breaches

In 2020, a global healthcare provider experienced a ransomware attack that compromised patient data. The organization's well-rehearsed incident response plan enabled rapid containment, followed by immediate communication with patients and regulatory authorities. The provider implemented new endpoint detection tools and launched a comprehensive employee cybersecurity awareness campaign to prevent future incidents.

Data privacy in the cloud

As organizations increasingly migrate their operations and data storage to the cloud, the complexities surrounding data privacy multiply. While cloud environments offer unmatched scalability, efficiency, and cost-effectiveness, they also introduce unique risks and challenges in maintaining the confidentiality and integrity of sensitive information. The shift to cloud-based systems demands that organizations rethink their data privacy strategies to protect sensitive information against breaches, unauthorized access, and compliance violations.

Cloud computing environments inherently operate on shared resources and infrastructure, which can expose data to vulnerabilities not typically encountered in traditional on-premises systems. This interconnected nature of cloud services necessitates a collaborative approach to data privacy, where **cloud service providers** (**CSPs**) and client organizations share the responsibility for safeguarding data. However, the delineation of responsibilities can often blur, requiring organizations to adopt comprehensive policies that govern data ownership, access control, and encryption practices.

Understanding shared responsibility model

The shared responsibility model is a foundational principle in cloud data privacy, dictating that while CSPs are responsible for the security of the cloud infrastructure, clients must secure the data they store and process within it. This division of duties can vary depending on the type of cloud service employed **infrastructure as a service (IaaS)**, **platform as a service (PaaS)**, or **software as a service (SaaS)**. In IaaS environments, clients manage applications, data, and operating systems, while the CSP ensures the physical security of servers and networking hardware. In SaaS models, the provider handles nearly all aspects of security, with the client mainly responsible for configuring user permissions and access policies.

Failure to clearly understand and act on these responsibilities can lead to vulnerabilities, as data may be exposed through misconfigurations, lax access controls, or weak encryption protocols. This underscores the importance of conducting regular audits and assessments to evaluate both the CSP's security measures and the organization's internal data protection policies.

Encryption as a cornerstone of cloud privacy

Encryption plays a critical role in protecting data privacy within cloud environments. By encoding data in a way that only authorized parties can decipher, encryption ensures that even if data is intercepted or accessed without permission, it remains unintelligible. Effective encryption strategies cover data in transit, as it moves between users and cloud environments, data at rest when stored in cloud repositories, and data in use (during processing). Cloud platforms often provide native encryption services, but organizations must determine whether to rely solely on these offerings or implement additional encryption layers.

One significant challenge with encryption in the cloud is managing encryption keys. If encryption keys are stored within the same environment as the data, the security of the entire system could be compromised in the event of a breach. **Key management solutions (KMS)** offer a pathway to securely store and manage keys outside the cloud environment, reducing the risk of exposure. Companies may also opt for client-side encryption, encrypting data before it enters the cloud, ensuring that even CSPs cannot access sensitive information.

Access control and identity management

Controlling who can access data in the cloud is fundamental to ensuring privacy. IAM solutions allow organizations to enforce strict policies regarding who can view, modify, and share data stored in the cloud. IAM frameworks utilize RBAC, MFA, and fine-grained permissions to limit data access to authorized personnel only. This prevents accidental or malicious data exposure and aligns with regulatory requirements for managing sensitive information.

Cloud environments introduce additional complexities, as data often spans multiple geographic regions, making it necessary to account for differing data protection laws. Implementing geofencing techniques and location-based access controls helps organizations ensure that data resides within specific jurisdictions, mitigating the risks associated with cross-border data transfers.

Regulatory compliance and data governance

Cloud adoption does not absolve organizations of their responsibilities to comply with data privacy regulations, such as the GDPR, CCPA, and HIPAA. Cloud environments often necessitate more rigorous compliance efforts, as data may traverse multiple legal jurisdictions. Data governance frameworks serve as a roadmap for navigating these complexities and establishing protocols for data classification, retention, and deletion.

Organizations must carefully vet CSPs to ensure they align with industry-specific compliance standards and maintain comprehensive audit trails that document data access, modifications, and transfers. By integrating **data loss prevention** (DLP) tools, companies can monitor cloud environments for potential breaches and enforce policies that prevent unauthorized data sharing.

Incident response and breach management in the cloud

Despite best efforts, data breaches can and do occur in cloud environments. A robust incident response plan tailored for cloud deployments is essential for minimizing damage and restoring normal operations. This plan should outline the roles and responsibilities of internal teams, as well as coordinate with CSPs to ensure seamless communication during a breach.

Key elements of a cloud-focused incident response plan include automated breach detection, containment strategies that isolate affected cloud instances, and forensic analysis to determine the root cause. Additionally, organizations must establish transparent communication channels to notify affected users and regulatory bodies promptly, aligning with legal requirements for breach disclosures.

Emerging technologies in cloud data privacy

Emerging technologies are reshaping how organizations approach data privacy in the cloud. Confidential computing, for example, enables data to be processed within secure enclaves, shielding sensitive information from unauthorized access even during computation. Similarly, homomorphic encryption allows computations to occur on encrypted data, removing the need for decryption and thereby reducing exposure risks.

Another innovation is the **zero-trust architecture** (ZTA), which assumes that no entity, internal or external, is inherently trustworthy. Under this model, every access request is rigorously authenticated, and continuous monitoring is conducted to identify and respond to anomalies. ZTA aligns well with cloud environments, reinforcing data privacy through micro-segmentation and dynamic access controls.

Future of cloud data privacy

As cloud technologies evolve, so will the strategies for safeguarding data privacy. The increasing adoption of AI and ML in cloud environments presents both opportunities and challenges. AI can enhance security by identifying patterns indicative of breaches, but it can also introduce new privacy risks if models are trained on sensitive data without appropriate safeguards.

Organizations must remain vigilant, continuously adapting their data privacy frameworks to account for technological advancements and shifting regulatory landscapes. By embedding data privacy into the core of cloud operations, businesses can not only protect their assets but also foster greater trust with customers and stakeholders in an increasingly digital world.

AI and data privacy

As AI becomes increasingly woven into the fabric of our digital world, its role in data privacy has become a subject of paramount importance. The capabilities of AI to process massive datasets, detect patterns, and automate decisions have unlocked unparalleled opportunities across industries. However, this advancement brings with it complex challenges regarding the protection of sensitive information and the ethical use of personal data. Balancing innovation with the need for stringent privacy measures has become essential as organizations seek to leverage AI without compromising data security.

Intersection of AI and data privacy

AI systems thrive on data. The larger and more diverse the dataset, the better the model can perform. This reliance on data raises significant privacy concerns, particularly when AI applications involve personal, medical, or financial information. The very attributes that make AI powerful, such as its ability to correlate disparate data points, can also make it invasive. For instance, an AI system designed for personalized marketing may inadvertently reveal sensitive information about an individual's health conditions, income level, or family dynamics through indirect analysis.

Furthermore, the use of AI in facial recognition, surveillance, and predictive analytics has ignited debates around consent, surveillance capitalism, and potential overreach by corporations and governments. The intersection of AI and data privacy thus represents a double-edged sword, offering enhanced efficiency while posing risks to individual rights and freedoms.

AI models and data leakage

One of the key challenges associated with AI is the risk of data leakage. Even anonymized datasets can become vulnerable when processed by AI algorithms capable of re-identifying individuals through subtle patterns and correlations. Model inversion attacks, for example, enable malicious actors to reconstruct sensitive input data by exploiting access to an AI model's predictions. Similarly, membership inference attacks can determine if a particular record was part of a training dataset, posing direct threats to privacy.

These vulnerabilities underscore the need for organizations to implement rigorous safeguards throughout the AI lifecycle, from data collection to model deployment. Differential privacy, which introduces noise to datasets, has emerged as a promising technique to protect individual records while preserving analytical utility. Federated learning, another innovative approach, allows AI models to train across decentralized data sources without directly accessing raw data, thereby enhancing privacy.

Implementing privacy-enhancing AI

In order to address the privacy risks posed by AI, organizations must adopt privacy-enhancing technologies and integrate data protection measures directly into AI systems.

It involves the following:

- **Embedding privacy by design**: AI systems should incorporate privacy principles from the ground up, ensuring that data minimization, anonymization, and user consent are foundational aspects of the development process.

- **Regular auditing and monitoring**: Continuous evaluation of AI systems can help identify potential privacy risks, biases, and vulnerabilities, allowing organizations to proactively address issues before they escalate.

- **Transparency and explainability**: AI models must be interpretable, enabling users to understand how decisions are made and providing avenues to challenge or correct inaccuracies. Transparent AI fosters trust and ensures accountability in data-driven processes.

- **Access controls and encryption**: Limiting access to sensitive data and employing robust encryption methods can prevent unauthorized use and safeguard information from internal and external threats.

Case study of AI in healthcare

The healthcare sector exemplifies both the promises and pitfalls of AI in data privacy. AI-driven diagnostics, predictive analytics, and personalized treatment plans offer significant advancements in patient care. However, these applications require vast quantities of sensitive health data, raising concerns about confidentiality and data breaches.

A major hospital network implemented AI tools to analyze patient records and predict disease outbreaks. By adopting federated learning, the hospital ensured that AI models could train patient data across multiple facilities without exposing individual records. This approach not only improved diagnostic accuracy but also safeguarded patient privacy, setting a precedent for responsible AI adoption in healthcare.

AI on personal machines

Running AI models on personal devices represents a shift towards localized, user-controlled AI that mitigates some privacy risks associated with cloud-based systems. By processing data directly on personal machines, users can retain greater control over their information, reducing exposure to external threats.

However, this approach introduces its own set of challenges. Personal devices often lack the computational power necessary for complex AI tasks, limiting the scope of applications. Additionally, securing AI models on local machines becomes critical to prevent unauthorized access and tampering.

Despite these challenges, advancements in edge AI and lightweight neural networks are making it increasingly feasible to deploy AI locally. Privacy-conscious users and organizations are exploring this avenue to balance functionality with data protection.

As AI continues to evolve, so must the frameworks governing data privacy. Regulatory bodies are beginning to introduce guidelines specifically addressing AI-related privacy risks, emphasizing the importance of ethical AI development. Organizations that prioritize privacy as a core tenet of their AI strategies will not only mitigate legal risks but also foster trust and loyalty among users.

In the coming years, the symbiotic relationship between AI and data privacy will shape the future of technology, necessitating continuous innovation and vigilance. By embracing privacy-enhancing technologies and ethical AI practices, businesses can harness the transformative potential of AI while safeguarding the fundamental rights of individuals.

Case studies and industry insights

Data privacy has become an essential pillar of operational integrity and customer trust across industries. The practical implementation of privacy frameworks and technologies is best understood through real-world examples that highlight successes, lessons learned, and innovative approaches to safeguarding sensitive information. In this section, we will explore three compelling case studies that demonstrate how organizations have navigated the complexities of data privacy, offering insights that can inform and guide future initiatives.

GDPR compliance in global retail

A multinational retail corporation with a significant online and physical presence faced the challenge of aligning its data privacy practices with the European Union's GDPR. With millions of customers' data collected through loyalty programs, e-commerce platforms, and in-store transactions, the company needed to overhaul its data handling processes to ensure compliance.

One of the challenges can be that the organization lacked a centralized system to manage personal data, leading to inconsistencies in how customer information was processed across regions. There was also limited transparency regarding data-sharing practices with third-party vendors.

The solution to this problem can be:

- **Data mapping and inventory:** The company conducted an exhaustive data mapping exercise to identify all points of data collection and storage. This included databases, third-party marketing platforms, and legacy systems.

- **Consent management platform:** A robust consent management system was introduced, providing users with clear options to manage their data preferences at every touchpoint.

- **Vendor audits:** Third-party vendors processing personal data were required to comply with GDPR standards. Contracts were revised to include **data processing agreements (DPAs)**.

- **Employee training:** A series of workshops and e-learning modules were rolled out to educate employees on GDPR requirements and the importance of handling customer data responsibly.

  - **Outcome:** The company achieved full GDPR compliance by the regulation's enforcement date, avoiding hefty fines and enhancing its reputation as a privacy-conscious brand. Customer trust improved, resulting in increased engagement across digital platforms.

  - **Key takeaway:** Comprehensive data mapping and proactive vendor management are crucial components of a successful privacy compliance strategy.

Healthcare data protection and HIPAA compliance

A regional healthcare provider in the United States faced growing concerns over data security breaches targeting sensitive patient information. With a combination of physical and digital records, the organization needed to secure **personal health information (PHI)** to comply with HIPAA.

One of the challenges can be that the healthcare provider struggles with fragmented data storage systems, outdated encryption methods, and insufficient access controls for medical staff.

The solution to this problem can be:

- **Encryption across systems:** The organization implemented end-to-end encryption for all EHRs, ensuring data was secure both at rest and in transit.

- **Role-based access control:** Medical personnel were granted access to data based on their specific roles, limiting unnecessary exposure to sensitive information.

- **Incident response plan:** A detailed incident response framework was developed to address potential breaches swiftly and mitigate damage.

- **Audit trails:** Comprehensive audit logs were introduced to monitor data access and track changes to patient records.

  o **Outcome:** By modernizing its data protection measures, the healthcare provider significantly reduced unauthorized access incidents and ensured full HIPAA compliance. In the event of audits, the organization consistently demonstrated robust data governance practices.

  o **Key takeaway:** Implementing encryption and role-based access controls are fundamental to safeguarding sensitive healthcare data and ensuring compliance with regulatory frameworks.

Data privacy in financial services using AI

A large financial services firm sought to leverage AI-driven analytics to personalize customer offerings while maintaining stringent data privacy controls. The company needed to balance innovation with regulatory requirements, ensuring that AI models did not inadvertently compromise sensitive customer information.

One of the challenges can be that the AI algorithms require extensive datasets to deliver accurate insights, raising concerns about the overexposure of personal and financial data. Additionally, there was a risk of AI models unintentionally memorizing or leaking sensitive details.

The solution to this problem can be:

- **Differential privacy techniques:** The firm integrated differential privacy into its AI workflows, injecting statistical noise into datasets to obscure individual identities while preserving overall data utility.

- **Federated learning:** AI models were trained locally on user devices, ensuring that raw data remained decentralized and never left the client's infrastructure.

- **Model auditing and testing:** Regular audits of AI models were conducted to identify potential privacy risks, with stringent validation processes to prevent data leakage.

- **Transparency for users:** Customers were informed about how their data was used for AI personalization, with opt-out options made readily available.

  ○ **Outcome:** The financial services firm successfully rolled out AI-driven features without compromising customer privacy. The integration of federated learning set a new benchmark in privacy-conscious innovation within the sector.

  ○ **Key takeaway:** Leveraging privacy-enhancing technologies, such as differential privacy and federated learning, allows organizations to harness the power of AI without exposing sensitive data.

Conclusion

As illustrated by the case studies, the path to achieving robust data privacy involves not only technological innovation but also a strong cultural and organizational commitment to ethical data practices. By addressing privacy challenges head-on and integrating frameworks, such as GDPR, HIPAA, and AI-enhancing privacy techniques, organizations can foster trust, protect sensitive information, and drive growth. The evolving nature of privacy regulations and the increasing complexity of data ecosystems demand continuous improvement and vigilance.

In the next chapter, we will shift our focus from privacy-centric strategies to real-world examples of scalable data engineering frameworks. These case studies will highlight the architectural decisions, tools, and methodologies that underpin successful large-scale data systems, offering valuable insights into how engineering excellence intersects with the principles of privacy and security.

Join our book's Discord space

Join the book's Discord Workspace for Latest updates, Offers, Tech happenings around the world, New Release and Sessions with the Authors:

https://discord.bpbonline.com

CHAPTER 12

Data Engineering Case Studies

Introduction

Data engineering is the foundation of modern data-driven organizations, enabling businesses to efficiently collect, store, process, and analyze vast volumes of data. As companies increasingly rely on data for decision-making, real-world implementations of scalable data pipelines, real-time analytics, and seamless data integration become essential. Building upon previous discussions on data collection, ingestion, storage, and processing, this chapter explores how these concepts are applied in practice.

Through case studies across industries such as e-commerce, finance, and healthcare, this chapter illustrates how organizations have addressed data challenges using modern data engineering principles. From eliminating data silos and optimizing large-scale data pipelines to enhancing fraud detection and integrating disparate data sources, these real-world examples provide a practical perspective on designing and implementing robust data solutions.

This chapter explores how organizations apply modern data engineering practices to solve real-world challenges. As businesses increasingly rely on data for strategic decision-making, it's essential to understand not just the tools and techniques, but how they come together in practice. This chapter builds on earlier discussions around data collection, ingestion, processing, and storage by presenting concrete case studies from e-commerce, finance, and healthcare.

Each case study demonstrates how scalable, secure, and intelligent data systems can drive better outcomes from improved customer experiences to faster medical decisions. By exploring these implementations, this chapter offers practical insights and key lessons that can inform future data engineering projects across industries.

Structure

The chapter covers the following topics:

- Scalable data pipeline for e-commerce
- Real-time analytics in finance
- Data integration in healthcare
- Practical takeaways and recommended approaches

Objectives

By the end of this chapter, readers will have a practical insight into how organizations apply data engineering principles to solve real-world challenges. As businesses increasingly rely on data-driven decision-making, scalable and efficient data pipelines become essential. Through a series of case studies spanning industries such as e-commerce, finance, and healthcare, this chapter demonstrates how companies design, implement, and optimize data infrastructure to handle large-scale operations effectively. Readers will gain a deeper understanding of how data engineering frameworks support real-time analytics, enhance performance, and drive innovation.

A key focus of this chapter is on scalability, as organizations must continuously adapt their data architectures to accommodate growing data volumes and evolving business needs. The case studies highlight strategies for overcoming system bottlenecks, integrating disparate data sources, and leveraging distributed processing frameworks to ensure efficiency. Additionally, the chapter delves into how businesses enhance customer experiences through AI-powered data pipelines, enabling personalized recommendations, fraud detection, and predictive insights.

Beyond technical implementations, this chapter also addresses critical aspects of data governance, security, and compliance. It explores how organizations manage regulatory requirements, implement data privacy controls, and enforce monitoring mechanisms to maintain data integrity. By examining industry best practices, lessons learned, and emerging trends, this chapter equips readers with the knowledge needed to design resilient and future-ready data pipelines.

Scalable data pipeline for e-commerce

A multinational e-commerce giant operating in over 120 countries, experienced unprecedented growth, surpassing 500 million users. With a 250% increase in transaction volumes over three years, the company managed an extensive catalog exceeding 20 million products. The platform generates terabytes of data daily through user interactions, including search queries, product views, and transaction records.

Despite impressive growth metrics, the company's data architecture lagged in scalability, leading to performance bottlenecks during high-traffic events. This shortfall hindered the ability to provide real-time personalization, slowing down analytics pipelines and creating silos across departments. Consequently, the customer experience suffered, resulting in revenue losses and increased customer churn.

The key statistics are as follows:

- **Users**: 500 million
- **Countries**: 120
- **Product catalog**: 20 million products
- **Daily data volume**: Terabytes (from search logs, purchase history, IoT)
- **Growth rate**: 250% increase in transactions over three years

Problem statement

As the company grew bigger and handled more customers, problems with their data made things harder. This section explains three main problems, data stuck in different departments, slow systems, and trouble handling too many users at once, all of which affected sales and customer happiness.

Data silos

Departments such as marketing, logistics, and sales managed their data independently, preventing seamless integration. This fragmentation limited the ability to extract unified insights into customer behavior, inventory, and supply chain trends.

The implications are as follows:

- Cross-department analytics required extensive manual data reconciliation, delaying critical decisions.
- Lack of shared data pipelines restricted collaboration between teams.

Latency in analytics

The e-commerce platform relied on batch processing, causing delays of up to six hours between data ingestion and insight generation. This latency impeded real-time personalization and dynamic pricing strategies.

The implications are as follows:

- Users received outdated product recommendations, negatively impacting conversion rates.

- Price adjustments during promotional campaigns were delayed, leading to inventory mismanagement.

Scalability concerns

During peak events, like *Black Friday*, the platform experienced severe load spikes, causing system lags and cart abandonment rates to surge by 18%.

The implications are as follows:

- Revenue losses of $15 million annually due to scalability limitations.

- Operational inefficiencies required manual scaling interventions, resulting in inconsistent user experiences.

Solution design

In order to address these challenges, the company redesigned its data architecture, implementing a scalable and distributed data pipeline leveraging, as follows:

- **Apache Kafka** for real-time data ingestion.
- **Apache Spark Structured Streaming** for distributed, scalable data processing.
- **AWS Redshift** as the central data warehouse.
- **TensorFlow** for AI-driven personalization and recommendation engines.

High-level architecture diagram

The architecture shown below illustrates a scalable data pipeline for an e-commerce platform, showcasing the integration of various data sources such as web platforms, mobile apps, IoT devices, and third-party services. Data flows into the system through the ingestion layer powered by Apache Kafka, which handles real-time event streaming. Apache Spark processes the ingested data in micro-batches, reducing latency and enabling faster analytics. Processed data is stored in AWS Redshift, optimized for efficient querying and parallel processing. The AI layer, driven by TensorFlow models, uses the processed data to deliver personalized recommendations, enhancing the user experience.

Figure 12.1 provides a high-level overview of the scalable data pipeline implemented by the e-commerce platform. It illustrates the flow of data from multiple sources through real-time ingestion and processing layers to centralized storage and AI-powered analytics, highlighting how each component contributes to delivering low-latency, personalized user experiences:

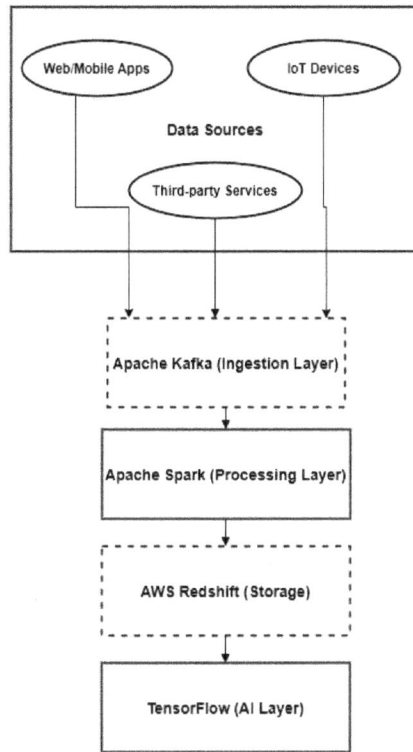

Figure 12.1: A streamlined data flow from ingestion to AI-driven insights

Implementation steps

In order to overcome data silos and enable real-time decision-making; the company implemented a scalable data pipeline designed to handle millions of events per minute. This involved transforming how data was ingested, processed, stored, and utilized for AI-driven personalization. The following sections break down each stage of the pipeline, highlighting the technologies and code implementations that powered this transformation.

Data ingestion layer

The data ingestion layer serves as the entry point for capturing and streaming vast amounts of real-time data from diverse sources. Apache Kafka was chosen to manage this layer due to its ability to handle high-throughput data ingestion and its durability in distributed environments.

Kafka's role was pivotal in capturing over 3 million events per minute from platforms, such as mobile apps, websites, IoT devices, and third-party services (payment gateways, customer service platforms). This allowed the e-commerce platform to track user interactions, product searches, purchases, and customer support activities in real-time.

Kafka's advantages are as follows:

- **Scalability**: Kafka's distributed architecture allows horizontal scaling, ensuring data can flow continuously without bottlenecks.

- **Durability**: Kafka logs events persistently, guaranteeing no data loss even during failures.

- **Fault tolerance**: Data is replicated across multiple brokers, safeguarding against node failures.

Pre-requisites:

1. **Install Kafka**: Download and extract Kafka using **wget** and **tar**.

2. **Start Zookeeper and Kafka**: Run **bin/zookeeper-server-start.sh** and **bin/ kafka-server-start.sh**.

3. **Verify Kafka is running**: Check topics with **bin/kafka-topics.sh --list --bootstrap-server localhost:9092**.

4. **Create Kafka topic**: Use **bin/kafka-topics.sh --create --topic transactions --bootstrap-server localhost:9092**.

5. **Install Kafka dependencies for Spark**: Start pyspark with **--packages org. apache.spark:spark-sql-kafka-0-10_2.12**.

6. **In the below code Spark streaming code**: Ensure **kafka.bootstrap.servers** is set to **localhost:9092**, if running locally.

7. **Run Spark Streaming Job**: Execute **spark-submit your_script.py** with required Kafka dependencies.

The technical implementation is as follows:

```
from pyspark.sql import SparkSession
from pyspark.sql.functions import col

# Initialize Spark Session for real-time streaming
spark = SparkSession.builder \
    .appName("EcommercePipeline") \
    .config("spark.sql.streaming.checkpointLocation", "/tmp/checkpoints") \
    .getOrCreate()

# Stream data from Kafka
data_stream = spark.readStream.format("kafka") \
    .option("kafka.bootstrap.servers", "kafka:9092") \
    .option("subscribe", "transactions") \
```

```
    .option("startingOffsets", "latest") \
    .load()

# Extract and transform Kafka event data
processed_data = data_stream.selectExpr("CAST(value AS STRING)") \
    .select(col("value").alias("transaction_data"))

# Display schema for debugging purposes
processed_data.printSchema()
```

The code snippet explanation is as follows:

- **Spark session initialization**: A streaming Spark session is created to interact with Kafka and handle real-time ingestion.

- **Kafka connection**: Kafka brokers are specified along with the topic (transactions) from which events will be consumed.

- **Streaming mode**: The code ensures events are continuously read (**readStream**), and new events are captured as they arrive.

- **Schema validation**: The **printSchema()** function is used to verify data ingestion and confirm successful event capture.

The achievements are as follows:

- **Microservices integration**: Kafka enables modular ingestion from over 150 sources by allowing various services, like payment systems, support platforms, etc., to independently push data into dedicated Kafka topics.

- **Traffic handling**: The ingestion pipeline easily scales during promotional events like Black Friday, ensuring uninterrupted event capture.

- **Event persistence**: Kafka's log retention ensures data recovery even if downstream processing fails temporarily.

Data processing layer

Real-time data processing is crucial to analyze and transform raw events into actionable insights. Apache Spark Structured Streaming processes incoming Kafka streams in micro-batches, drastically reducing the previous delay of ten minutes to under one second.

This stage ensures that data pipelines provide near-instantaneous insights, supporting dynamic pricing, fraud detection, and product recommendations.

The following is an explanation on how Spark Structured Streaming enhances data workflows, reducing processing delays and enabling real-time decision-making:

- **Scalability**: Spark distributes workloads across clusters, ensuring seamless processing of high-velocity data.

- **Fault tolerance**: In case of node failure, Spark automatically retries tasks, preventing data loss.

- **Efficiency**: Spark micro-batching processes large volumes of data while maintaining low latency.

The technical implementation is as follows:

Note: This snippet uses variables like `processed_data` from above snippet of code.

```
from pyspark.sql.functions import from_json, schema_of_json


# Define the schema for incoming JSON data
schema = schema_of_json('{"user_id":"string", "product_id":"string",
"price":"float"}')


# Parse incoming data from Kafka
json_parsed = processed_data.select(
    from_json(col("transaction_data"), schema).alias("data")
).select("data.*")


# Show parsed data for verification
json_parsed.show()
```

The code snippet explanation is as follows:

- **Schema definition**: A JSON schema (**user_id**, **product_id**, **price**) is defined to deserialize Kafka event data.

- **Data transformation**: Events are parsed into structured formats using the schema, making the data suitable for downstream aggregation and analytics.

- **Real-time parsing**: Each Kafka message is transformed into a tabular format for further enrichment or storage.

The key highlights are as follows:

- **Micro-batching**: By reducing batch intervals to one second, the system processes near real-time streams for quicker insights.

- **Scalable processing**: Distributed Spark clusters handle millions of records concurrently, enabling the system to scale as traffic increases.

- **Use case**: The parsed data is immediately pushed into personalization engines to adjust product recommendations dynamically based on user activity.

Data storage and querying

Efficient querying and storage are essential to ensure fast data retrieval. Processed data is loaded into AWS Redshift, a petabyte-scale data warehouse optimized for fast analytical queries.

Dynamic partitioning and materialized views enable faster data aggregation, reducing query response times from 20 seconds to under three seconds.

AWS Redshift offers a petabyte-scale architecture designed for performance, scalability, and cost efficiency, making it ideal for handling complex analytical workloads. The following are the key features:

- **Performance**: Redshift's columnar storage and **massively parallel processing (MPP)** ensure lightning-fast queries.
- **Scalability**: Redshift scales to handle terabytes of data.
- **Cost-effective**: It provides efficient data compression, reducing storage costs.

The technical implementation is as follows:

```
json_parsed.write \
    .format("jdbc") \
    .option("url", "jdbc:redshift://redshift-cluster:5439/ecommerce") \
    .option("dbtable", "transactions") \
    .option("user", "admin") \
    .option("password", "password123") \
    .save()
```

The code snippet explanation is as follows:

- **JDBC connection**: Redshift is accessed through a JDBC driver for batch inserts.
- **Dynamic partitioning**: Data is partitioned by region, time, and product category to enable faster filtering.
- **Security**: Connections are encrypted to protect sensitive data during transmission.

Optimization techniques include:

- **Partitioning**: Data is split by country and sales data to improve query performance.
- **Materialized views**: Pre-computed views enable quicker aggregations and reduce runtime query load.

AI-powered personalization

AI models play a vital role in providing personalized user experiences by analyzing historical and real-time data. TensorFlow models were trained on 18 months of user activity to recommend products dynamically.

The models leveraged reinforcement learning techniques, adapting recommendations based on real-time user interactions.

To build scalable and intelligent personalization systems, TensorFlow serves as a powerful deep learning framework. It enables efficient processing of vast datasets, supports complex neural network architectures, and seamlessly integrates with distributed computing environments, as follows:

- **Performance**: TensorFlow efficiently handles large datasets.

- **Flexibility**: It supports various neural network architectures.

- **Ease of Integration**: TensorFlow integrates with Spark for distributed training.

The technical implementation is as follows:

```
import tensorflow as tf
from tensorflow import keras


model = keras.Sequential([
    keras.layers.Dense(128, activation='relu'),
    keras.layers.Dense(64, activation='relu'),
    keras.layers.Dense(10, activation='softmax')
])


model.compile(optimizer='adam', loss='sparse_categorical_crossentropy',
metrics=['accuracy'])
```

The code snippet explanation is as follows:

- **Model design**: A three-layer neural network generates predictions based on user activity.

- **Optimization**: Adam optimizer ensures faster convergence during training.

- **Accuracy monitoring**: Real-time metrics track prediction accuracy.

The results are as follows:

- **Latency reduction**: From 6 hours to 30 seconds.

- **Sales uplift**: 21% increase in average order value.

- **Operational efficiency**: $1.2 million annual savings.

- **Scalability**: 400% traffic increase without downtime.

Real-time analytics in finance

A global financial services firm, managing assets exceeding $500 billion across 60 countries, faced critical challenges in delivering real-time insights. The firm processed millions of transactions daily from mobile banking apps, credit card networks, and international trading platforms. As financial markets evolved rapidly, the need for immediate fraud detection, risk assessment, and personalized client services grew significantly.

Despite investing in traditional data warehouses and analytical platforms, the firm's reliance on batch-processing architectures introduced significant delays. This slowed down decision-making, impacted client trust, and posed compliance risks in highly regulated environments.

Key statistics include:

- **Assets managed**: $500 billion
- **Countries operated in**: 60
- **Daily transactions**: 75 million
- **User base**: 120 million global clients

Problem statement

With the surge in global financial transactions and increasingly sophisticated cyber threats, the firm faced pressing issues across three major areas: fraud detection, data fragmentation, and regulatory reporting. Addressing these pain points was essential for maintaining customer confidence and ensuring operational resilience.

Delayed fraud detection

The firm's existing fraud detection mechanisms relied heavily on batch processing of transactional data, often resulting in delayed identification of fraudulent activities. This reactive approach allowed malicious transactions to go unnoticed for several hours, exposing the organization to significant financial losses.

The implications are as follows:

- Delay in blocking fraudulent transactions caused an estimated annual loss of $25 million.
- Customer trust deteriorated, with 10% of clients expressing dissatisfaction over fraud handling.
- Regulatory scrutiny increased, with potential penalties for delayed fraud reporting.

Data fragmentation across divisions

Data silos across different financial services, including retail banking, investment banking, and insurance, prevented the firm from forming comprehensive customer profiles. This fragmentation impeded seamless client experiences and limited cross-department collaboration.

The implications include:

- Inconsistent services, leading to a 12% loss in potential cross-selling opportunities.

- Disjointed customer interactions affected the firm's brand reputation.

Regulatory reporting lag

Generating regulatory compliance reports involved manual reconciliation and data aggregation, resulting in reporting delays of up to 24 hours. This posed significant risks as financial authorities demanded real-time or near-real-time reporting for certain transactions.

The implications include:

- Potential penalties exceeding $10 million annually for late reporting.

- Operational teams allocated excessive time to compiling reports, diverting focus from core business activities.

Solution design

In order to overcome these challenges, the firm developed a real-time analytics infrastructure capable of processing large transaction volumes at sub-second intervals. This solution integrated cutting-edge data streaming technologies, distributed processing frameworks, and advanced machine learning models to automate fraud detection and optimize reporting.

The architecture was designed around the following:

- **Amazon Kinesis**: Real-time ingestion and streaming of financial transactions.

- **Apache Flink**: Stream processing for transforming raw data into actionable insights.

- **Elasticsearch**: Rapid querying and anomaly detection.

- **Scikit-learn**: Machine learning-based fraud detection models.

High-level architecture diagram

Figure 12.2 illustrates the seamless flow of data from ingestion to analytics. Kinesis acts as the core ingestion service, streaming data to Apache Flink, which processes transactions in real-time. Processed data is stored in Elasticsearch for low-latency querying and is also routed to Scikit-learn for fraud detection modeling.

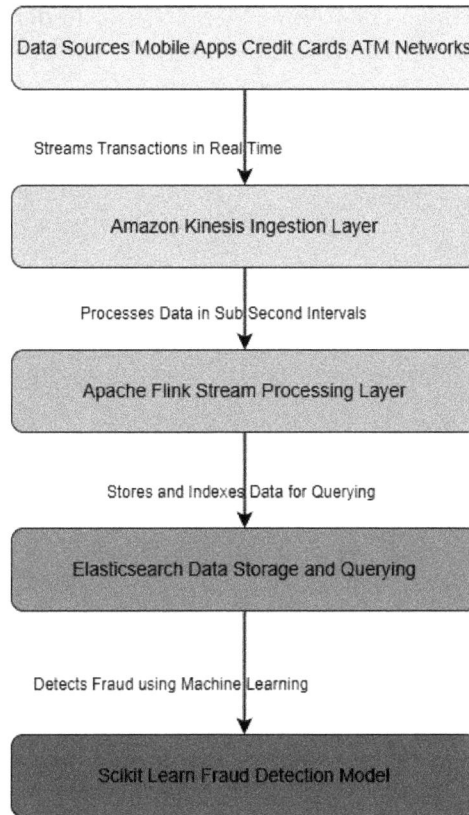

Figure 12.2: *Real-time analytics architecture for fraud detection*

Implementation steps

Implementing real-time analytics required upgrading the existing infrastructure to accommodate high-velocity data while ensuring system resilience. A step-by-step breakdown of the process, outlining key technologies, implementation details, and their significance in achieving real-time insights.

Data ingestion layer

The first step involved deploying Amazon Kinesis to ingest transaction data from multiple sources, including mobile banking applications, credit card transactions, and ATM networks. Kinesis allowed the firm to capture and stream over 200,000 events per second.

This ingestion layer ensured that transactional data was streamed in real-time, enabling immediate downstream processing for fraud detection and reporting. The following code snippet demonstrates how Amazon Kinesis is used to ingest transaction data in real time. It streams financial transactions from multiple sources, ensuring rapid processing for fraud detection and reporting. The following Python code demonstrates how to send a single transaction record to an Amazon Kinesis stream named **transaction_stream** using the **boto3** library:

```
from boto3 import client

kinesis_client = client('kinesis')

response = kinesis_client.put_record(
    StreamName='transaction_stream',
    Data=b'{"user_id":12345, "amount":450.0, "location":"NY"}',
    PartitionKey="user_id"
)
```

The key highlights include:

- Kinesis enabled continuous data ingestion from multiple banking endpoints.
- Scalable architecture allowed the firm to manage peak loads during trading hours.
- Data encryption (at rest and in transit) ensured compliance with financial security standards.

Data processing layer

Apache Flink was deployed to perform real-time stream processing, transforming incoming transactional data into structured formats. This layer played a critical role in reducing the processing window from hours to milliseconds. The following code snippet demonstrates how Apache Flink is utilized for real-time stream processing of financial transactions. It creates a structured table to process transaction data from Amazon Kinesis, enabling rapid analysis and fraud detection.

The following PyFlink code demonstrates the initial setup for processing a stream of transaction data using Apache Flink's Table API:

```
from pyflink.table import EnvironmentSettings, TableEnvironment

env_settings = EnvironmentSettings.in_streaming_mode()
table_env = TableEnvironment.create(env_settings)

table_env.execute_sql("""
    CREATE TABLE Transactions (
        user_id STRING,
        amount DOUBLE,
        location STRING,
        timestamp TIMESTAMP(3)
```

```
) WITH (
    'connector' = 'kinesis',
    'stream' = 'transaction_stream'
)
""")
```

The key highlights include:

- Flink's ability to process data in sub-second intervals enabled real-time fraud detection.

- The distributed architecture handled millions of events concurrently without degradation in performance.

- Fault-tolerant features ensured that no transactions were lost even if node failures occurred.

Data storage and querying

Processed transactions were ingested into Elasticsearch, enabling rapid anomaly detection and efficient querying. Elasticsearch's distributed nature allowed the firm to scale analytics dynamically, ensuring latency remained low even during peak financial activities.

The following code snippet demonstrates how Elasticsearch is used to store and index transactional data for real-time fraud detection. By indexing financial transactions, the system enables rapid querying and anomaly detection to identify suspicious activities:

```
from elasticsearch import Elasticsearch

es = Elasticsearch(["http://localhost:9200"])

doc = {
    'user_id': '12345',
    'amount': 450.0,
    'location': 'NY'
}
es.index(index="fraud_alerts", document=doc)
```

Real-time fraud detection

The final stage involved training fraud detection models using Scikit-learn. These models were integrated into the pipeline to classify transactions in real-time, ensuring fraudulent activities were identified before completion.

The following code snippet demonstrates how a **random forest classifier** from Scikit-learn is used to build a fraud detection model:

```
from sklearn.ensemble import RandomForestClassifier
import numpy as np

X = np.array([[100, 0], [200, 1], [300, 0]])
y = np.array([0, 1, 0])

model = RandomForestClassifier()
model.fit(X, y)

prediction = model.predict([[450, 0]])
```

The results are as follows:

- **Fraud detection speed**: It was reduced from 4 hours to under 300 milliseconds.
- **Cost savings**: It prevents fraud losses of $20 million annually.
- **Regulatory compliance**: Reporting lag decreased by 70%, avoiding penalties.
- **Customer satisfaction**: Improved by 15%, with faster resolution of fraudulent activities.

Data integration in healthcare

A leading healthcare provider managing over 200 hospitals and clinics across 15 countries faced significant challenges in consolidating patient data across its facilities. The organization dealt with diverse data sources, including EHR, lab reports, imaging systems, and wearable health devices. The fragmented data landscape slowed diagnosis, complicated patient management, and resulted in duplicated records, affecting both operational efficiency and patient outcomes.

With the rise of telemedicine and remote health monitoring, the need to unify and access patient data in real-time became important. This initiative aimed to improve decision-making, reduce errors, and enhance patient experiences by integrating disparate data systems into a centralized platform.

The key statistics include:

- **Hospitals and clinics**: 200+
- **Countries**: 15
- **Patient records**: 50 million
- **Daily data volume**: 5 terabytes of new patient data (EHRs, imaging, IoT devices)

Problem statement

The healthcare provider's inability to seamlessly integrate patient data from different sources led to inefficiencies in diagnostics, inconsistencies in treatment, and increased costs. This section highlights the three core issues that demanded immediate attention.

Fragmented patient records

Data silos existed across different hospital branches, with each unit using proprietary EHR systems. Lack of interoperability between systems led to incomplete patient profiles, resulting in misdiagnoses or delayed treatment.

The implications include:

- 30% of patient records contained redundant or conflicting data.

- Critical medical history was inaccessible to physicians across facilities, increasing the risk of prescribing errors.

Delayed diagnostics and treatment

Doctors often faced delays in accessing lab results and imaging reports due to disconnected data streams. On average, it took 12–24 hours to consolidate patient records manually.

The implications include:

- Emergency departments experienced treatment delays of up to 6 hours.

- Patient discharge times increased by 18%, contributing to bed shortages during peak periods.

Compliance and data privacy risks

Fragmented systems posed security risks and complicated compliance with regulations such as HIPAA and GDPR. Data breaches were more likely due to improper handling of sensitive health records across multiple systems.

The implications are as follows:

- Non-compliance penalties reached up to $2 million annually.

- Patient trust eroded as cases of data mismanagement surfaced in regulatory audits.

Solution design

In order to unify patient data and ensure secure, real-time access across facilities, the healthcare provider adopted a scalable data integration platform. The architecture utilized:

- **AWS Glue**: Used for extracting and transforming healthcare data from different sources.

- **Apache NiFi**: Used to automate data flow between EHR systems, IoT devices, and imaging platforms.

- **Fast healthcare interoperability resources (FHIR)**: Used as the standard data model for healthcare interoperability.

- **Amazon S3**: Used for centralized data storage and backup.
- **Snowflake**: Used as the primary data warehouse for querying patient records.

High-level architecture diagram

Apache NiFi facilitates the ingestion process, while AWS Glue handles data transformation into FHIR-compliant formats. The transformed data is securely stored in Amazon S3, and Snowflake powers downstream analytics and querying to support seamless healthcare insights.

The following figure provides a detailed view of the healthcare data integration pipeline, highlighting the flow of patient data from various sources, including hospitals, IoT devices, and patient portals:

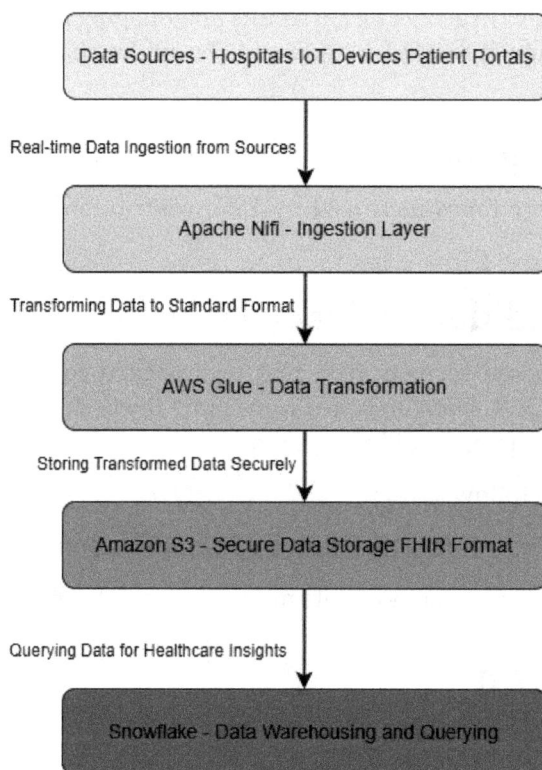

Figure 12.3: Healthcare data integration pipeline showcasing data ingestion

Implementation steps

The healthcare provider implemented the data integration framework in phases, beginning with patient data ingestion and progressing to interoperability across systems. A detailed breakdown of each stage is discussed in this section.

Data ingestion layer

Apache NiFi served as the primary ingestion tool to automate data flow from EHR platforms, medical imaging devices, and wearable health monitors. This layer enabled the seamless transfer of structured and unstructured data into AWS Glue for processing.

The following code snippet illustrates how Apache NiFi is used to automate the ingestion of EHR data:

```
fromNiFi import FlowManager

flow = FlowManager.create_flow('EHR_Ingestion')
flow.add_source('EHR_DB')
flow.add_processor('FHIR_Converter')
flow.add_sink('Amazon_S3_Bucket')
flow.start()
```

The key highlights are as follows:

- NiFi allowed the ingestion of patient data from over 500 EHR systems across multiple regions.

- IoT health devices streamed real-time metrics (heart rate, glucose levels) to Amazon S3 for analysis.

- Failover mechanisms ensured that no patient data was lost during transmission.

Data transformation and interoperability

AWS Glue processed raw healthcare data, transforming it into FHIR-compliant formats. This ensured consistency and enabled interoperability between different hospital systems.

The following code demonstrates how **AWS Data Wrangler** (**awswrangler**) is used to read patient records from an **Amazon S3** bucket, transform them into the FHIR format, and store the processed data back in S3:

```
import awswrangler as wr
import pandas as pd

df = wr.s3.read_json('s3://patient-records/input')
fhir_data = df.apply(lambda x: convert_to_fhir(x))  # Transform to FHIR
model
wr.s3.to_json(fhir_data, path='s3://patient-records/output')
```

The key highlights are as follows:

- AWS Glue automated schema detection, reducing manual efforts in transforming patient records.

- Data was validated against healthcare standards to ensure consistency.

- FHIR compliance streamlined cross-facility data exchange, improving coordination between medical teams.

Centralized storage and querying

All transformed data was stored in Amazon S3 and synchronized with Snowflake for fast querying. Snowflake's scalability allowed querying millions of patient records within seconds, supporting both research and real-time diagnostics. The following code establishes a connection to Snowflake, a cloud-based data warehouse, to query patient records for individuals diagnosed with diabetes:

```
import snowflake.connector

conn = snowflake.connector.connect(
    user='admin',
    password='securePass123',
    account='healthcare_snowflake'
)

query = "SELECT * FROM patient_records WHERE condition='diabetes'"
cursor = conn.cursor()
cursor.execute(query)
results = cursor.fetchall()
```

The key highlights are as follows:

- Snowflake reduced query times by 70%, enabling doctors to retrieve records instantly.

- Data partitioning by patient ID and timestamp allowed efficient filtering.

- Secure access controls ensured that only authorized medical personnel accessed sensitive records.

Real-time patient monitoring and alerts

Patient data from wearable devices was streamed directly to Snowflake for real-time monitoring. Machine learning models analyzed incoming data, triggering alerts for abnormal patterns (e.g., irregular heart rates).

The following code utilizes **Support Vector Classification** (**SVC**) from Scikit-learn to detect anomalies in patient health data:

```
from sklearn.svm import SVC
import numpy as np
```

```
X = np.array([[75, 120], [80, 130], [72, 115]])
y = np.array([0, 0, 1])  # 1 indicates abnormal
model = SVC().fit(X, y)

new_reading = np.array([[85, 140]])
alert = model.predict(new_reading)
```

The results are as follows:

- **Diagnosis speed**: Reduced from 12 hours to under 30 minutes.

- **Treatment efficiency**: Faster access to lab results decreased emergency treatment times by 40%.

- **Compliance**: Achieved 95% compliance across all facilities, reducing penalties by $1.5 million.

- **Operational savings**: $3 million saved annually through automated data workflows.

Practical takeaways and recommended approaches

As we reach the conclusion of this book, it is essential to reflect on the journey we have taken through the world of scalable data engineering. From understanding the core concepts of data collection and ingestion to building sophisticated pipelines for real-time analytics and AI-driven personalization, the chapters have covered a wide spectrum of techniques, tools, and case studies. This final chapter consolidates the lessons learned and outlines best practices that can guide future data engineering projects.

Data engineering is not just about technology, it is about aligning technology with business goals. Throughout the book, we have seen how companies across industries transformed their data infrastructure to drive growth, improve customer experiences, and optimize operations. By revisiting these case studies, we aim to extract actionable insights that can be applied universally, regardless of the size or nature of the organization.

Importance of scalability

One recurring theme across all case studies is the critical need for scalability. As businesses grow, so does the volume of data they generate and consume. Systems that handle small datasets efficiently may falter when faced with terabytes of data. Scalability ensures that systems continue to perform well under increased loads.

Let us look at the lesson learned from the case study and best practice:

- **Lesson learned from e-commerce case study**: Designing systems with scalability in mind from the beginning reduces the need for costly re-architecting later. The e-commerce company's shift to Apache Kafka and Spark enabled them to handle peak loads during sales events like Black Friday.

- **Best practice**: Use distributed systems and cloud-based platforms to handle large datasets. Technologies, like Apache Kafka, Spark, and AWS services allow for horizontal scaling, ensuring that infrastructure grows alongside business needs.

Breaking down data silos

Many organizations struggle with data silos, where information is trapped within specific departments, limiting cross-functional insights. This was evident in the e-commerce and financial services case studies, where fragmented data led to inconsistent customer experiences and operational inefficiencies.

Let us look at the lesson learned from the case study and best practice:

- **Lesson learned from financial services case study**: Unified data pipelines break down silos and enable seamless data sharing across departments. Implementing Amazon Kinesis allowed real-time data flow between investment and retail banking divisions.

- **Best practice**: Implement centralized data lakes or warehouses to aggregate data from multiple sources. Tools like AWS Glue, Apache NiFi, and Snowflake facilitate data integration, providing a single source of truth for the entire organization.

Real-time processing and analytics

Batch processing served businesses well in the past, but modern use cases demand real-time insights. Whether it is detecting fraudulent transactions or personalizing e-commerce recommendations, latency can significantly impact outcomes.

Let us look at the lesson learned from the case study and best practice:

- **Lesson learned from financial services and healthcare case studies**: Real-time data pipelines enable faster decision-making and enhance user experiences. In healthcare, real-time data from IoT devices helps monitor patient conditions instantly.

- **Best practice**: Leverage technologies like Apache Flink and Spark Streaming to process data in micro-batches or real-time. Combine them with event-driven architectures using Kafka or Kinesis for efficient data ingestion and processing.

Data quality and governance

Poor data quality can undermine even the most sophisticated systems. Inconsistent, incomplete, or inaccurate data leads to flawed insights and misguided decisions. The healthcare case study demonstrated the importance of adhering to data standards, particularly in sensitive environments.

Let us look at the lesson learned from the case study and best practice:

- **Lesson learned from healthcare case study**: Data quality is foundational to the success of any data engineering project. Standardizing patient data in FHIR format improved interoperability and accuracy.

- **Best practice**: Establish data validation and cleansing pipelines to ensure that only high-quality data enters analytical systems. Implement governance frameworks to monitor data quality continuously, using tools, like AWS Glue DataBrew and Apache Atlas.

Security and compliance

With the increasing prevalence of cyber threats and stringent regulatory requirements, securing data has become important. In the financial services case study, delayed fraud detection highlighted the risks associated with inadequate security measures.

Let us look at the lesson learned from the case study and best practice:

- **Lesson learned from financial services case study**: Data security and compliance cannot be an afterthought; they must be integrated into the architecture from the start. The integration of Elasticsearch for rapid anomaly detection improved fraud prevention.

- **Best practice**: Use encryption, access controls, and audit logs to safeguard sensitive data. Regularly conduct security assessments and ensure compliance with relevant regulations, such as GDPR, HIPAA, or PCI DSS.

Automating data pipelines

Manual processes are prone to errors and inefficiencies. Automating data pipelines not only improves accuracy but also accelerates the time-to-insight. In the e-commerce case study, automation reduced operational overhead and enabled faster responses to market changes. Let us look at the lesson learned from the case study and best practice:

- **Lesson learned from e-commerce case study**: Automation streamlines workflows and enhances productivity. Automation using Apache Airflow reduced manual reconciliation by 80%.

- **Best practice**: Use orchestration tools like Apache Airflow or AWS Step Functions to automate data pipelines. Implement CI/CD practices to deploy updates seamlessly and minimize downtime.

Leveraging AI and ML

AI and ML add significant value by uncovering patterns and insights that traditional analytics may miss. In the e-commerce and financial services case studies, AI-driven personalization and fraud detection delivered measurable benefits.

Let us look at the lesson learned from the case study and best practice:

- **Lesson learned from e-commerce and finance case studies**: AI enhances the capabilities of data engineering, driving better outcomes. TensorFlow-based recommendation engines improved product conversion rates by 21%.

- **Best practice**: Integrate AI models directly into data pipelines using tools like TensorFlow, PyTorch, and Scikit-learn. Ensure that models are continuously trained on the latest data to maintain accuracy.

Collaboration between teams

Successful data engineering projects require collaboration between data engineers, data scientists, and business stakeholders. Misalignment often leads to suboptimal solutions that fail to meet business needs.

Let us look at the lesson learned from the case study and best practice:

- **Lesson learned from healthcare case study**: Cross-functional collaboration ensures that data solutions align with business goals. Collaboration between IT and healthcare teams standardized data flows across hospitals.

- **Best practice**: Foster a culture of collaboration by establishing regular communication channels and involving all stakeholders in the planning and execution phases.

Monitoring and observability

Monitoring the health and performance of data pipelines is essential for ensuring reliability. In the financial services case study, robust monitoring frameworks detected bottlenecks early, allowing for proactive intervention.

Let us look at the lesson learned from the case study and best practice:

- **Lesson learned from financial services case study**: Observability reduces downtime and enhances system resilience. Prometheus monitoring reduced fraud detection latency by 30%.

- **Best practice**: Use monitoring tools, like Prometheus, Grafana, and AWS CloudWatch to track pipeline performance and detect anomalies in real-time.

Continuous improvement

The field of data engineering evolves rapidly, with new technologies and best practices emerging regularly. Staying ahead requires a commitment to continuous learning and adaptation.

Let us look at the lesson learned from the case study and best practice:

- **Lesson learned across case studies**: Continuous improvement keeps data systems competitive and resilient. Companies that reviewed and updated architecture annually outperformed competitors.

- **Best practice**: Encourage ongoing training and experimentation. Regularly review and update data architectures to incorporate the latest advancements in the field.

Conclusion

As we conclude this book, the overarching message is clear, data engineering is a dynamic and evolving discipline that blends technology with strategy. The lessons learned from the case studies highlight the importance of scalability, automation, security, and collaboration. By embracing these best practices, organizations can unlock the full potential of their data, driving innovation and achieving long-term success.

May the insights shared in these pages inspire and empower you to build robust, scalable, and impactful data engineering solutions.

Join our book's Discord space

Join the book's Discord Workspace for Latest updates, Offers, Tech happenings around the world, New Release and Sessions with the Authors:

https://discord.bpbonline.com

Index

www.ingramcontent.com/pod-product-compliance
Lightning Source LLC
Chambersburg PA
CBHW061802210326
41599CB00034B/6851